Metronome

Place de Clichy

Lamarck — Caulaincourt

Abbesses

Barbès-Roc

Blanche

Pigalle

Anvers

Saint-Georges

Gare du Nord

Rome

Notre-Dame-de-Lorette

Liège

Trinité
D'Estienne-d'Orves

Le Peletier

Poissonière

Gare de
l'Est

Europe

illiers

nceau

14 Saint-Lazare

Château
d'Eau

Saint
Lazare

RER E

Chaussée
d'Antin
La Fayette

Grand
Boulevards

Bonne
Nouvelle

Strasbourg
Saint-Denis

es

Saint
Augustin

Richelieu
Drouot

Réaumur
Sébastopol

Miromesnil

Havre
Caumartin

A RER

Opéra

Quatre
Septembre

Bourse

Sentier

Tem

Philippe
du Roule

Madeleine

Pyramides

Les
Halles

Etienne
Marcel

Franklin D.
Roosevelt

Concorde

Louvre
Rivoli

Châtelet

RER A B D

Ra

Champs-Elysées
Clémenceau

RER

Palais Royal
Musée du Louvre

Pont
Neuf

11 Châtelet

Hôtel de Vi

Invalides

Assemblée
Nationale

Cité

Pont Marie

Varenne

Solférino

Saint-Michel

Sully — Morland

La Tour
Maubourg

Rue du Bac

Odéon

RER B C

Saint
François-Xavier

Mabillon

Cluny — La Sorbonne

Sèvres — Babylone

Saint-Germain
des Prés

Cardinal Lemoine

Jus

Rennes

Saint-Sulpice

Maubert
Mutualité

Place
Monge

Ségur

Duroc

Saint
Placide

Notre-Dame-des-Champs

Centre
Daume

etronome

A History of Paris from the Underground Up

Lorànt Deutsch

With assistance from Emmanuel Haymann

Translated from the French by Timothy Bent

St. Martin's Griffin   New York

www.stmartins.com

Design by Steven Seighman

Library of Congress Cataloging-in-Publication Data

Deutsch, Lorànt, 1975–
    Metronome : a history of Paris from the underground up / Lorànt Deutsch; with assistance from Emmanuel Haymann; translated from the French by Timothy Bent. — First U.S. edition.
        Pages   cm
    "First published in France by Éditions Michel Lafon"—Title page verso.
    ISBN 978-1-250-02367-4 (trade paperback)
    ISBN 978-1-250-02368-1 (e-book)
    1. Paris (France)—History—Miscellanea.   2. Paris (France)—Description and travel.
3. France—History—Miscellanea.   4. Subways—France—Paris—History.
5. Subway stations—France—Paris—History.   I. Haymann, Emmanuel, 1946–   II. Title.
    DC707.D521713 2013
    944'.361—dc23
                                                            2013026916

St. Martin's Griffin books may be purchased for educational, business, or promotional use. For information on bulk purchases, please contact Macmillan Corporate and Premium Sales Department at 1-800-221-7945, extension 5442, or write specialmarkets@macmillan.com.

First published in France by Éditions Michel Lafon

First U.S. Edition: December 2013

10 9 8 7 6 5 4 3 2 1

To Eddy Mitchell, whose Final Lecture *first got me interested in history. And to my sister and my parents, who for my sake found a way to catch the weekly shows.*

Contents

Introduction

Before the Crossing

My love for its history began many miles from Paris, in a village along the Sarthe River in the Loire Valley where I spent my childhood. My family and I left the village for vacations, but most special of all were the trips to the French capital with my grandparents. When we reached the outskirts of the city—the *boulevard périphérique,* or ring road around it—I would gaze into the distance at its lights. Then into it we would plunge, and immediately be swept up in a whirl of hurrying pedestrians and swirling colors. I remember the bright neon signs—the green ones for the pharmacies and the red carrots for the *tabacs,* or tobacco shops. It was like Christmas, even in summer. Paris seemed to me a jungle, and being inside it both frightened and excited me.

At the age of fifteen I went to live in Paris, and took with me my love of its history. The city that had seemed so anonymous and impersonal, so beyond the scope of my comprehension, was now an open book. I knew almost no one; the names of the streets were my first companions. Most of all, it was through the subway system, the Métro as it is known, short for Métropolitain, that I discovered Paris. The Métro introduced me to and took me through this enormous, humming hive of activity. It was a country boy's ticket to ride, and I took full advantage, crossing, recrossing, and crisscrossing the city. At each stop I asked questions. Why was it called *Les Invalides*? What was *Châtelet*, exactly? What *République* were they referring to, anyway? Who was *Étienne Marcel*? What did *Maubert* mean?

The Paris Métro map represents the city's central nervous system; you can use it to trace its beginnings, when it was little more than a small island in the Seine. Each stop evokes some part of the past—not simply of Parisian history but of French history as a whole. From *La Cité* to *La Défense*—oldest to newest—the Métro serves as a moving time line, each station punctuating one of the twenty-one centuries of the city's history. Riding it carried me from the past to the present. And sometimes it went ahead of me, transforming the city into France's capital before I had quite caught up with it.

In short, I learned history by riding the subway. While I was doing that I was also becoming involved in theater and then film, both of which are in their own way forms of time travel. By entering into the world of La Fontaine, for example, or Fouquet, Mozart, and Sartre, what I did was relive history—or, perhaps better, reenact history.

As a kid I channeled my love for French history through toy soldiers on the field of battle. Not much has changed. History remains the engine that drives my life and my desires; it is an endlessly rewarding archaeological site to which I keep returning, again and again, unearthing more mysteries and paradoxes and posing more questions.

This book will seek to serve as a sort of timekeeper, a metronome, measuring history's tempo, moving through time by means of Métro stops. The subway lines, like Ariadne's thread, will guide you, just as they guided me, through tunnels echoing with the city's hopes, fears, and dreams. Watch the closing doors, please. First stop, Lutèce.

Metronome

2. The remains of Lutetia, discovered beneath the suburb Nanterre. **3.** The only positively identified Gallic remains on Île de la Cité, twenty feet below Square du Vert-Galant **5.** The Eiffel Tower, sitting on what used to be the plain of Garanella, where thousands died in the battle for Lutetia. **6.** The Pillar of the Boatmen. **7.** The Place Dauphine on the Île de la Cité, the birthplace of Paris.

First Century

Cité

Caesar's Cradle

"Aren't you getting off at the next stop?" This question was posed to me in a timid voice by a diminutive lady who had nudged me gently.

The subway car's brakes squealed loudly and metallically. *Get off here? Actually, yes, I will get off here.* Île de la Cité is the ideal place to start: this island sits at the very heart of Paris and is its birthplace; appropriately enough, it has the shape of a cradle. "The head, the heart, the very marrow of Paris," as Gui de Bazoches wrote in the twelfth century.

The Île de la Cité stop consists of a series of wells dug deep into the city's entrails—almost fifty feet (some twenty meters) below the water level of the Seine, and, as in Jules Verne's *Voyage to the Center of the Earth*, when you go down into it you have the feeling that time moves in reverse. No need of a volcano shaft to get down into the depths, or a *Nautilus* to dive leagues down below the surface. The Cité stop will do.

I vaulted up the metal circular stairs four at a time and headed toward the light, leaving the nice lady far behind. Once outside I ran smack into a scraggly cypress tree. I extricated myself only to find that now I was tangled up in the branches of an olive tree. *Aha!* I thought. *An olive tree! A trace of the South, a faint echo of the*

Italian countryside. Actually, however, I was in the middle of the Cité's flower market, which crowds right up to the edge of the subway entrance, as if both nature and history were trying to reclaim what once was rightfully theirs. Their success at this is illusory, for on one side the cars hum along in their endless descent down Boulevard Saint-Michel; on the other there is the same flood of cars heading in the other direction, climbing Rue Saint-Jacques.

After a few steps I reached the quays. A little farther along are the green boxes of the *bouquinistes*—the vendors of secondhand books and old prints. I can never resist plunging in and always resurface with something, on this occasion two dog-eared histories of Paris. I sometimes think that the city is my wife. It is most definitely a woman, as André Breton put it in *Nadja*, his Surrealist novel: the triangle formed by the Place Dauphine represents the delta of Venus from whose womb it all emerged. I wanted to go in, not out; I wanted to return to a time before cars and the gray façades of the buildings, back to when the banks of the Seine were verdant slopes presiding over a muddy bog and the island was forested.

It is the 701st year following the founding of Rome and fifty-two years before the birth of Jesus Christ. Île de la Cité is empty—there are no houses, no structures, nothing. There's also as yet no sign of the Lutes of which Julius Caesar spoke in his *History of the Gauls*. "Lutetia, town [*oppidum*] of the Parisii, located on an island in the Seine." Not very precise, of course, and indeed the proconsul had spent all of one day in the place, a day on which he was far more preoccupied with the gathering of the Gaul chiefs than he was with exploring the boundaries of this *oppidum*. In fact, when he came to write his history, Caesar knew it only through secondhand sources, relying on rumors and on hastily written military reports. He repeated what he had heard bruited about by his legionaries, whose descriptions were very sketchy.

Here's the thing. Just where you might expect to find something there was . . . nothing. The future Île de la Cité—the very heart of Paris—consisted of six or seven little islands on which sat a small temple and several simple huts with reddish thatched roofs. It was no hive of activity. You might see a handful of fishermen casually casting their nets into the waters. On the Right Bank, stretching westward, were swamps and a dense forest. On the Left Bank, still more wetlands, and, farther along, a rocky promontory referred to as a "mountain," which one day would be called "Montagne Sainte-Geneviève."

To find the significant-sized Gallic town the Roman legionaries referred to as the great city of the Parisii, you had to go downriver, to the west. At the time, the river offered the only way of getting around. Roads would come later and be built by the Romans. To get anywhere you were forced to clamber down the bank at one of the launch sites favored by the Gauls, climb into a long, delicate craft made of tree limbs, and venture out into the water.

The boat was the ancestral mode of transportation for the Parisii. Predictably, the earliest remnants of settlements here, dating back to the Neolithic period (five thousand years before Christ) were dugout canoes. They were discovered in Bercy, the little suburb that was the protocrib of Paris. Today these primitive boats can be found in the Musée Carnavalet, the museum that conserves the city's history.

To find the real Gallic Lutèce, which is what we French call Lutetia, you have to travel west down the Seine for twenty or so miles, to a spot where the river bends back upon itself so dramatically that it nearly forms a circle. Some Romans might understandably have confused it for an island. And in this enormous bend a city came to life, with streets and shops and neighborhoods and a port. Here was Lutèce, or, more exactly, in the Gallic tongue, *Lucotecia*, a name as fluid as its location. Caesar shortened *Lucotecia* to Lutetia, more closely approximating the Latin *lutum*, meaning "mud," and the Gallic *luto*, meaning "swamp." The city emerged from the swamp; name and place correlated perfectly.

Originally from the north, the tribe that settled on the banks of the river depended upon it. To the members of this tribe, the

Where was the original Lutèce located?

Over the centuries, historians have repeatedly tried to claim that Lutèce was located on Île de la Cité. There was but one small and vexing problem with that. No matter how deeply they dug, and dug, and dug, none could find even the smallest trace of the legendary Gallic city.

"Big deal," said some among them. "The Gauls built straw huts, and they simply disappeared during all the invasions and migrations."

It certainly is the case that the island was frequently destroyed, rebuilt, and redestroyed, and that all trace of the original has disappeared. And when you consider the last great urban transformation of Paris, undertaken by Baron Haussmann in the nineteenth century, during which older buildings were either razed or modified nearly beyond recognition, there would be no way of uncovering a single trace of its past. The only positively identified remains would be the ones you would find if you went to the Place Vert-Galant (referring to Henri IV of Navarre, whom we'll meet later). Dig down twenty or so feet and you would find yourself at the level where the Parisii once lived. That means that twenty feet of detritus have accumulated over two thousand years.

(Cont.)

river was a goddess—Sequana—capable of curing disease, and she gave her name to the waters that ran along the length of Lutèce, the Seine. The river offered very tangible benefits to these people, for not only did it provide the fish that fed them and the water that helped them grow wheat, and which sustained the humans and animals, it served as their means of contact with the outside world. Their coins were among the most beautiful in all of Gaul, golden and bright, one side featuring Apollo and the other a horse in full gallop. Farther away, beyond the city, the fertile soil helped the Parisii—who were farmers, herders, metalsmiths, and woodcutters—prosper.

The "Kwarisii," the Celtic people of the quarries, became the Gallic "Parisii" sometime in the third century B.C. (The Celtic *k* was transformed into the Gallic *p*.) These people had done so much navigating in their boats before settling the area that later their origins would become mixed up with those of other peoples and other legends. To glorify their ancestors, and therefore themselves, the descendants of these rock breakers and humble fishermen would clothe their genealogical forebears in all kinds of bright costumes.

The Parisii would become nothing less than the descendants of the Egyptian goddess Isis, or, better yet, the children of Paris, the prince of Troy and youngest son of King Priam. Paris, as we all know, had run off with Helen, the wife of Menelaus, leading to a terrible and protracted war between the Greeks and the Trojans. He escaped death at the hands of the jealous husband thanks to Aphrodite, who hid her protégé in the protective fog of the heavens and whisked him out of Troy. Troy, however, was not spared. Helen was reunited with Menelaus. Paris fled to the banks of the Seine, where he would give rise to a new people.

It was a pretty tale, if one with absolutely no basis in fact, but it gave to succeeding generations of Parisii a gloriously divine heritage of which to be proud. Much later, in the thirteenth century, Saint Louis strongly encouraged belief in this myth, which thrived during the entirety of the Capetian reign. "Our civilization was not descended from a band of wandering Celts. We share a noble ancestry with the Romans." That was also what most of the Frankish kings had thought.

So it's completely disappeared? Well, not quite. To help with traffic flow, city engineers designed the A86, a so-called *super-périphérique*. The idea was to create an even wider ring road around Paris. When they were digging at one of the construction sites in 2003, located beneath the city of Nanterre, in the western suburbs of Paris, workers came across the remains of what clearly had been a large and prosperous settlement. It had everything—houses, streets, wells, a port, even some graves.

Archaeologists also identified a large field bordered by ditches and fences; in it they found a spit used for roasting and a caldron fork. This led them to think that it must have been set apart and used for community cookouts. Setting Lutèce in the fluvial bend of Gennevilliers—which was far more visible then than it is today—served two needs: the location meant that the river and Mont Valérien afforded them greater security; more importantly, it gave them two ways of accessing the water, which was the source of riches and the axis of exchange.

Painful though it might be for Parisians, they may have to accept the fact that the original Lutèce was located not in their city but in its suburbs.

But we're getting way ahead of ourselves. For in the time in question the Romans had the upper hand in this part of the world, imposing their language and culture and appropriating myths and legends that justified their having conquered the world. Of course, the Romans were themselves merely descendants of some Indo-European tribe that had settled in what would become Italy in the seventh century B.C. They chose to believe otherwise. "We are descended from gods and heroes," their leaders declaimed.

This line of reasoning in turn followed from Homer's *Iliad* and *Odyssey*, which legitimated the supremacy of the Greeks in the Mediterranean. Then in the first century B.C., Virgil wrote the *Aeneid*, a tale that was a carbon copy of its illustrious Homeric predecessors, with the difference being that the heroes were now Roman rather than Greek. The Trojan Aeneas, a son of Aphrodite, fled Troy as it was being destroyed by the Greeks and founded Rome, taking with him his son Iulius, the ancestor of Caesar ("Julius" is the family name for anyone called "Caesar," coming from "Julia," as the Latin *i* and *j* are interchangeable). Caesar had the right to rule the world because he was descended from the gods.

In this year, 52 B.C., the Romans arrived to attack the humble Parisii and to occupy their lands along the banks of the Seine. This people had had, well, the gall, to be among the first to resist. They rallied behind a certain Arvernian chief named Vercingetorix, who was determined to unite the Gallic tribes and together repel the Roman invaders. Julius Caesar, keen to bring order to the distant borders of the empire, sent in his best general, Titus Labienus.

Titus Labienus came with four legions and a cavalry regiment, sending the Lutetians into a panic. How were they going to defend themselves? They sent an urgent message to the town of Mediolanum Aulercorum—today, Evreux—where lived an elderly chief whom the entire Gallic world respectfully referred to as Camulogenus, which means "son of Camulus," who was himself the son of the god of war. With a name like that, the man had no choice but to come and defend the city from the Romans. The citizens placed their fate in his hands. Camulogenus would organize the counterattack and push back the enemy.

What could the poor old man do? He was placed at the head of a small and poorly trained army whose soldiers were more courageous than effective and who tended to fight naked to the waist, armed only with a few axes and some heavy swords made of poor-grade metal.

Labienus and his legionaries advanced inexorably. Camulogenus prepared his defense. He didn't wait in the city for the Romans to arrive, however; he set up his camp in a swamp, in the heart of the moist zone that surrounds Lutèce.

Soon enough Labienus arrived and the war began. The impeccably disciplined Romans, with their bronze helmets and their steel chest plates, advanced in tight formations. The legionaries were used to fighting on solid ground, having trained on open plains; now they found themselves getting sucked into the shifting terrain between water and land, a place where even small boats went aground and men drowned. The cavalry was useless; the horses' hooves stuck fast in the mud.

The Gauls, on the other hand, were right at home in this kind of wetland. They descended upon the enemy troops and slaughtered the proud soldiers of Rome, who were unable to defend themselves against this onslaught. By the time night had fallen, Roman blood reddened the stagnant water. Labienus faced reality and had the trumpets blast a long mournful note of retreat. Lutèce erupted in joy. The city was saved and the invaders pushed back!

Labienus, enraged, decided to wreak revenge on these stubborn Gauls and, pushing along the edges of the Seine, moved to attack Metlosedum—what is today Melun—another city built in the bend of the meandering Seine.

Metlosedum was defenseless, most of its men having joined Camulogenus at Lutèce, and was inhabited mainly by women and old men. They tried to push back the legionaries with their bare hands. What occurred wasn't even a battle worthy of the name but a cold-blooded affair of throat-cutting and disembowelment. The Romans rammed their lances into the guts of anyone who looked as if they might oppose the new order, pillaging reserves of wheat and desecrating the altars of the divinities, sacking the wealthier houses. And then they left, leaving behind them a city in ruins.

It was on Lutèce that Labienus wanted to exact his revenge, however. He had no intention to return to Caesar and admit to the shame of his defeat. In the middle of the night, he gathered his officers together in his tent and gave them a speech worthy of a virile Roman general.

"We cannot expect reinforcements. It's up to our legions to crush the Gauls and take their city. You will conquer these barbarians for the glory of the empire and Rome will crown you with the laurels of victory."

The Roman camp sprang to life. The troops massed themselves along the right bank of the Seine, swung around the swampy region and headed north of the bend in the Seine that protected Lutèce, then spiked southward toward the city. Meanwhile a small Roman flotilla, consisting of fifty ships, managed to make their way to the level of the capital of the Parisii.

Before the arrival of the Romans, those who had managed to survive the massacre at Metlosedum, disheveled and traumatized, had come to warn Camulogenus.

"The Romans are heading toward Lutèce!" they cried.

To avoid being surrounded, Camulogenus decided to burn the city and move upriver along the left bank.

"Burn the two bridges across the Seine, and burn your houses! The goddess Sequana will protect us!" he decreed.

By the early hours of the morning, Lutèce was little more than an empty field of ashes. All that remained were the ruins of the homes that but a day earlier had risen over the banks of the Seine; the network of streets that divided the modest hovels of wattle and daub walls; and the storehouses of wheat and wine that had stretched along the heights.

In this fateful dawn, everyone prepared for the final battle—over a city that effectively no longer existed. The Gaul chief and his cohort moved up along the Seine, invoking Camulus, the god armed with a spear and a shield, a mighty master of war and violent death. Dying for one's country was a glorious fate, and the

Gauls approached combat determined to sacrifice themselves to the bloody appetite of the terrible Camulus. The Roman legions were close behind them, invoking Mars, their god of war. But they had no intention of sacrificing themselves to him. They would fight to the best of their abilities, defeat the Gauls, and gain the spoils of victory.

The Romans met the Gauls on the plain of Garanella, located on the banks of the Seine. Garanella, or "little *garenne*"—meaning "rabbit warren"—was so called because in happier times it had been a place to hunt. Called today the field of Grenelle, it would witness an entirely different kind of hunt on this day, a horrific clash of arms.

The whistle of arrows and javelins cut the air. The Roman infantry threw their deadly spears and the horsemen used their superior height to decimate the Gauls' ranks. Every arrow seemed to find its target; warriors perished in the hail of deadly projectiles. The arrows seemed endless; dense clouds of them temporarily stalled the advance of the Parisii. Wounded or not, these men yearning for death got up and pressed on, seemingly indifferent. Hundreds more collapsed as death rained down upon them.

His sword in his hand, old Camulogenus rallied his troops, calling upon them to die for Camulus. For a moment, the Gauls succeeded in breaking through the Roman lines. Protected by their large shields they penetrated the armored squares of Romans, who seemed to hesitate and then began to retreat.

At that moment a Roman legion, its standards unfurled, approached from the back of the plain. Four thousand mercenaries held in reserve attacked the Gauls from behind. Retreat was impossible. The carnage can scarcely be described. The poor-quality Gallic sabers were broken by the Roman swords, which were both lighter and stronger. Blood soaked the ground. The groan of the wounded rose from the plain of Garanella.

Both sides fought furiously—the Parisii seeking death and the Romans their spoils. The Gauls didn't surrender. Survival wasn't contemplated. By the time the sun had set, the plain of Garanella was littered with the bodies of thousands of Gauls. Camulogenus,

Where lie the remains of the Gallic warriors?

The plain of Garanella became the village of Grenelle, which in turn became part of the city of Paris during the Second Empire in the nineteenth century. The Romans, impressed by the valiant defense mounted by the Gauls, called it "Champs de Mars," the name it carries to this day.

Much, much later, at the same spot where the Gallic chief and his men perished, would rise the Eiffel Tower, as if in towering memorial. Here is where Parisians come to spend their Sunday afternoons, either ignorant of or indifferent to the fact that they are walking on ground on which thousands of Parisii made the supreme sacrifice to their people.

also, was killed in this last stand. All in defense of a Lutèce that was no longer even there.

Several months following the burning of the first Lutèce, a decisive battle was fought between the troops led by Julius Caesar and those led by the Vercingetorix. In the height of summer, the proconsul came up north with his six legions to join them with those of the triumphant Labienus. Vercingertorix's cavalry attacked the Romans but German mercenaries, who were used to bolster the ranks of the legionaries, repelled them.

Vercingetorix drew back to the heights of Alésia, in what is today Burgundy. He had an impressively large army that included eight thousand Parisii fighters. A dozen Roman legions lay siege to Alésia but the besieging army was smaller than the one being besieged, and the Romans for the moment had to give up the offensive. Instead, they tried to starve the Gauls out by encircling the *oppidum* with a double line of fortifications.

When the summer wound down, a Gallic army arrived as reinforcements. In the darkness of night this new contingent launched an assault, and though they fought valiantly they couldn't break through the Roman lines. Another Gallic army attacked the larger camp of Romans, while Vercingetorix left the city with his men. The fierceness of the assault forced the Romans to fall back. Caesar sent in fresh troops. Eventually he succeeded in halting the advance of the Gallic troops. This turned into a full retreat. Those not fortunate enough to die on the field of battle tried to flee. The Roman cavalry cut off their retreat, prelude to a horrific massacre. Hope was extinguished. The next day Vercingetorix emerged from his camp on horse and came to place his arms at Caesar's feet. Three years later the proud chief of the Arverni tribe was strangled deep within his Roman prison.

In this Gaul that was now "Gallo-Roman," the Romans rapidly undertook the construction of what they henceforth called Lutetia. A new location was chosen, one that was more defensible than the original setting in the bend in the river. What could be more ideal than a real island? And indeed a stone's throw from the Champs de Mars where Labienus had achieved his victory was a group of small river islands. In the largest of them sat a small temple built to the Gallic gods: Cernunnos, the master of abundance; Smertios, the protector of herds; and Esus, the spirit of the forests. Flocks of seagulls flew above the humble structure, swarming and squabbling over the crumbs of the offerings left by the believers.

The remaining Gauls of Lutèce regrouped around this place of faith and devotion. The small islands, soon to be connected by bridges, already contained the outlines of a new town. And thus it was that the Gallo-Roman city of Lutetia emerged from this spit of land that would one day become Île de la Cité.

As in the past, the Parisii made their living near and by the river, which continued to confer prosperity. The new Lutetians exacted tribute from voyagers who wanted to use the bridges or get their boats through. Lutetia thus became a city-bridge, a tollbooth on the Seine. Later, the city's motto, *Fluctuat nec mergitur*—"It floats but runs not"—reflected the heritage of this early and crucial bond with the river.

In the first century A.D., the little islands were already oriented around the symbols of terrestrial authority and heavenly power: to the west was built a fortified palace, seat of Roman power; to

What happened to the Pillar of the Boatmen?

In 1711, while digging under the choir of the cathedral of Notre-Dame in order to excavate a tomb for the archbishops of Paris, workers found the pillar, which was brought to light and integrated into the masonry of two walls. Restored between 1999 and 2003, it is today on exhibit at the Musée de Cluny.

The sacred places remain, however much the divinities chanted. It was no coincidence that this monument was discovered deep in the foundations of Notre-Dame, and it was no coincidence that the cathedral remains the primary symbol of French Catholicism: on this very spot on Île de la Cité rose the first temple votives of the Gauls, which became Gallo-Roman and then, ultimately, Christian.

the east, the places of worship of the Parisii. The temple was enlarged and embellished, and opened as well to worshipping the Roman pantheon of gods, thereby mixing the two religious cultures. It was here that the future city's first significant monument was built. The boatmen, the brotherhood of mariners who navigated the Seine, showed their gratitude by driving in a support column of a building, a pillar that was fifteen feet high and made of cubic blocks sculpted to represent the Gallic divinities Cernunnos, Smertios, and Esus, as well as the Roman Vulcan and Jupiter. The pillar was in fact dedicated to these Roman gods and to the Emperor Tiberius, who ruled from A.D. 14 to 37: "To Tiberius Caesar Augustus and to Jupiter, both so good and so great, the mariners of the territory of Parisii, with funds from their community treasury, have erected this monument." Henceforth the Gallo-Roman civilization was set in stone.

Lutetia was established, and the history of Paris begun.

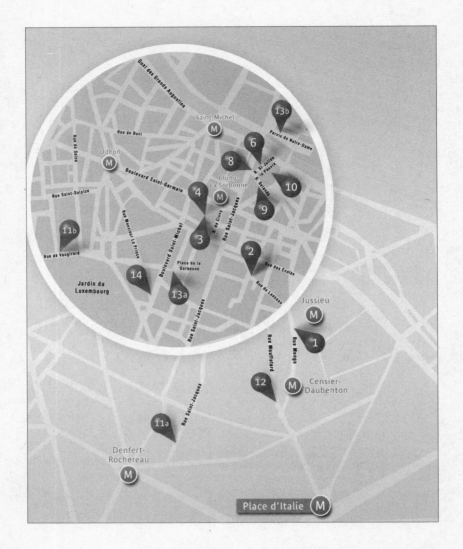

1. The Lutetia arena. **2.** The oldest cellar in Paris, below the restaurant Coupe-Chou. **3–4.** The Cluny Baths. **6.** The last tile of the *Via Romana*, preserved outside the church of Saint-Julien-le-Pauvre. **8.** Rue Saint-Jacques, the original crossroads between the *Via Romana* and the path leading to Saint-Jacques-de-Compostelle. **9.** At 42 Rue Galande, a small bas-relief sculpture representing St. Julien l'Hospitalier that dates from the fourteenth century. **10.** The oldest tree in Paris, in Viviani Square: a native North American locust, planted in 1602. **11a–11b.** The *cardo maximus* / Rue Saint-Jacques. At 254 Rue Saint-Jacques, there is still a kiln, a miraculously salvaged vestige of one of the pottery workshops established along the road. **12.** Le Rue Mouffetard. **13a.** On the Place de la Sorbonne, the remains of wells that belonged to two *insulae* (high Roman dwellings). **13b.** Further remains of Roman houses in the archaeological crypt of the square in front of Notre-Dame. **14.** The remains of the forum, at 61 Boulevard Saint-Michel.

Second Century

Place d'Italie

All Roads Lead to Rome

It has always seemed to me that there's something not quite right about the Place d'Italie. When you come out of the Métro and look around, nothing seems to work, or be where it should be. Even the nineteenth-century *mairie*—mayor's office, or local town hall—for the Thirteenth Arrondissement (as the twenty administrative districts of Paris are of course known) even looks as if it is backing away from it, repulsed by the endless flow of cars that go around the traffic circle in an awkward and poorly choreographed ballet. Facing you, on the roofs of the studiously hypermodern-looking commercial center, futurist "assemblages" involuntarily mimic the fossilized cranes of an abandoned construction site. On the other side of the avenue, fast-food stands disgorge their nauseating smell of rancid fries at the foot of a collection of gray-colored cubes. Farther along, the sad outlines of soulless-looking building towers spread out into the distance.

The one thing that seems fitting is the blue-and-green-enameled plaque that reads "Place d'Italie." In the second century, when the Lutetia envisioned by the Roman occupiers was established on Île de la Cité, the road to Rome passed through here. This was the time of the *Pax Romana* and the new city of the Parisii, for reasons we'll see, was growing south of the Seine. Direct lines of communication were established in the direction of Rome, to connect the distant corners of this far-flung empire. The Place d'Italie found itself on this *Via Romana,* which led first to what is today Lyon and thence to Rome.

Basically the square might as well be renamed "Place de Rome," in recognition of the debt that the Paris that we know and love owes to those who came north to conquer Gaul two millennia ago.

Of course those same Romans also destroyed the roots of Paris. We should not underestimate the cataclysm that was the burning of Lutèce and the defeat of Alésia. They represented nothing less than the death of a culture and the disappearance of a language. Nearly every trace of an entire way of life, with its stories, histories, divinities, its passions and mysteries, was simply wiped away—closed like an unfinished book. And what did manage to survive has been transmitted by the Romans. Genial as they were, the Romans used their histories to control the memory of these barbarians whom they forced into submitting to their power. In the process they essentially destroyed the Gallic identity, destroyed it so completely, in fact, that for a long while historians either regarded the existence of this ancient nation with skepticism or condescendingly dismissed it altogether. At best the Gauls were treated as a slightly savage people, with long droopy moustaches and brightly colored clothes, fond of roasting wild boar. How lucky it was for us all that Julius Caesar came along and brought civilization to these brutes. Now, however, historians are starting to revise this perception. While it's true that the Gauls produced no great literary masterpieces and built no grand monuments, at least of the sort that delight tourists of the third millennium, it doesn't mean they were complete rubes. They were part of a highly developed civilization, one with its own rites, divinities, myths, and heroes.

We might equally ask what might have become of the Parisii— and their city—had the Romans not come and conquered them.

Would the people of the Seine have retained their independence and identity? Probably not. Tribes were on the move in the east. In the north another conquest was under way, and without Julius Caesar the Gauls would surely have become Germanic. There lay the alternatives for the Parisii: Latinate versus Teutonic. History and Caesar's military force decided the matter. The Gauls became the Gallo-Romans.

The city that got built was no longer purely a Parisii settlement but, rather, one designed by the Roman worldview. This was perhaps why the Place d'Italie took on a slightly disproportionate irrational importance in my imagination. We are actually quite far from where the first Lutetian houses were huddled together on the banks of the Seine, here in this spot across which Roman legionaries, merchants, and builders made their way. The square once echoed with the sound of wheat wagons bumping along on the uneven stones and the rhythmic march of soldiers. From here the Gauls directed their steps toward Rome, the capital of the world.

In the confusion of cultures, what is certain is that this is where the road starts. And what a road it

Were the Gauls always considered the ancestors of the French?

No, actually, they weren't. Under the Romans, the history of France begins in 481, with the sanctification of Clovis, the Christian king of the Franks. This religiously pure and indisputably monarchic beginning satisfyingly invested the country's sovereigns with divine right. This changed in the nineteenth century during the Second Republic, when Napoleon III wanted to ground his empire in a different kind of family tree, one less marked by religion. What was needed was a schism, a break in the chronology, and the Gauls provided him with one. So passionate was he about these hypothetical ancestors that he undertook a study of them—in several volumes—called *History of Julius Caesar*. Despite the title, the scope of what the French emperor had to say went far beyond a discussion of the Roman dictator.

In fact, Napoleon III returned the Gauls to their rightful place in history. In 1861, he ordered archaeological digs to be undertaken on the spot in Burgundy where Alésia was thought to have been located, and the experts did everything they could to oblige him. To Napoleon it *(Cont.)*

was a matter of finding out whether any real vestiges of this famous battle, which suddenly had become one of the major events of French history, could be found. And the searchers came through. They unearthed more than five hundred pieces of Gallic money, two bronze pieces stamped with "Vercingetorix," one hundred and forty-four Roman coins, some ditches, fences, and a stele on which was written "ALI-SILA." It was actually quite a rich archaeological haul. Some wondered whether it wasn't a little too rich.

In any case, the emperor henceforth ruled over Alésia. In 1865, a large statue of Vercingetorix rose over the battlefield that was now an archaeological site. The sculptor, Aimé Millet, saw to it that the leader of the Arverni bore a striking resemblance to Napoleon III.

was, connecting Gaul with its new identity. We might mourn the disappearance of Gallic culture. However, rather than shed tears over that which was lost, let us focus on what the Gauls gained from Romanization—what the Romans did for the Gauls. From total and abject defeat emerged a revived culture and a new nation.

In Lutetia, the changes were set, literally, in stone. The century opening up ushered in an era of peace, reconciliation, and growth, and indeed for that growth to take place Lutetia needed a break from the seemingly endless troubles. History seemed to be smiling benevolently down on the future Paris. No one was being slaughtered, nor were there armies on the move; the era of death in combat, glorious or otherwise, was past, and both Parisii and Romans could devote themselves to building something new. Never again would the city enjoy such an extended period of peace.

Let's follow the footsteps of someone arriving in Lutetia from Rome. He would have first passed through what is today the Porte d'Italie, then taken what used to be called the Avenue Italie, which led him across the future site of Place d'Italie before arriving at the location of the current Avenue des Gobelins, then headed up to Place Saint-Médard, where, by means of what is now Rue Mouffetard, he would have begun the ascent up the hill.

For the Roman, Lutetia was a city upon a hill. It would not be subject to the whims of the river, as had been the earlier settlements.

Indeed the specifically Roman part of the city would have been ill at ease with all those shifting and muddy wetlands. In the image of Rome and its seven hills, it sought the higher ground. Therefore to reach the Roman Lutetia we must, like our Roman citizen, climb Mount Sainte-Geneviève, then known as Mons Cetarius—the "mountain of fish tanks," proving at least that the Seine's influence had not entirely evaporated.

The *Pax Romana* turned Lutetia into an open city, one without fortifications. The traveler to the summit of Mons Cetarius would therefore have had an unobstructed view of the city spreading out below him.

By the second century A.D., Lutetia became a place where every kind of pleasure could be found—a place in which to find amusement and distraction. The Roman's gaze would immediately be drawn by an enormous construction site: the amphitheater. Stretched across a flat area between the hill and the river, slightly apart from the city, it would eventually hold as many as fifteen thousand people in rows rising gradually in an arc. The site had been chosen for its very specific topography, for it benefited from the light of the rising sun, and spectators could expect to enjoy an unobstructed view of the Bièvre bend in the river; in the distance were two wooded hills that would become Ménilmontant and Belleville. It was a glorious spot.

This amphitheater, the most beautiful and opulent in all of Gaul, was made of sculpted stones and fluted columns, with statues devoted to the adoration of the gods. The technical achievement was by itself impressive—the niches dug into the far wall, for example, provided perfect acoustics. Here was quite literally the height of comfort: a giant canvas covering protected spectators from the heat of the sun or the inconvenience of rain.

Gauls and Romans flocked there, and we can follow their path by redescending the hill a short way by means of the stairway on the Rue Rollin.

When you approached the amphitheater, you could feel the power of Rome emanating from its imposing façade, comprised of columns and vaulting archways. You entered through two large gates over which caryatids stood sentry, their stony gaze, impassive but not unkind, fixed upon the milling crowd.

Inside there was a great marriage in Roman fashion of giddy bacchanalia and the satisfaction of watching a well-acted tragedy. Colonizers and colonized shared the same passion for the ancient writers. When you wanted to laugh, you went to see a comedy by Plautus, whose *Pot of Gold* was a surefire hit; everyone loved the adventures of an old miser who is overjoyed to discover a caldron filled with gold only to have it turn into his torment, for he lives in fear that a thief will steal it.

There seems little doubt that Euripides's great play *Bacchae* played in the amphitheater, the spectators pressed together while the chorus, from the back of the arena, intoned their plaintive monody, its echoes rolling in waves up the rising rows of seats.

Sometimes blood was spilled in the Lutetia arena, and theater became circus. Rome's games were not always as peaceful and innocent as the comedies of Plautus or the tragedies of Euripides. Half-starved and enraged lions and tigers held in cages were set free across the sand only to be disemboweled by gladiators, whose swords and nets were sometimes not enough to protect them. The crowd emitted a low groan when a fighter was taken down by powerful claws and his throat ripped open.

Far better was when the gladiators were pitted against each other. There were the gladiatorial superstars the crowds rushed to see, men who personified power and virility. In a worthy battle, meaning one that was intended to offer a lesson in courage, these gladiators offered the spectacle of heightened violence that was played out at Lutetia just as it was across the empire. They fought to the last measure of their strength and ability until they succumbed to the sharp points of the victor's trident and their blood pooled on the ground. Finally their bodies were taken away through the gate of Libitina, the goddess of death. The crowd by this point would have been on its feet in ecstasy.

The next day there would be a play by Plautus, and the old miser would make them laugh again. That's what took place in the Lutetia arena.

The vast beauty of the arena spoke to the importance of Lutetia to Roman Gaul. After barely a century of existence, the town had become populous and thriving. During this golden age nearly ten thousand inhabitants had settled on the Île de la Cité and started to spread southward onto the Left Bank.

The Right Bank, on the other hand, didn't yet have much to show for itself. In the distance, on a hill that was dedicated to religious observance—the future Montmartre—sat a small temple and a few dwellings placed under the protection of the gods. This side of the river was mostly a working construction site and used for food storage. Here was where you looked for the silty clay used in the making of tiles; where the fields of wheat were planted and cattle were raised. It represented the antithesis of design and city planning; this was a place where you could scavenge for whatever was necessary to ensure the elegant and refined lifestyle that could be found on the other side of the river.

What remains of the arena today?

The arenas of Lutetia were destroyed during the barbarian invasions in A.D. 280. The amphitheater was first turned into a cemetery, and then filled in after the construction of a fortified wall by Philippe Auguste at the beginning of the thirteenth century. Then it was forgotten about until the nineteenth century and the rage for archaeology. During some excavation on the Rue Monge that began in 1860, workers came across very strange things while digging at number 49. They uncovered masonry, then more was found when the General Company of Omnibuses acquired the land next to it to use as their depot. Gradually the arena was brought to the surface. Officials fretted over the discovery, since the growing city needed a large street that ran straight. Holdovers from antiquity were simply impediments to progress, and a good part of the amphitheater was destroyed. Indeed the entire structure seemed destined for oblivion. Then in 1883 Victor Hugo, the venerated author of *The Hunchback of Notre Dame*, wrote this letter to the municipal council: "It is simply not possible that Paris, the city of the future, would ignore living proof of the city on which it is built. The past guides the future.

(Cont.)

The arenas are the mark of the great city and a unique monument to it. The municipal council that destroys them in some manner destroys itself. Preserve the arenas of Lutetia. Preserve them at any cost. You will perform a useful action and, of even greater value, you will offer a great example." The great man had spoken; the council approved funds to clear out the arenas, which were opened to the public in 1896.

In this new village, a number of Gauls, following the example of the Romans, had given up their frail huts with thatch roofs that had been their homes in ancient Lutèce and opted for more solid—and even opulent—accommodations. The high and the low began to find common ground, for in Upper Lutetia lived mainly the Romans and in Lower Lutetia, on the island, lived the Gauls. Gradually it became habitual to call this Lower Lutetia *Civitas Parisiorum*, meaning "the city of the Parisii." "Paris" was moving closer to coming into being.

What did the denizens of Lower Lutetia do? As I've mentioned, they lived off the Seine, and most of their jobs were connected directly or indirectly with water. There were those who loaded and unloaded boats, those who transported bundles of fluvial deposits, and of course the indispensable fishermen, fish preparers, and fish sellers.

Upper Lutetia was never a Gallic town. In the Roman mode, it was built on the higher elevations, above the cramped and swampy place down below. Nonetheless, it was well provisioned with water, for its inhabitants would never have simply bathed in the river.

Where can you find the ancient baths?

The vaulted cellar of the restaurant Le Coupe-Chou is a vestige of the second century A.D. baths, as well as being the oldest cellar in all of Paris. During construction they made this precious find: hot-water channels and a Gallo-Roman swimming pool.

A reservoir was built about fifteen miles away, one which provided water by means of the gradual slope of an aqueduct. The water flowed into the town through a network of clay or lead pipes that fed the fountains and most especially the thermal baths. To the Romans, the baths were both a necessity and the quintessence of luxury and comfort. No city could be considered great without public baths. Lutetia boasted three. Two were relatively small: one in the south and the other in the east, in the place where the Collège de France stands today, spread out beneath the Rue de Lanneau.

The most important of all the baths, also dating from the end of the second century, were the Cluny baths, which still exist. Their original name was "Northern baths."

Open to all and free of charge, these baths were a place to unwind, a combination of meeting spot and place for personal hygiene. Everything here was designed for the well-being of the citizen: mosaics, marble, frescoes depicting colorful seaside vistas. After a little exercise, one went into a warm room, known as the *tepidarium*, which literally means "warm room," and then into the "hot room," or *caldarium*, and thence into the *frigidarium*, which was of course the "cold room," and finally into the resting room, where you met up with friends for gossip and small talk.

Aside from a hint of Gallic influence, the town's architecture was prototypically Roman. The rectilinear streets produced right angles and created public spaces in which patrician villas and open areas could be found. The main street of this Roman Lutetia

Who built the Cluny baths?

These baths clearly reveal Roman influence. However, it would be a mistake to assume that they are the unadulterated implantation of the occupying force on an obedient populace. The Parisii themselves were involved in the construction of the building, which has endured for the ages. Decoration in the *frigidarium*, for example, shows boats loaded down with weapons and goods. This manner of signing the work shows clearly the influence of the sailors in the construction. These men who governed commerce on the river and represented a kind of municipal council did not want to give the Romans sole responsibility for the construction of such an important edifice. The Parisii were aware that they needed to take their fates into their own hands and get involved in the organization and governance of the town. It is without question due to this that Lutetia would become Paris.

Where were the *cardo maximus* and the forum located?

The *cardo* lies along what is today Rue Saint-Jacques, and extends into the Right Bank by Rue Saint-Martin. It is said that the route was originally made by woolly mammoths coming down from the hills to drink the water of the Seine. A pretty tale, to be sure, but there was indeed a path here long before the Romans arrived, long before Lutetia existed, a road that started in Spain and led to the North Sea.

The Roman paving stones along Rue Saint-Jacques have disappeared, but in front of the church Saint-Julien-le-Pauvre, at the intersection between the Roman path of Italy and the axial *cardo* of Saint-Jacques, an old paving stone was left behind the ancient well and on the edge, directly in front of the main door. There is what remains of Paris's oldest road.

In fact, right next door in Viviani Square, you will find the city's oldest tree, a locust originally from North America that was planted in 1602 by botanist Jean Robin (in French a locust is called a *robinier*), for whom it is named. This tree still seems green but don't be fooled: the first layer of leaves belong to a vine climbing the odd-looking concrete structure designed to hold up the venerable old locust.

(Cont.)

was the *cardo maximus,* which crossed through the Upper Lutetia and zigzagged down to a bridge and into the Lower Lutetia. This was the artery from the city's heart—hence the name—along which pumped its lifeblood. Everything that went into Lutetia did so by means of the *cardo,* and it was the path by which Parisii learned to build a city. The lessons that it imparted would not be lost later when it came to creating a far larger city.

Along this route were the two pottery workshops that served Lutetia. Situated between the town and the countryside on this busy thoroughfare, artisans who worked there provisioned the city's fancy shops, as well as the farmers from the surrounding countryside, and eventually even the occasional traveler.

By means of the *cardo maximus,* one climbed up to the heights of Mons Centarius. This was, as I've suggested, the town's epicenter: the forum, a vast esplanade bordered by columns. Here was where one was seen, and did business, and engaged in banter. The wall enclosing the road was bordered on two sides by a covered gallery lined with shops. Lutetians, then as now, went shopping, looking to buy olive oil, lotions, or jewelry.

To create this beating heart of Lutetia, the builders did not bend to circumstance; they shaped the hill in order to make its slopes more gradual and more gracious. The Romans were great builders and didn't hesitate to force nature to adhere to the demands of thoughtful city planning. One can imagine how dumbfounded were the Parisii when they looked up at these projects, which must have seemed simultaneously titanic and mysterious. Those who had spent their lives in towns subject to the whims of nature, in modest dwellings that were easily destroyed, must have gazed wondrously at the way in which the Romans built with an eye toward the centuries to come. The Parisii could not yet know that their town was being built for the ages.

Farther along, on the ancient *cardo*, at 254 Rue du Faubourg Saint-Jacques, is a pottery kiln, the miraculously preserved vestige of a craftsman who worked along the edge of the great street, which was an ancient version of an industrial zone.

Moreover, on the Place de la Sorbonne, a circular niche disrupts the symmetry of the square. This is the remains of wells that belonged to two *insulae* (high Roman dwellings).

As for the forum, it succumbed to the exigencies of men and time. What remains of it lies today at 61 Boulevard Saint-Michel, at the entrance to the Vinci parking garage: a piece of the retaining wall that somehow was preserved. Meager consolation.

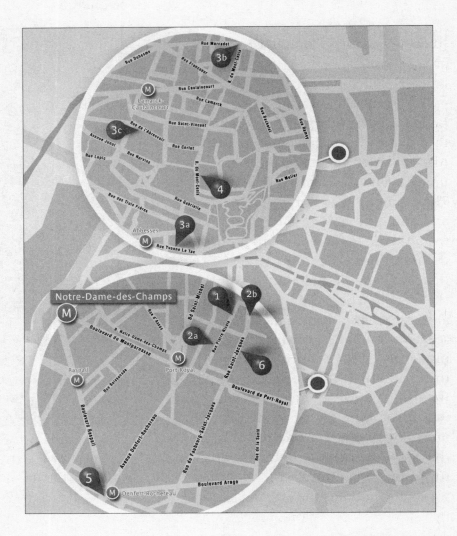

1. The Crypt of Saint Denis, the first cathedral in Paris. 2a–2b. The scattered remnants of Paris's first cathedral. 3a–3c. The long walk of Saint Denis. 4. The church Saint-Pierre-de-Montmartre (2 Rue du Mont-Cenis). The four marble columns here are the last remnants of the Temple of Mercury. 5. The catacombs. 6. The catacombs were once officially called *fief des tombes* ("stronghold of graves"). An engraved inscription, FDT, on the stone wall at 163 bis Rue Saint-Jacques, serves as a reminder.

The Martyrdom of Saint Denis

The escalator at the mouth of the Notre-Dame-des-Champs Métro stop disgorges subway voyagers right into the heart of Boulevard Raspail; pedestrians have no choice other than to disrupt the flow of traffic in an attempt to make it to the safety of the far sidewalk. I came here seeking a memory of ancient Lutetia, but nothing remains to evoke it. Straight in front of you, in a ramshackle little square, stands a statue of Captain Dreyfus, the Jewish military officer wrongly accused of espionage at the end of the nineteenth century. A little farther along, in Montparnasse, the church of Notre-Dame-des-Champs unfolds with its end-of-century rococo façade, a witness to the faith that animated the bourgeoisie of the Second Empire.

In these oddly shaped places away from the original center we enter into the domain of legend and mystique. Everything is hidden from those looking for obvious signs and dead certainties. To find what you seek you have to listen for the gentle breeze of credo and credulity.

By the middle of the third century, Lutetia had become an important center, important enough at least for Christians to dream of coming to convert the population. For this was a place of worship of Toutatis and Jupiter, Gallic gods and Roman gods sharing the same altars.

Meanwhile, in Italy, an energetic bishop named Dionysius burned with an inextinguishable fire for Christ and wanted to spread the True Faith, to extend the religion of the crucified God and to save those souls lost to paganism. He humbly placed himself at the feet of the bishop of Rome, the successor to Saint Peter, and implored of him a mission of catechization. The bishop had other things to preoccupy his thoughts, such as ensuring the survival of Christianity in the face of persecution. Spreading the Good Word was put off for better times. He thought he had gotten rid of this irritating neophyte by sending him on a mission to convert the Gauls, and good luck to him! It was well known that Gauls were resistant to all change and clung obstinately to their old idols. Their reputation did not deter Dionysius, who was happily willing to face any difficulties and if necessary to level mountaintops to help Christ the King triumph.

With two companions, the priest Rusticus and the deacon Eleutherius, Dionysius, now known as Denis, made his way to Lutetia in about A.D. 250. The three men made their way into the city by way of the *cardo maximus* and walked straight to the forum. They were appalled by what they found: a population given over to pleasures and to false idols. Everything disgusted the ascetic Christians: shops devoted to women's vanity and sacrifices made to stone statues. Those who dreamed of a just and beneficent God whose benevolent gaze could overturn the despair of the human soul simply could not understand how one could worship these vulgar superstitions.

So they put some distance between themselves and the town and sought refuge in the surrounding vineyards that stretched into the distance, there to practice and to teach this new religion. Eventually, Denis's devotion attracted small crowds who were willing to be converted. But danger was close behind; even here, Christians were persecuted. To protect themselves, they continued to evangelize but now in the secrecy of an abandoned quarry, or in an underground passageway from which the stone that went into the construction of Lutetia had been dug. The Christians held their ceremonies in secrecy, and the clandestine nature of it deepened fervency and suspicion.

The first furtive mass they held was sung in one of their hidden sanctuaries, and the name given it by tradition was "Notre-Dame-des-Champs"—Our Lady of the Fields—though actually rather than "fields," it should have been called "depths"—Notre-Dame-des-Profondeurs. Here in this improbable location the first believers affirmed their faith. Out of the darkness of this cave, which eventually became a cathedral, grew Paris's Christian future.

Trembling as they huddled around Denis were Gallic and Roman families determined to be baptized, whatever the risks. Enveloped in a darkness broken only by the flickering flames of the small oil lamps, Denis spoke. Wearing his white robes, his eyes flashing in the dim light, he spoke movingly about Jerusalem and Golgotha. And the great cross of dark wood barely visible in the shadows lent dramatic and tangible authority to what he was telling them.

To locate the spirit of Paris's first Christians, a better option is to visit the catacombs, whose entrance

What happened to Paris's first cathedral?

Given that Saint Denis was the first bishop of Paris, the secret church in which he catechized was indeed the city's first cathedral. To find the spot when you come out of the Métro, you have to walk up Rue Notre-Dame-des-Champs, for the key to the enigma can be found at the end. After having crossed Boulevard Saint-Michel, you find yourself on Rue Pierre-Nicole, a small and straight path that seems somehow sleepily provincial. Pushed up against the brick walls of a high school is an enormous structure of wood and flagstones of the type that tended to flourish in modernist architecture of the 1960s.

Impassive, the building's doorman refuses access to this wandering historian. This is private property, he explains. To gain access and to seek the trail of Denis will take persistence. Which paid off. Thanks to one of the building's co-owners I was able to visit the basement.

An elevator, a parking garage in which cars are neatly tucked into evenly spaced spaces marked with white paint, and then suddenly there was a partially concealed door. Once through, we've entered the past, a dark stairway taking us down by degrees into the depths of an ancient quarry. Descending

(Cont.)

gives the impression of going deeper into time. The vaults were stabilized and restored in the nineteenth century, but you can still find more ancient vestiges. Beneath a tombstone sleeps Saint Reginald, who died in 1220. It is said that a vision of the Virgin launched him on his priestly career. The long nave reaches the altar, on which sits the statue of Saint Denis. The centuries of devotion have consecrated the place where he once preached.

Guides for tourists from a century ago still mention the crypt. Later it was swallowed up in the foundations of the building that rose up above it. All that remains of Paris's first cathedral lies buried under this parking garage, partly integrated into the management company that maintains it but which also reserves it only for a select few. It is an absurd situation: the only vestige of the first Christian Parisians has survived because of the good faith of a few private citizens. And yet the history of this place is so rich.

The secret cathedral was replaced by an oratory in the seventh century, and by a church a hundred years following that, and then by a priory that was built in the twelfth century. Finally, at the beginning of the seventeenth century, the Carmelites of Notre-Dame-des-Champs took over the place. The *(Cont.)*

can be found on Place Denfert-Rochereau. Here you can enter into a vast necropolis, the largest in all of Paris, just as Saint Denis once did.

During his time, the necropolis was located beneath the *cardo maximus*, in spaces hollowed out by the ancient quarries. This was one of those lost places, ideal for Saint Denis and the other Christians for whom death was but a passage into the Kingdom of God before the Resurrection. The flesh inhabited the realm of shadows: "catacomb" comes from the Latin *cumbere*, "to rest." This place, which was called "fiefdom of the tombs," has left an enduring memory: we are reminded of it by the inscription FDT (*fief des tombes*) at 163a Rue Saint-Jacques.

The Denfert-Rochereau necropolis that one can now visit was created as late as 1785, and for sanitary reasons. It was located on the city's outskirts and designed to receive bones from the city's churches. The remains of six million people were transported there, including those of Fouquet, Robespierre, Mansart, Marat, Rabelais, Lully, Perrault, Danton, Pascal, Montesquieu, and so many others of note.

But we need to go back. The path that led us to the entrance of the ossuary is that of the foundation of an ancient Roman aqueduct that carried water from Arcueil. Following this path takes us back to the Roman period and to Saint Denis, praying in secrecy and in darkness.

One day in the year 257, Roman legionaries made their way into his underground church. They had come to arrest Denis, Rusticus, and Eleutherius. To the Romans these were troublemakers all. Having repeated the claim that the stone idols were not the true powers in the universe, these rebels had shaken the spirits of even the strongest souls. Were they allowed to continue to preach, the entire social order was at risk. The three men were forthwith led before the prefect Sisinnius Fesceninus, the Emperor Valerian's representative in Lutetia. Like his superior in Rome, the prefect could not abide the disorder that the Christians represented.

In the time of paganism, the emperor was the object of veneration and those who did not adhere to this imperial faith were persecuted, including but not limited to the Christians. For Christians, it was a matter of rendering unto Caesar what was Caesar's and unto God what was God's. They were not much concerned by the temporal; it was the heavenly that preoccupied them. In any case, Christians were not good subjects of the emperor and their loyalty was always in

Revolution ravaged the convent—as it did so many places of worship—but the tomb of Saint-Denis, hidden in the depths, escaped destruction. In 1802, when the sisters rebought the parcel of land above the tomb and built a more conventional space. These buildings were demolished when the convent closed definitively in 1908.

From this long stretch of history, a few scattered remnants are still visible today:

- The stone frame of one of the convent's entrances that was conserved but integrated into a store that was built on the ground floor of the modern building at 284 Rue Saint-Jacques.
- A small oratory enclosed in the private gardens of 37 Rue Pierre-Nicole.
- And of course, the tomb located beneath the parking garage of 14a Rue Pierre-Nicole, along with several fragments of the convent walls brought up during the new construction.

Where did Saint Denis's long walk lead him?

The hill on which Saint Denis was beheaded took the name Mont-des-Martyrs—Hill of Martyrs—which eventually became shortened to "Montmartre." The hill had already been sacred for quite some time. A temple dedicated to Mercury was almost certainly built there by the Romans. In 1133, Louis VI acquired the hill and founded a Benedictine abbey there. The abbey was ransacked during the Revolution and the last mother superior, elderly, deaf, and blind, was accused of having plotted "deafly and blindly against the Republic."

Today the white pastry dome of Sacré-Coeur recalls Montmartre's religious past. The building's foundation stone was set in place in 1875 and it is said that the dome was built to "expiate the crimes of the Commune" (about which more later in the chronology). That's actually not the case. The decision to restore Montmartre to its religious past had already been made a few years earlier, during the reign of Napoleon III.

As for Saint Denis, headless, he would have left the hilltop of Montmartre by means of Rue du Mont-Cenis. He would then have doubled back along Rue de l'Abreuvoir to wash his head in the fountain in Place de Girar-
(Cont.)

doubt, which was even more dangerous to the social order; they rejected the official religion and recognized only Jesus as the son of God.

Prefect Fesceninus was ready to make an example of these men, but equally prepared to be magnanimous in the event of repentance. He therefore offered the prisoners a choice: submission to the emperor or death.

"No man can force me to submit to the emperor, for it is Christ who rules," replied Denis.

He was speaking in a language with which Fesceninus was unfamiliar. The best that the prefect could do was to stop the man's ravings. To teach him to think in a more righteous manner the prefect ordered Denis's head to be separated from his body.

In their prison, awaiting the execution of their sentence, Denis and his two codisciples continued, despite the circumstances, to preach the great mystery of the Redemption of Humanity and together celebrated one final mass.

Soon the three men were taken from their cell and dragged to the top of the highest hill in Lutetia, from which their fate could be observed by one and all. A cross was raised on which Denis was tied and his head cut off. Then, a miracle! The lifeless body was transfigured by the apparition of the Savior. Headless, it came to life, undid the bonds that held it, and started to walk. Denis picked up his own head and carried it over to a fountain, where he washed it off, and then made his way back down the hill. He walked for about ten miles until, finally, he confided his severed head to a good Roman woman named Catulla. He then collapsed in a heap. Catulla respectfully buried the pious man in the very spot where he had expired. And on this spot instantly grew a single blade of white wheat, a final miracle.

What remains of Denis the martyr in Lutetia? The miracle was probably not even noticed. Heads were being removed at so rapid a clip at the time that no one paid much attention.

don, where a statue commemorates the occasion. Then he would have gotten back on Rue Mont-Cenis along which if you walk you can see at number 63, at the corner of Rue Maradet, the turret of a house that dates from the fifteenth century, the oldest construction in Montmartre. The turret offers a modicum more authenticity than Place du Tertre, which looks like it came out of Disneyland.

Saint Denis thus walked about ten miles holding his head in his hands. The place where he was buried is today Saint-Denis Basilica.

Around his tomb, which visitors can still admire in the cathedral's crypt, a mausoleum was built. In the seventh century, King Dagobert decided to found a monastery and to make the martyr's mausoleum into a final resting place for himself and his family. Thus Saint-Denis became the necropolis for the kings of France.

The Lutetians had other troubles. The city had enjoyed peace and prosperity for more than a century and now was about to lose them.

Nothing in Imperial Rome was working any longer. This had been happening for some time. One emperor was replaced by another and their followers tore at each other's throats; authority passed to whoever survived. It was an age of backroom deals, plots, and treason. Valerian fought in Mesopotamia but was defeated and taken prisoner by the Persians. No one mourned his loss. Romans didn't want this disgraced emperor to return and hence didn't engage in negotiations. The captive rotted in his

Persian dungeon and when he finally died in captivity it was to
the great relief of one and all. This worked out nicely for his son
and coemperor, Gallienus, who became the sole legitimate emperor.

In short, Rome was Rome no more. The emperor was no longer a man far above other men, feared and worshipped both. He
had become a subject for plots, enmeshed in corruption and petty
dealing. The degradation of political tradition and leadership
proved a disaster for the enormous empire, which required stability in order to survive. Into this void came chaos. The empire
was unraveling and the barbarians were at the gates. They could
sense what was happening: the Romans were weak; the time had
come to overwhelm them. The German tribes crossed the Rhine
and invaded Gaul, turning it into a site of savagery and rape. The
enemies pillaged the countryside and took back with them all of
its richest spoils.

Marcus Cassianus Latinius Postumus was a brilliant Roman
general of Gallic ancestry. Sometime around the year 260, when
the German tribes attacked Roman Gaul, Emperor Gallienus and
Postumus prepared to repel them. Each one wanted to go after a
different enemy. The emperor was determined to chase the Alamans back to the east, and the general to push the Franks back
north.

Postumus fought so valiantly that his stature among his troops
skyrocketed: the legionaries were prepared to proclaim their
general the next emperor. But emperor of what, exactly? Of Rome?
Of Gaul? Gallienus, who sensed that his dynasty was in trouble,
gave his son Saloninus the title of Augustus: he, and no one else,
would succeed his father. Thus they hoped to moderate the ambitions of the Gallic general.

But these were hard times for the son of an emperor. Postumus could not abide the thought that one day Roman authority
would be assumed by this dullard Saloninus and attacked Cologne, capturing Augustus Saloninus and promptly executing him.
All that remained for him to do was assume the imperial symbols. His soldiers pronounced him emperor of Gaul. His image

became familiar to one and all—his handsome visage, full beard, and golden crown were set on the coins minted to regulate the economy of his new domain.

As far as Rome was concerned, Postumus was nothing but a usurper, of course, but one whose ambitions, happily, seemed rather limited. He apparently did not have in mind toppling the Roman emperor, nor crossing the Rubicon, nor trying to make himself legitimate in the eyes of the Senate, and did not seem to call into question his "Romanness."

He did finally want to rule, even though he avoided assuming the supreme title and preferred to refer to himself more modestly as "Restorer of the Gauls." Still, by unifying the Gauls under his power he was effectively separating them from the Romans. For the first time in a long while, Gaul and Rome were separate political entities, no longer responding to the same authority.

As for Gallienus, while such insubordination galled him, the Alamans were just then giving him all that he could handle; the German tribe was attempting to cross the borders, which needed constant supervision. So a kind of tacit agreement rose up between the emperor of Rome and the Restorer of the Gauls, one from which each gained something: Postumus was in charge of defending the Rhine and in exchange was given control of Brittany, Spain, and a major part of Gaul.

Things eventually ended badly for Postumus. Having overcome so many obstacles on his rise to power he ended up being killed by his own soldiers. In 268, when the town of Mogontiacum revolted against his authority, Postumus tried to bring the seditious town under control and put the leaders of the mutiny to death. This justice, though expedited, was not enough for the Gallic troops, who wanted to pillage the city. What was the point of going to war, after all, if you couldn't gain something from doing so.

Postumus refused to let them. He was not willing to see a town in his empire pillaged, particularly a town as valuable as Mogontiacum, which was critical to the defense of the Rhine. The boorish soldiers would have none of this line of reasoning; they wanted to enrich themselves and nothing else would satisfy them.

The Restorer of the Gauls stood in their way; he would simply have to be brought down. Postumus and his son and his personal guards were all massacred. Thus, Postumus passed from this life. He had reigned over the Gauls for ten years, succeeded in pushing back the invaders, and brought to the region financial prosperity.

These events, which had repercussions from Brittany all the way down to Spain, shook Lutetia profoundly. Tension was palpable on the banks of the Seine. Hordes of German barbarians wearing helmets and carrying hatchets were roaming the countryside, destroying the harvest and pillaging. Out of caution these tribes left Lutetia alone. On the other hand, the part of Lutetia that extended onto the Left Bank was beyond the city gates; it was wealthy, vulnerable, and ripe for the taking. Hordes suddenly descended upon it and then disappeared just as quickly.

When the Germanic tribes had moved off, they left the field to *bagaudes,* armed brigands (from the Celtic term *bagad,* meaning "band"). These bands, comprised of thieves, deserters from various armies, and dispossessed peasants, avoided attacking the Roman legions and let the cities be, but they spread terror throughout the countryside.

The hills were no longer merely home to wild beasts and spirits. A ragtag army lived in the crevices. Surviving on the remains of the empire, these bandits ravaged villages and rural dwellings, massacring and raping, carrying off anything of value. Thus sometimes could be seen on these distant paths cohorts comprised of bloodthirsty men, loaded down with golden cups and various weapons, carrying jars filled with the finest wines, pushing before them fattened sheep and cattle and dragging behind them terrified women with bound hands who stifled their tears so as not to awaken the cruelty of their new masters.

Between the double threat of barbarians and *bagaudes,* the Roman aristocracy abandoned Lutetia sometime around 270. The elegant and prosperous city that had stretched along the Left Bank was deserted. The *cardo maximus* on which beautiful Roman women had paraded became rutted and potholed, the houses that lined the road were abandoned and fell into ruin. A bit lower down, the forum—in which only shortly before the flames of sacrifices made to the gods had burned, the forum where merchants sold rich jewels and sweet-smelling ointments—was nothing but an empty shell.

Against every expectation, the empire of Gaul did not collapse with the death of its "restorer." A successor rose up, replaced the slain leader, and assured continuity: Tetricus, a Roman senator born to a Romanized Gallic aristocratic family, seized the reins of power. Unlike his predecessor he was not a military man but a "politician." Tetricus knew that Gaul would one day soon again fall under the sole authority of Rome. The empire of Gaul was condemned to rejoin the Roman escutcheon. His job was essentially limited to that of preserving Gaul at a moment when it was being attacked along several fronts, and while the regime on the Tiber River was showing real signs of weakness.

And indeed, in 273, the emperor Aurelian undertook the reconquering of lost provinces. Near Châlons-en-Champagne, Tetricus and his troops capitulated without great resistance. Aurelian celebrated his triumph with great pomp. At last the empire was reunited. Meat was roasted and prisoners from all the barbarian nations were paraded in the streets. Tetricus was led through the streets of Rome. The Gaul was the silent living symbol of the all-powerful Aurelian, the emperor who had turned into the "restorer of the Roman world."

After his unrivaled triumph, the victorious emperor quickly pardoned Tetricus, and the former chief of Gaul was not only *not* treated as a defeated enemy but named governor of Lucania in the south of Italy, and given back his place in the senate.

Meanwhile the barbarians continued to threaten Lutetia, which was reduced once again to the Île de la Cité. It was decided that the city, already protected by the river, would be safer still were it surrounded by a fortified wall. All the materials necessary to construct it were at hand. Houses, monuments, and even tombs were despoiled of their ornaments and stones, which were integrated into the ramparts that encircled the island, absorbed the port, and swallowed up the riverbanks.

Henceforth, posted at the extremities of the Cité, guards watched the river. At the slightest suspicious movement the alert was sounded. Lutetia was prepared to defend itself. It seemed impregnable. With access to the water, the woods, and the fields, it would be able to gather together everything necessary to survive a long siege. An army was formed to inhabit the city, and a flotilla sat ready in the river harbor. Lutetia had become an integral part of the defense system of northern Gaul.

By reason of its own precariousness and location, the settlement became a stronghold. However, now deprived of its Left Bank expanses, it no longer had the resources to match the greatness of other places in the empire. Its population was reduced to a bare minimum; its most beautiful edifices were gone. Compared to Poitiers, for example, it paled.

Lutetia, once a great Gallo-Roman city, had become the Gallic city that henceforth would be called Paris, from the name of the *Civitas Parisiorum* that alone survived within its fortified walls. Paris did not, alas, possess the architectural elegance of Lutetia. It was but a small town hunkered down defensively on an island in the middle of a river, trembling in expectation of fresh attacks from the German tribes massing in the north and in the east.

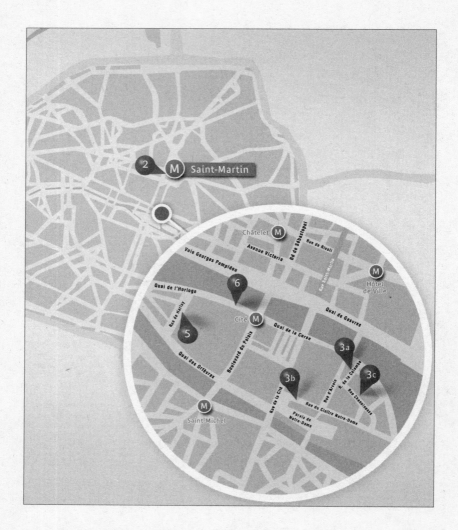

2. Rue Saint-Martin, formerly the *Via Romana* north, the principal axis of the right bank. **3a–3c.** Remnants of the fortified city wall at 6 Rue de la Colombe; in the archaeological crypt under the square in front of Notre-Dame; and at 18 and 20 Rue Chanoinesse. **5.** The royal residence of Julian. **6.** The four towers along the Seine.

Paris, Imperial Residence

The Saint-Martin Métro stop is actually no longer even a stop; it was closed in 1939. Run today by the Salvation Army, its platforms are now intended not for passengers but for the poor. When the city goes through a cold snap, the homeless (who are called the "SDF," or *Sans Domicile Fixe*) can go and find refuge and a little warmth, putting themselves thus into the care of Saint-Martin, the apostle of the Gauls, the man who devoted his life to the poor.

During the winter of 338–339, Martin—a young soldier in the Roman army stationed in Amiens—passed a beggar on his knees who asked for alms. Martin had already given away all that he had, alas, so he drew his sword and cut his cape in the middle and handed half of it to the man. The next night, Christ appeared to Martin. He was carrying the part of the cape that Martin had given to the beggar, and said to him, "Martin the neophyte gave to me this cloth."

It was simply coincidence that the name of the Métro station dedicated to caring for the poor would bear Martin's name—it was chosen for location and logistics, not as a symbol—but the coincidence is nonetheless haunting.

I also find fascinating the contrast between Saint Denis, the underground persecuted priest, and Saint Martin, the legionary who became a bishop and gained a multitude of disciples. Between them a century had passed. The first lit a spark and the second started a fire. By the time of Martin the Church no longer needed to hide itself in the deeps; it could operate in broad daylight, build for the future. Emperor Constantine had shifted the lines. Christians were no longer a persecuted minority.

Starting at the end of the third century, barbarian invasions forced Emperor Constantine to deploy forces along the entire length of the Roman Empire's borders. He realized that he was therefore constrained to delegate a part of his power to various little caesars, territorial emperors. The empire began to break up slowly, and an east-west division began to appear.

Concerned above all about keeping the empire in one piece, Constantine had to fight Roman dissidents before pushing back the barbarians. A certain Maxentius had risen up and announced that he was the only true ruler of the empire. Constantine, under pressure to eliminate this rival, would be forced to fight him and his army at Milvian Bridge, near Rome. In this, the year 312, faced with Maxentius's troops, Constantine had a vision: a cross appeared in the sky above the battlefield where men were tearing each other apart. And the vision came to life, and made these words clear to Constantine, *In hoc signo vinces!* ("By this sign will you conquer!").

Constantine won an overwhelming victory at the Milvian Bridge. Maxentius was killed, drowned in the waters of the Tiber. Now sole emperor, Constantine eventually established his new capital in Byzantium, which he rebaptized Constantinople. The new imperial city would become the heart of the eastern part of the Roman Empire.

Constantine believed that he had been favored and protected by Christ, and thus could do nothing less than renounce the anti-Christian persecution practiced by his predecessors; he relied upon this same new religion to consolidate the unity of the emperor. A year after his triumph at Milvian Bridge, Constantine adopted an "edict of tolerance" in Milan that rallied the Christians to him: ". . . to give to Christians as to everyone the freedom and the possibility to follow the religion of their choice in order that everything that is divine in heavenly rest might be good and right, to ourselves and to all who find themselves under our authority . . ." It was both a prudent strategy and good common sense: the Christians had become predominant in the empire.

After thirty-one years of rule, Constantine died on Sunday, May 22, in the year 337. On his deathbed he asked of the bishop of Nicomedia, "Is there any method of absolving me of all my sins?"

"None," replied the bishop. "Apart from Christian baptism."

The emperor accepted the truth of this and allowed himself to be baptized, hoping thus to be expiated for his crimes and accepted into the paradise promised by the Son of God. However, Constantine's deathbed baptism did not create unanimity and did not establish, once and for all, the new faith. For quite some time to come, Christianity and paganism existed side by side.

About twenty or so years later, Constantine's nephew, the future emperor Julian, took the opposite spiritual path. Born and raised as a Christian but passionate about philosophy, Julian was persuaded that Plato's wisdom exceeded that of biblical monotheism. He returned to worshipping the divinities who peopled the Greek pantheon and wrote a book, *Against the Galileans,* in which he expressed his violent opposition to the Christian "sect": "It is, I think, expedient to set forth to all mankind the reasons by which I was convinced that the fabrication of the Galilaeans is a fiction of men composed by wickedness. Though it has in it nothing divine, by making full use of that part of the soul which loves fable and is childish and foolish, it has induced men to believe that the monstrous tale is truth." His line of argument leaned heavily upon the symbolic value of ancient myths: "Plato gives the name gods to those that are visible, the sun and moon, the stars and the heavens, but these are only the likenesses of the invisible gods.

The sun which is visible to our eyes is the likeness of the intelligible and invisible sun, and again the moon which is visible to our eyes and every one of the stars are likenesses of the intelligible. Accordingly Plato knows of those intelligible and invisible gods which are immanent in and coexist with the creator himself and were begotten and proceeded from him. Naturally, therefore, the creator in Plato's account says 'gods' when he is addressing the invisible beings, and 'of gods,' meaning by this, evidently, the visible gods. And the common creator of both these is he who fashioned the heavens and the earth and the sea and the stars, and begat in the intelligible world the archetypes of these."

In fact the dogma of a single God, preached by those whom Julian calls the "Galileans," brought with it the unavoidable consequence of "insulting the other gods." That is precisely what the young philosopher refused to allow. He would perhaps agree to consider the Father, the Son, and the Holy Ghost as divine forms, but only on the condition that he could accord them a small place alongside the innumerable gods of paganism. For him, monotheism, that of the Christians as well as the Jews, was the product of an intolerance that he could neither understand nor accept. To demonstrate this, he broke with the religion in which he had been raised, embraced the ancient faith of the Greeks, and settled in Athens. Here on philosophy's ancient ground he hoped to find a fruitful end to his thoughts and to lift his spirits to the level of those who had inspired him.

Alas, Julian would soon enough be forced to abandon his cherished studies: the emperor Constantius, who preferred to occupy himself with the eastern part of his empire, named Julian vice-emperor and ordered him to settle in Gaul to govern the country and to fight against the barbarians threatening it. For Julian, this handsome promotion seemed a catastrophe. He would have to enter into real life, putting aside his meditations on the position of the gods in the sky, abandoning his reading of the dialecticians of the past. He would have to strap on the armor, get back on the horse, and command the legions. Distraught, Julian went up to the Parthenon and implored Athena to intervene, to alter the course of earthly events. To this the goddess remained silent, and thus the disappointed young man sadly went on his way to take up his duties as the assistant emperor.

A strange destiny watched over this philosopher-turned-warrior. As it turned out, Julian proved an energetic, brilliant, and highly effective military leader. Against every expectation, the ethereal theorist turned out to be really good at waging war. He was daring enough to take his legions deep into the heart of the Germanic forests, into which no Roman army had ventured for three centuries and no one would risk going afterward. He crushed the Alamans at the Battle of Argentoratum (what today is Strasbourg), pushed Rome's enemies to the far side of the Rhine, and put an end to the pillaging raids. What seemed to be his divine inspiration spread across the empire: the young man who once had been seen as a prince lost to the contemplative life had saved Rome by means of arms. His soldiers carried him in triumph and would willingly have sacrificed their lives if he gave the word.

Between battles and expeditions, Julian went to relax in the cozy little capital formerly known as Lutetia, which he had chosen as his home since January 358. He was alone: his wife, Helen, had stayed in Rome to give birth. The general's stay in Paris was punctuated by forced departures—he had to go out and be a warrior from time to time—but as soon as he was able he returned to the banks of the Seine.

At the extreme end of the Île de la Cité a Roman villa stood, fortresslike, a small piece of Italy located in the middle of Gaul. Ocher-colored walls and black columns surrounded a square courtyard in which fig trees were planted around a pool in which ran clear water. In the middle of this luxurious residence, the banquet hall, watched over by golden eagles and frescoes depicting Bacchus, banquets of an opulence that would have astounded even a Roman were held. Here the cream of Roman society gathered, each member wearing a multifold toga. Julian knew how to entertain these men. Each dinner consisted of three courses: first

When did Paris become Paris?

Paris will always be Paris, of course, but at what point did Paris *become* Paris? Beginning at the end of the third century the city had in large part been abandoned by the Roman population and become the exclusive city of the Gauls. From that moment onward, it would appear that the name Lutetia became increasingly abandoned. The first indication emerged when a Roman military marker dating from 307 was discovered in 1877. It didn't bear the name Lutetia but *Civitas Parisiorum*, or "city of the Parisii." Here is therefore when Paris emerged from Lutetia. This marker, which was reused for a sarcophagus from the Merovingian period, can today be seen in the Musée Carnavalet.

Beginning in the third century, Paris was concentrated on the Île de la Cité and encircled by fortified walls. In the archaeological crypt of the square in front of Notre-Dame, we can see that a fragment of this rampart has miraculously been conserved. Another sign is the thickness of the walls of the building at number 6 Rue de la Colombe.

eggs and olives accompanied by honey wine, then meats, and finally fruit.

This center of power extended to an adjoining building in which Julian's administration busied itself. Julian in effect surrounded himself with a group of councillors and aides who comprised a solid hierarchy on which his authority depended. Pretorian prefect, quaestors, the great chamberlain, military commanders, senior secretaries, they all milled around and saw to the business of governing Gaul, extending from Brittany to the north all the way to Spain in the south. Julian was recognized as the absolute leader of this realm.

To preserve his power, the vice-emperor had first and foremost to be a warrior. He regularly participated in the military exercises of his legions. One day, when he was doing maneuvers, a blow from a blade broke off his shield, such that all he was left holding was the strap. Not a big deal—were it not for Roman superstition. The soldiers around him were in despair, for they saw this as a sinister omen. Julian would have none of it. He turned to his men and, in a firm voice, said, "Be reassured, I did not lose my grip!"

His words overcame doubts and conquered fears. Julian knew how to handle power, and the philosopher in him understood what that power meant. What he loved above all was to walk in the city that he stubbornly referred to as Lutetia, in the Roman manner, though the inhabitants themselves were already referring to it as Paris.

Julian was thus one of Paris's first strollers, among the first to love the city for more than simply the contingencies of military tactics or the exigencies of imperial power. He loved Paris for its main island, so near to the shores and yet protected from them. He loved Paris when the river was calm. He loved Paris when suddenly the waters swelled and rose up to the level of the houses along its banks. He loved Paris when he walked about, dressed as a simple legionary, through the muddy alleys, when the shops that were largely open-air overflowed with ham haunches, sausages, pig heads, when the fish that had been freshly caught and newly made cheeses covered the shelves, when the sweet scent of fermented barley and mint wafted out the windows of a place where they were preparing the *cervesia*, the Celtic beer so passionately embraced by the Parisii. He loved Paris for the merchants.

"Shopkeeper, have you got some wine spiced with pepper?"

"I do."

"Well then, there's a good fellow, fill my gourd with it."

The seasoned soldier that Julian now was also appreciated the warships that crossed in front of the Île de la Cité and troops that were encamped on the Right Bank. The constant deployments of this military force reassured him. They helped him feel protected, beyond the shocks of the world, happily ensconced in his own little world. It was a small world, to be sure, located at a terrestrial and fluvial crossroads, but it was to him an enchanting one.

Not only was Julian the first lover of Paris, he was its first bard. He spent his evenings writing feverishly about Lutetia: "It is a small island lying in the river; a wall entirely surrounds it, and wooden bridges lead to it on both sides." As for the Seine, to Julian it was little less than the source of life and purity. "The river supplies quiet water that is very pleasant and very pure, both to look at and to drink, if one wants. Actually, given that one lives on an island, it is mostly from the river from which one takes water."

Julian loved everything in Lutetia, aside, that is, from "the rusticness of the Gauls and the harshness of the winter." The Gauls did not exactly offer the kind of sophistication the young man was accustomed to; they used a strange language and practiced strange customs, and they prayed to gods that were unknown to the Roman nobility. There was thus a barbarian element to them that only a great Latin civilization might succeed in rooting out.

On the other hand, as far as the winters went, Julian was right to be wary. The second winter he spent in Lutetia was exceptionally glacial, as we can see in an apocalyptic portrait he made of it: "The river carried giant slabs of marble . . . massive frozen great white blocks that smashed into one another and nearly formed a continuous passage, a road on the current."

It was therefore necessary to heat the house on the Île. *Braseros*—braziers—were lit regularly. One night Julian asked for more of them to help fight off the frigid temperatures. Eventually he was able to fall asleep—only suddenly to wake up, shaken by a coughing fit. His room was filled with smoke and he was suffocating; gasping for breath, his eyes stinging and his throat rasping, he screamed as loudly as he could, then blacked out. His cries for help were heard; slaves burst into the smoke-filled room and dragged out his inanimate body into the courtyard. The fresh air revived Julian, whose rise to power had nearly been cut short by the braziers. What would have happened to Paris had he asphyxiated that night? It would have become and remained an accursed Gallic town feared by the superstitious Romans.

Of course Julian survived the accident, and when spring arrived and finally melted the ice on the river he set off for the Rhine, to strengthen the fortresses and to deal with the little barbarian kings who had sprung up in the borderland between the Alamans and Burgundy. He returned to Lutetia at the end of fall. It was said that henceforth he would not leave his residence. Helen had joined him there and he would content himself from then on with living a peaceful life on the banks of the Seine. Perhaps this might have come to pass, had politics not thrown the region into turmoil.

Because Julian had been so effective in securing Gaul's stability, his soldiers would soon be sent to the East, in order to wage war against the Persians. But the idea of leaving the safe confines of Lutetia to wander around in the deserts of Mesopotamia was unacceptable. Starting in the month of February in the year 360, the legionaries revolted. They crossed the city, swearing that they would never leave Julian. (Protests in the streets of Paris? Now that's something new!)

The vice-emperor asserted his authority and addressed his Gallic soldiers, telling them that he would do what he could to see that they would not leave for the East.

"Let your anger cool for a bit, I beg you, and it will be a simple matter to get what you wish without rebellion and without revolutionary means. The pull of your native land is so strong, and you fear foreign cultures to which you are not habituated. So go home. You will never go beyond the Alps, since you do not wish to. I will personally see to your exclusion by means of appropriate measures with Emperor Constantius, who is a very wise prince and capable of seeing reason."

Julian's words calmed his soldiers somewhat, but, come spring, tensions rose again and a mix of Roman and Gallic legionaries decided to force the issue.

"Julian Augustus!"

They called out his name in unison, as if hailing an emperor. To them, he was their emperor, distant as they were from the intrigues of an emperor whom they never saw but who seemed a constant threat.

The soldiers burst into Julian's residence and asked their general to seize the diadem and crown himself. There was no diadem, however. They looked around for something that might stand for one. Someone suggested the necklace worn by his wife, Helen. Julian refused. Her jewels were not to be touched. Someone else suggested a gold plate that was part of a horse harness. Julian grimaced at this. It seemed unworthy of his greatness. There seemed no solution to the problem.

Then a centurion by the name of Maurus undid his necklace

What remains of Julian's imperial residence?

Of the actual residence, nothing remains, but the location has remained a palace across the centuries. Today it is the location of the city's Palais de Justice. Like most of the rest of the Île de la Cité, the current building dates from the works of Baron Haussmann, in the second half of the nineteenth century. The neo-Gothic southern façade only dates from the beginning of the twentieth century and yet it contains the traces of history, given that it shows the gouges and holes made by bullets fired during the liberation of the city in August 1944.

Before that, in the period of the Franks, the palace had become a royal palace, where at least according to medieval tradition, the king's room contained the bed of Justice. The throne was consolidated during the reign of Saint Louis, who would add Sainte-Chapelle, the oldest structure still standing in the spot.

The four towers along the Seine each have a name. The first, which is square-shaped, is the Clock Tower, as one side of it featured the first public clock, a gift of Charles V to Parisians in 1371, but the one in place now dates from 1585. At the top of this tower is a vaulted room in which Charles liked to go to look out *(Cont.)*

of golden braid and placed it on Julian's head. And so it was accomplished. By means of this simple gesture, supported by the entire army of Gaul, Julian was made emperor.

"I promise you each five pieces of gold and a livre of silver!" announced the new sovereign.

Instantly strong arms seized him and lifted him onto a soldier's shield and he was carried off by four soldiers. This was how Julian appeared before the crowd of Parisians, some of whom welcomed their leader joyously.

What about Emperor Constantius? Well, he was quite simply dethroned.

The question was whether Julian would make Lutetia the capital of his new empire. The first pressing problem facing him was his face—he needed to grow his beard, considered a manly attribute and indispensable to his high position. Once that was accomplished, he left Lutetia at the beginning of the summer to lead a new military campaign—his fifth—to the lands beyond the Rhine. Though he didn't know it at the time, he would never return again to the banks of the Seine.

Lutetia the imperial city would become in this same year of 360 an ecclesiastical city. The Gallic bishops decided to convene an important council there whose essential goal was to unify the flock and condemn Christian heresies, and in particular Arianism, which recognized neither the divinity of Christ nor the authority of the pope. Paris thus became in an instant the most dogmatic center of Roman Catholicism.

During this time, Julian led his troops into combat. That he was emperor changed very little. He was fighting against the Franks, the Attuaries, and the Alamans.

over the city, and which contains a bell that rang for three days and three nights to announce the birth or death of a king. After that is Caesar's Tower (a modern designation to recognize the palace's Roman ancestry); the Silver Tower (to signify the wealth of kings); and the Bonbec Tower—roughly "good beak"—the oldest of them all and decorated during the time of Saint Louis. This is where the torture chamber was located, the place where beaks were made to open and confessions spilled out.

For his part, Constantius was not deeply impressed by Julian's military victories and took no action against this puny little philosopher whom he had lifted up to the greatest responsibilities, and who had repaid him by betraying him in order to gain the favor of a few legionaries. Eventually Constantius determined that he wasn't simply going to relinquish power without a fight and decided to quash this upstart. His imperial army marched on Julian's imperial army, pitting emperor against emperor. There was to be no fight, for along the way Constantius very opportunely delivered up his soul and his scepter to the Eternal Father.

Now the sole emperor, uncontested and venerated, Julian called for an edict of toleration, but that did not make everyone happy. The former philosopher authorized all religions and banned measures against the pagans, Jews, and dissident Christians. At the same time he revealed his preference for paganism, for he had no confidence in the Christians, and to humiliate them he forbade them from teaching classical poetry, under the pretext that it contained verses about gods that they maintained they had renounced. Nonetheless he also refused to persecute the disciples of Christ.

"I hope that the Christians will recognize their own errors without my having to make them."

Finally Julian established himself in Antioch in the East, to prepare for battle against the Persians. In the spring of 363, he led a victorious military campaign that reached Ctesiphon, the Persian capital. But he had gone too far too quickly and had to retreat, and in the process was mortally wounded on June 26. He died at the age of thirty-one, very far indeed from his beloved Lutetia.

In Gaul, the emperors changed but not their worries. The Alamans were threatening yet again. Valentinian, coemperor with his brother Valens, put himself into Julian's slippers. While Valens was playing at being emperor in Constantinople, Valentinian took up residence in the city of the Parisii in 365. There he occupied the Roman palace. He already knew it well, having served there under Julian and often visited it. By doing so, he was giving notice that he was taking the place of the dead emperor. Lutetia was thus promoted to the ranks of putative capitals of the Western Empire. For two years, Valentinian would work on reconstructing the area around the palace, though he was frequently called away from it.

Despite being an adopted son of Paris, Valentinian deserves no less recognition. From his residence on the Île de la Cité were issued imperial edicts that spread the fame of the city far and wide. And in the city's streets he welcomed with great pomp General Jovinus, who had crushed the Germanic tribes. Dressed in his red toga and riding a white horse, Valentinian approached the conquering general, who entered Paris on his war steed. The two men dismounted and walked together to receive the city's welcome. Who at this point could question that the city of the Parisii had become the center of the world?

Valentinian believed that he had done enough to emulate Julian, though from the point of view of the Parisii, he was but a pale reflection of the former emperor. He imitated the attitudes and passions of his predecessor but lacked the range and the quality of his thought, and therefore his attachment to the city was somewhat less than sincere.

Nonetheless Valentinian went there as often as possible. He spent some time in Reims to quell a revolt there, and then returned to Paris, only to leave shortly for Amiens, which had signaled the presence of Saxon pirates. He returned again to Paris but immediately fell ill. He had barely recovered when he left and thereafter took up residence for good in Trier, on the banks of the Mosel River, a large city that he probably thought would be more easily transformed into a capital.

It was, in fact, while on his way to Trier that Martin stopped in Paris at the beginning of the winter of 385. He was no longer the young soldier who had impulsively cut his cloak in half at the gates of Amiens; he was older and more substantial. Now he was the bishop of Tours and lived in a monastery that he himself had founded in Marmoutier, where he adhered to a routine that involved vows of poverty, mortification of the flesh, and prayer.

In a Gaul that had adopted Christianity, the friend of the poor had become a considerable figure. When he entered Paris he was followed by a large crowd who carried and jostled him, sensing that the spirit of Christ had arrived with him.

The bishop walked the length of the northern Roman road, and the faithful pushed in to kiss the hem of his robe. But his eye was fixed upon a ragged leper lying with his back against the ramparts not far from the city's northern gate. The man's face was disfigured; his arms and legs were covered in lesions and sores. He approached the man; the crowd held its collective breath. Martin leaned over him and kissed him tenderly on his scrofulous cheek, then held the man's head in his hands and blessed him. The next day, the leper entered the church and the assembled beheld a miracle, for the man's face, which the day before had been ravaged, was today smooth and soft. Word spread that Martin had the power to heal. So along his path, people tore off bits of his robe and from it made bandages and compresses that were, it was believed, capable of repelling demons and curing disease.

Martin never again returned to Paris, but his miraculous cure was not forgotten, and an oratory was constructed on the very spot where it had taken place. The small structure was spared by the fire that ravaged the city in 585. This, too, was deemed a miracle (though of course it was made of stone). Veneration for Martin grew for centuries. Modern Paris has not erased all memory of the saint. Today, the northern Roman road on which the leper was once cured is called Rue Saint-Martin.

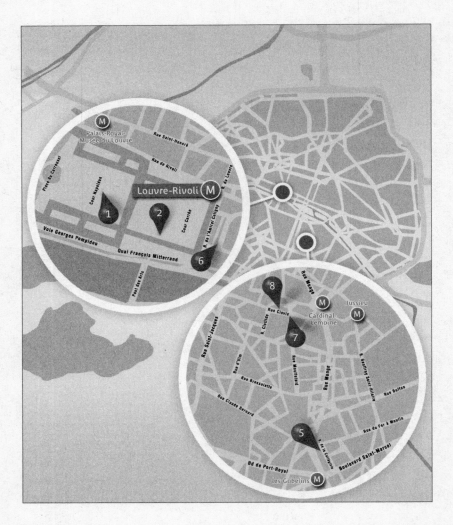

1–2. The foundations of the Louvre. **5.** The town of Saint-Marcel. **6.** Reminders of the saint of Auxerre. **7.** "Clovis Tower," the oldest vestige (dating from the eleventh century) of the church constructed by the first Christian Frankish king, still visible in the courtyard of Lycée Henri-IV. **8.** The sarcophagus of Saint Geneviève.

Fifth Century

Louvre-Rivoli

Paris, Capital of the Franks

The Louvre-Rivoli Métro stop is decked out in the finery of the palace. Not the "Louvre" of the former fortress or even the "Louvre" of the opulent royal residence, but the "Louvre" of the museum that houses today some of the most beautiful works of art created across the centuries—and the most visited museum in the world. In 1968, André Malraux, minister of culture under General de Gaulle, came up with the idea to have art brought down into the subway passageways. While paving stones were flying through the air above—it being the time of the student demonstrations—the subterranean walls of the number 1 Line were being refitted in Burgundian stone and niches were being dug out into which would be placed reproductions of the museum's masterpieces. Assyrian bas reliefs, Egyptian pharaohs, and Renaissance nymphs greeted the astonished and delighted subway passengers. The astonishment was all the more justified given that today this station is no longer the one that actually serves the museum.

In the years since then, everything has changed. The glass pyramid that former president François Mitterrand had built has altered the entrance to the Louvre. Today, in order to buy a ticket to the museum, you'd be better served getting off at the Palais-Royal stop.

For my purposes I could have gotten off at either stop, and it made little difference which one. What I had come to find was not the museum, which very much exists, but that which no longer exists—leaving behind almost no trace, and barely even a memory.

We have finally made it to the Right Bank. At the Louvre stop, we left the Roman world and entered that of the Franks. Coming from the south, the Romans had colonized southern Paris, meaning the Left Bank. The Franks were from the north and therefore settled in the northern part of the city, and that means the Right Bank.

At the end of the fifth century, one would have found in this place a fortified camp guarded by the Franks, who were laying siege to Paris. From this fortress—*loewer* in the Frankish language—we get "Louvre."

Today the Louvre is one of the vastest structures in all of Paris, and seemingly has no connection to the fort built by the invading Franks. A castle replaced the fort, a palace replaced the castle, and the museum replaced the palace. Nonetheless the original purpose of this place can still be found deep-down. Certain remains, well, remain. They date back not to Clovis but to Philippe Auguste, king of France at the end of the twelfth century. Going down in the Louvre's crypt, you can make out the walls and discover the foundations of the dungeon and the towers of the ancient fortress.

Under Philippe Auguste, this fortress was still a military installation, even a prison. Only at the time of Charles V, around 1370, did the location become a royal residence, with a number of embellishments (a scale model can be seen in the crypt).

Then the Hundred Years War took the kings of France away from Paris. Not until François I did the Louvre become a palace, ready once again to welcome its rulers.

———

The menacing Franks and their *loewer* facing Paris were one consequence of the gradual decline of the Roman Empire, whose death throes could be felt from the beginning of the fifth century onward. It was breaking up into pieces. First it was definitively divided in half. On the left was the Western Empire, which could not defend itself against the Visigoths who sacked Rome in 410. On the right was the Eastern Empire, powerful but also so far away. The Franks became auxiliaries in the Roman army. Merovech, their king and the founder of the Merovingian dynasty, was a general in the imperial militia formed under orders from Rome.

During this period of confusion and disorder, Gaul was somewhat forgotten and Lutetia/Paris completely forgotten. Valentinian III, emperor of the Western Empire, was almost entirely uninterested in the northern territories. In 425 he entrusted Aetius, a cavalry leader whom he held in high esteem, to rule Gaul in his name. In fact, as always, it was a matter of keeping the Germanic tribes on the other side of the Rhine, and it took all of Aetius's skill to push back the invaders as best he could, while avoiding the supreme catastrophe—allowing them to cross the Seine, which would have opened up all of Gaul to them. Aetius sent the Franks back into Germanic territory, crushed the Burgundians, who were also threatening them, and defeated the armed bands that had come from Armoric.

In Paris it was the hour of Christianization, and Bishop Marcel played the part of catalyst. To find any trace of this venerable prelate, we have to turn our eyes toward the Gobelins intersection, which branches off Boulevard Saint-Marcel. At the time, in the parts of town that were outside the city walls, the swamps were inhabited by animals that were more or less harmless. Nonetheless it seems as if some evolutionary throwback lived there. In the basin formed by the banks of the Bièvres, a serpent was terrorizing the inhabitants, who considered it to be a demon. The beast had already devoured a woman of royal blood but bad reputation, proving what came of sinfulness. Bishop Marcel, who was particularly vigorous—or just plain courageous—didn't falter. In

What became of the Saint-Marcel Cemetery?

Tombs were still being added to the cemetery until the end of the sixteenth century. After that it was closed because it was impeding the development of the neighborhood. Today nothing of it remains, either of the cemetery or of the oratory, though a number of tomb sculptures were discovered in 1873 by the great archaeologist Théodore Vacquer. Today they can be found in the Musée Carnavalet.

So we have to be content with memory. And the memory remains alive. Informational plaques can be found next to the Café Le Canon des Gobelins, which sits on the spot of the ancient tomb.

The oratory and congregation associated with it gave birth to an entire settlement, the town of Saint-Marcel. Though no vestige of this hamlet remains, one can try to imagine it. A path descended toward the boulevard and now is called the Rue de la Collégiale, the name of the church formed around the original oratory (and which remained standing until the Revolution): you are now standing on the old Place de la Collégiale Saint-Marcel, the religious center of the town. If you walk back up the Rue de la Collégiale, you will find, on your left, the Rue du Petit-Moine, or "street of (Cont.)

the name of Christianizing Gaul, and to demonstrate the power of the True God, he gave the monster two mortal thwacks on the head with a cross, and the animal thereby became part of religious legend as an authentic dragon. The pagans who were converted by this miracle—or simply relieved that the beast was gone—generously attributed several other miracles to Marcel. Canonized for having rooted out the Evil of the Marais—as the swampland is now called, a fashionable location—and freed the river people from the monster that had terrorized them, Saint Marcel became their protector. If you lived in the neighborhood you could ask anything of him.

After his death in 436, the bishop was buried near the place where he had performed his miracle, and very quickly the tomb became a holy spot. People from all over the city came to touch his tomb, to ask for good luck or for health. In homage to the saint an oratory was constructed with a small altar. Some of the faithful even went so far as to be buried next to their venerated protector, and little by little the grounds became a cemetery: the first Christian cemetery not only in Paris but in all of Gaul.

Fifteen years after the death of Bishop Marcel, a foe greater even than the Marais Monster rose up. Attila the Hun swept in from the Asian plains and was threatening to overwhelm Paris.

the little monk." This also serves as a reminder that the religious members of the Collégiale once walked here.

The king of the Huns had already tried and failed to devour the Eastern Empire. Using a combination of diplomacy and warfare he had tried every possible means of taking Constantinople. Brilliant war chief though he might have been, he was a hopeless diplomat; his dream slipped away. The Eastern Roman Empire eluded his grasp. The cost of the siege and his attempts at diplomacy were enormous, and yet he had come away with almost nothing. He had, however, one last card to play, in the form of a ring, a pledge sent to him by Honoria, the sister of the Western emperor Valentinian.

Honoria of the velvet eyes was deeply unhappy because her brother, who was both austere and inflexible, jealously guarded over her purity. She had, nonetheless, succeeded in finding a lover. The emperor immediately had the rascal executed, but it was too late; Honoria was pregnant. She was quickly engaged to an elderly senator and, while awaiting the marriage ceremony, shut away in a convent. One could not be too cautious.

Honoria, who was really not the religious type, sent Attila a ring. She would agree to anything that he wanted and anything he could imagine if only he came and liberated her. Attila took the proposal seriously, and deemed himself betrothed to the beautiful Honoria. But he also wasn't the type to let love overwhelm his wits; the most important thing was what kind of dowry he might obtain. And what would a king of the Huns demand as a wedding gift from a Roman emperor? Why, Gaul, and nothing less.

Valentinian was taken aback by this monumental naïveté on the part of the barbarian king. Give Gaul as a gift? For a marriage that would never even take place? The notion was absurd.

News of Attila's approach created panic in Paris. The citizens were convinced that he would burn the place to the ground. The terror was fed by rumors that his Asiatic warriors wore the skins of bears, ate raw meat that they kept under their saddles, had monstrous faces covered with scars, and that they were in general merciless killers and rapists. Faced with such a cataclysm, the Parisians had but one option: to flee. They started to pack up their things, collect a few valuables, and, with women, children, slaves, and cattle in tow, began to head out of town.

"Let the men run for it if they want to and if they are incapable of fighting. We women will pray to God so much that He will heed our prayers."

The woman of twenty-eight who made this announcement to the Parisian population was named Geneviève. She was neither a military strategist nor a firebrand agitator but a devout Christian woman immersed in the perfect faith, a lamb of the Church. Born in Nanterre, she had settled in Paris for a dozen years following the death of her parents, and consecrated her life to religious ecstasy and the sensible management of property inherited from a Roman father and a Frankish mother.

Geneviève was among the wealthiest Parisians, though material concerns meant nothing to her. What mattered was heaven. She devoted herself entirely to Christ, but to her way of thinking He didn't exist apart outside those monasteries open to women. The young woman had to be content with wearing the "virgin's veil," a veil of consecration that distinguished her from the common folk and commanded respect. She became a deaconess and remained in the world, of course, but chose to live in silence, prayer, and fasting. She ate only twice a week, on Sundays and Thursdays, when she felt she had no choice but to nourish the all-too-human body that cried out in protest.

The news of Attila's arrival changed Geneviève's destiny. Paris did not have need of saints; with Denis, Martin, Marcel, and several others, they had plenty of them. What the city needed, and badly, were brave souls willing to act. This young lady of the veil would be Paris's heroine.

In the general panic by which the inhabitants were seized, Geneviève was the only one to keep a level head. With the self-assurance of the believer, she knew that God was watching over her and over the entire population. She asked Parisians to join with her in prayer, and spoke to them about Esther, the biblical figure who once upon a time in Persia saved the Jewish people from extermination through her prayers and her fasting. Geneviève wanted to be the Esther of Paris, the savior of a nation, the standard-bearer of a people. And the women followed her. They gathered together and prayed, they fasted and pleaded with the Almighty to deliver them from the evil that menaced them. The men laughed cynically. What needed to be done, they said, was to get out of town and take shelter behind the walls of a city that was better defended than this one.

"Why do you talk about taking refuge in other cities?" demanded Geneviève. "Will their walls be better at keeping out the barbarian hordes than those of Paris? If Paris escapes carnage it will be because of Christ's protection."

"Silence, prophetess of misery!" the cynical and blackened souls spat back.

Some of them now talked about throwing Geneviève into a well, which admittedly would have been a rather radical means of silencing her. But just then the archdeacon of Auxerre arrived in town, wearing his coat of gold. He looked with benevolence upon the populace and forgave their folly and the excesses of men. He came with a message. Germain, his bishop, had died while giving proof to his followers of the Christian election of Geneviève. This constituted a kind of ecclesiastical guarantee.

"Citizens, do not commit this crime! We have heard from our sainted bishop Germain that she whose murder you plot has been elected by God since she emerged from her mother's womb."

From the moment they heard the message from the archdeacon, the Parisians were persuaded: how could they not believe

What memories remain of the saint of Auxerre who saved Saint Geneviève?

At the place where the archdeacon confronted the Parisian mob would be built a small oratory, then a church, one of the oldest on the Right Bank: Saint-Germain-l'Auxerrois, dedicated to the protector of the future protectress of Paris (it's located in the First Arrondissement, facing the Louvre). The Place de l'École reminds us that here future Christians received instruction. The current church came much later, but on the Rue des Prêtres-Saint-Germain-l'Auxerrois, archaeologists have found a number of sarcophaguses dating from the Merovingian epoch.

the final words of one of Gaul's most illustrious and holy bishops? They unanimously rallied behind the courageous deaconess. Their defense took the form of either destroying or constructing barricades on the bridges that would have allowed Attila and his hordes to cross the Seine. Arms were taken up and people prepared, courageously awaiting the arrival of the barbarians.

But there would be no battle, after all. Perhaps believing in the miracle was enough to make what they so desperately hoped for happen. Did Attila know that the city would defend itself? Or had someone perhaps whispered in his ear that the city was gripped by an epidemic of cholera? In any case the leader of the Huns turned his gaze away from the city and, along with his troops, retreated from the banks of the Seine. The city was spared.

Attila turned instead toward Orléans; occupying that city assured him of control of the bridges along the Loire, with the possibility of conquering Aquitaine. He would have a fight on his hands. At the beginning of the summer of the year 451, Aetius was at the head of a large army made up of Gallo-Romans, Franks, Visigoths, Burgundians, Saxons, Armoricans, and Bretons. All the peoples of Gaul were united under the Roman banner to repel this Asiatic invader.

This unexpected and slightly unbelievable force was united in a military fervor reminiscent of Roman days past. It attacked the Huns west of Troyes. What resulted was a fearsome battle, starting in the afternoon and lasting until the middle of the night.

At daybreak, Attila and his men were forced back to their camp; the shoe was on the other foot. A great fire was lit. The king of the Huns pledged to throw himself into it rather than become a Roman prisoner. Attila succeeded in avoiding this fate: wisely, Aetius did not push his success, and was content to watch the enemy armies retreat as they made their way across the plains until eventually they reached the valley of the Danube.

In Paris, Geneviève was credited with the victory. She had saved not only her city but all of Gaul. How could anyone now refuse what she was asking? She wanted a basilica constructed at the place where Saint Denis had collapsed, his decapitated head in his hands. She wanted to levy a special tax for the project, established the lime ovens necessary for the construction, and followed its progress with close attention. This would be more than a simple basilica, after all. The goal of the cult of Saint Denis, of which Geneviève was the head priestess, was first and foremost to anchor Parisians in the Catholic faith. With her deaconess companions, Geneviève patrolled the worksite, inspecting the work at night by the light of a candle held up for her by one of the pious young women. When the wind made the flame flicker and threatened to put it out, the holy woman took the candle in her own hand and lo! The flame was immediately restored.

The current location of Saint-Denis's crypt corresponds generally to this early church, built during Geneviève's lifetime.

Paris viewed its own somewhat modest history within the context of the life of this venerated woman, a saint to whom its citizens already attributed miracles: restoring sight by placing holy water on eyes; restoring to their wits a dozen pitiful souls possessed by demons; bringing back to life a little boy who had been killed by falling down a well.

And while Paris was agog at these miraculous accomplishments, the great events of history were taking place elsewhere. In Ravenna (which he had made his capital) Valentinian, the emperor of the Western Roman Empire, was seething: in Gaul, Aetius had robbed him of a part of his glory; so successful was the general that he could envision taking the throne for himself or his son. Valentinian needed to make Aetius disappear, to cut this potential rebellion off at the root before it grew. On September 21 in 454, Valentinian, having invited the victorious Gaul to his palace, proceeded to assassinate him. It was a foolish thing to do, both from a military and political standpoint, but driven by the most powerful of feelings: jealousy.

The people of Gaul mourned the loss of Aetius, henceforth known as "the last of the Romans." And it was true that the crime that took place in Ravenna brought about the end of the empire, which would collapse entirely in another twenty years, and from which a new world would emerge.

On September 4, 476, Romulus Augustulus, the last emperor of the West, was forced to abdicate, having been conquered by the Germanic leader Odoacer. Roman glory survived elsewhere, thanks to Zeno, the emperor of the East. Odoacer assumed the title of "king of Italy," while the Roman Senate, in a final gesture, tendered its resignation to Constantinople and sent its imperial seals. The Western Roman Empire now ceased to exist.

Paris was no longer the city of empires, or a citadel of Roman military might. It was entering a new period that we call the Middle Ages.

Paris could now count only on itself for its defense, meaning that it was defenseless. But who would take it? The situation in Gaul had become singularly complicated. Childeric, the Frank king who lived in Tournai, in the north, submitted himself to Odoacer, the king in Italy. Syagrius, the last Roman general in charge of Gaul, tried to maintain the law of the now-defunct empire. The Visigoths ruled in Aquitaine, while the Burgundians dreamed of extending their empire all the way to Marseilles. And of course there were the complex and short-lived alliances that linked various rulers.

Childeric, who was the son of King Meroveus, viewed all this

intrigue as a means to assure his lineage, that of the Merovingians, by taking Gaul and, in particular, Paris. He approached the
Seine with his mercenaries and seemed a redoubtable figure: his
name, Hilde-Rik, meant "mighty in war" in Frankish.

But Geneviève, Frank by her mother and therefore a speaker
of Frankish, went immediately to parlay with the man laying siege
to Paris. She dissuaded Childeric from entering Paris. Her bold-
ness initiated open war against Syagrius, who ruled the region
between the Somme and the Loire.

Childeric bided his time, hesitated, taking one step forward
and then one back. Would he or would he not lay siege to Paris?
No one really knew, but his troops were still encamped around the
city, blockading it and cutting off all the roads leading in or out,
starving the population. He wasn't entering Paris but he was at
least going to prevent his enemies from doing it. This *drôle de
guerre*, this silent confrontation, this suspended hostility, this
pointless blockade lasted for no less than ten years. Starting in
476, Childeric toyed with Paris, like a fat old cat might enjoy terrorizing a mouse that it has no interest in devouring.

The Frankish king built his camp on the Right Bank, directly
opposite the Île de la Cité, and constructed a tall watchtower, a
loewer, from which he could observe the city and everything going on inside. The Parisians became used to seeing this towering
menace that had risen up on the bank of the river, a constant reminder of their precarious situation.

The might of arms stood at the door but didn't come in. This
ridiculous situation permitted Geneviève to dominate Paris entirely with her charisma, her faith, her authority, and her wealth.
She controlled the curates just as she did the city council and
safeguarded the population's well-being.

When Paris began to starve, she intervened. Actually, it wasn't
a miracle that saved the city but an audacious move. While the
city was in the throes of hunger, Geneviève attempted to escape,
not by means of the roads, which were blocked, but by the river.
She mobilized a small flotilla of eleven boats and steered them upriver toward Arcis-sur-Aube in Champagne. The passage became

blocked with vegetation which Geneviève went at with her hatchet. The stunned and relieved sailors imagined that the saint was being attacked by a foul-smelling monster. Actually these were felled trees placed in the river by their enemies to prevent passage.

Once in Champagne, Geneviève started off by curing a woman from a local tribe who had been suffering for four years by making the sign of the cross over her. She bought wheat with her own money and returned, boats laden with grain. But navigating the river in boats piled high with grain was a dangerous proposition, and while the oarsmen were confident they were also inexperienced and clumsy. Prayer came to their rescue; they rowed to the rhythm of a hymn from the Book of Exodus: "I will sing to the LORD, for he is highly exalted. Both horse and driver, he has hurled into the sea. / The LORD is my strength and my defense; he has become my salvation."

In Paris, Geneviève distributed the wheat to those in need. To the poorest, who didn't have either an oven or wood, she offered bread that she herself had baked.

Childeric turned a blind eye to this transgression of his blockade. Perhaps he had grown weary of this nonconfrontation that seemed to go on forever. He had gotten nowhere; he hadn't taken Paris and he hadn't conquered Syagrius. The Gaul was in a bind, a trap of his own construction. And thus it was, bitter and disillusioned, that he left this world in 481 for Valhalla, the paradise of German warriors, leaving his son Clovis the task of completing what he had started.

Clovis, a young man of sixteen, was suddenly now king of the Franks, and decided with admirable filial piety to continue his father's politics. He opted to do battle against Syagrius and continued to lay siege to Paris. He kept up the pressure on the city, but he also had no illusions. He knew that if he wanted to rule Gaul he would first have to conquer the Roman general. From the top of his *loewer*, he regarded the city planted in the middle of the river, determined at some point soon to end the Gallo-Roman influence and turn Paris into a Frankish city.

For the moment Syagrius settled down behind the powerful walls of Soissons, on the banks of the Aisne River, from where he surveyed and blocked incursions of the Franks. The general commanded the last forces of the defunct Roman Empire. Facing his legions were the troops of Clovis. These were less numerous but better armed. It was Clovis's good fortune that Syagrius turned out to be filled with hot air. He put on the airs of a real soldier, looking the part for all the world, but his military talents were pitiful. Moreover, his legionaries had become discouraged; nonetheless, the general insisted that they fight for a cause that was already lost.

In 486, Clovis judged the time had come to have done with this Roman. He sent him a challenge and headed toward Soissons with his army, pillaging several churches along the way, because waging war was a good way of lining one's pockets.

Syagrius was worried that his city would be placed under siege, so he came out from behind the walls of Soissons and galloped to meet the king of the Franks. It was a slaughter. The hooked lances and double-sided hatchets of the Franks proved grimly effective.

And thus on the Soissonais Plain did the last Roman legionaries meet their end. Syagrius took flight while Clovis entered Soissons as a conqueror; he immediately made the city his capital. He took residence in the abandoned palace and drained the treasure recently acquired by his enemy. Several more battles would be necessary, but from this point onward the Frankish kingdom would extend across northern Gaul.

The siege of Paris could not be lifted. Geneviève, pious Christian though she was, submitted to the authority of the pagan Clovis. She didn't have much choice, of course. Nonetheless, ten years later, Geneviève would get her own back, when Clovis would submit to

What became of Geneviève?

Saint Geneviève died in 502, nine years before her Christian king was entombed in Saint-Pierre-et-Saint-Paul on Mount Lucotitus (today Mount Sainte-Geneviève). While she was alive, the saint had adopted the habit of climbing the hill to pray there; she gave her name to the pathway, which later became Rue de la Montagne-Sainte-Geneviève. The bell tower of a church is still visible within the courtyard of Lycée Henri-IV and bears the name Clovis Tower. This is the oldest vestige (the base dates from the eleventh century) of the church constructed by the first Christian Frankish king. Saint Geneviève's tomb, as well as that of Clovis and his wife, was located somewhere near the entrance to the school.

The church became an abbey in the twelfth century, and in 1744 was replaced by Sainte-Geneviève Church, at the command of Louis XV. Today it is the Panthéon, the mausoleum of the greatest figures in French history.

The coffer containing the relics of the patron saint of Paris was regularly carried in a procession through the streets. It was said that miracles happened when this took place. Alas, the reliquary was destroyed in 1793 and Geneviève's remains were burned in the Place de Grève.

(Cont.)

the arguments of his wife, Clotilda, a loyal Catholic, and renounce the pantheon of Germanic gods. He had promised he would convert to Christ in the event he defeated the Alamans, which he did at the Battle of Tolbiac in 496. The king of the Franks thereafter recognized the Father, the Son, and the Holy Spirit, and then permitted his baptism to take place in Reims in a grandiose ceremony that in the centuries to come would fill the pages of edifying works.

Clovis would institute a new line of kings but also engage in a series of conquests. He defeated the Burgundians at the Battle of Ouche in 500. In 502, to mark the arrival of a new era, he left Soissons and settled in Paris. The city still resembled the Roman city from the time of Julian, and the king delighted in walking in the footsteps of the former emperor. He moved into the city's palace, to which he added shaded gardens that descended down the gentle slope to the Seine. Along with him came an entire administration, which moved either into the palace or into the adjacent buildings. A handful of loyal followers hovered around the king and advised him—bishops and abbots took over control of the royal chapel, and several ministers, not yet numerous, were given particular responsibilities. The count of the palace led the tribunal's proceedings; the prefecture saw to taxes; the mayor of the palace acted as an attendant. In short, the king was already surrounded by a small band of courtiers.

The stone sarcophagus that contained the body of the saint was spared the destructive rage of the French Revolution, however. Rediscovered in 1802, it was transferred to the Saint-Étienne-du-Mont Church, located across from the Panthéon. Today the sepulcher is covered with a cloak of inlaid gold that partly conceals it.

Paris, the Gallo-Roman burg, the fortress city, became the capital of the Frankish kingdom in 508, in celebration of a great victory over their final rivals, the Visigoths, in 507 in Vouillé.

From his new capital city, Clovis could cast his eye over his accomplishments: he had conquered all of Gaul, with the exception of Provence and Languedoc-Roussillon. Now he could die in peace.

And indeed in the month of November in 511, Clovis suddenly became ill and died, despite bleedings and prayers. He was forty-five years old and had reigned for twenty-nine years. What was to be done with the remains of a Frankish king who had died in Paris? Should he be buried in Tournai, next to his father Childeric? Instead it was determined that the body should remain in Paris and be placed in the crypt of the new church Saint-Pierre-et-Saint-Paul. The presence of the tomb of the first Christian king was sure to increase the prestige and grandeur of the capital. Nonetheless, the French people's distant ancestors did not display any great reverence for the royal tomb; it completely disappeared, and no one knows where it went. A few optimistic archaeologists hope one day to find it, perhaps when they are allowed to dig more deeply in the area around the famous school Lycée Henry-IV.

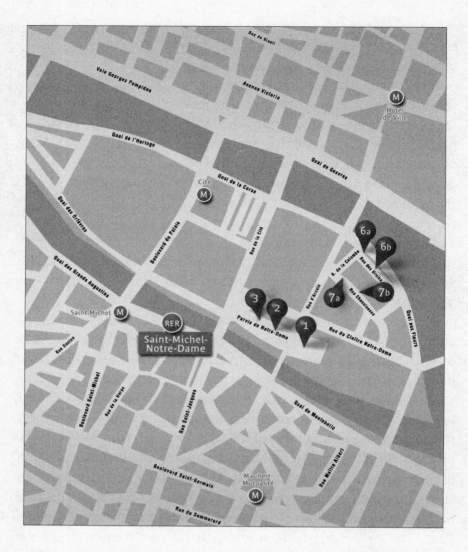

1. Notre-Dame—the secret of Biscornet. **2.** Notre-Dame—ground zero of all the roads of France. **3.** One can find traces of the original square in front of Notre-Dame (six times smaller than it is today), before Haussmann expanded it in 1865. **6a–6b.** The best way of imagining the Île de la Cité as it once was is to stand on Rue de la Colombe, kitty-corner from Rue des Ursins. At number 19 Rue des Ursins is the Saint-Aignan chapel, which is the last of the twenty-three churches that once surrounded Notre-Dame. **7a.** 18 and 20 Rue Chanoinesse, the barber and the pastry chef. **7b.** At 22 and 24 Rue Chanoinesse, beautiful houses dating from the sixteenth century.

● —— ● —— ●

The Merovingians, Elder Sons of the Church

Notre-Dame—the cathedral, the novel by Victor Hugo, and also, since 1988, the utterly charmless train station through whose passages people hurry to find fresh air—opens out into the wide expanse of the cathedral square.

That square today is six times larger than it was in the past. To get a sense of how it has changed, look at the markings on the ground: they reveal the winding trail of the old streets that surrounded the cathedral before 1865, when Baron Haussmann gave it the appearance that we know today.

Notre-Dame square is the ground zero of all of the roads of France. This is partly because it was the site of an ancient wooden post known as the bishop of Paris's Ladder of Justice. At the foot of this ladder the accused were brought to make amends before the sentence upon them was carried out. They approached in their shifts, a rope around their neck, a candle in their hand, bearing on their chest and back a sandwich board detailing their crime; they kneeled before the Ladder of Justice and publicly admitted to their crime and pleaded for forgiveness for their sins.

Walking in the neighborhood around Notre-Dame, one can find a number of rather moving vestiges of what was there before. The best way of imagining the Île de la Cité as it once was is to stand

What Notre-Dame's square inspired

At the beginning of the 1970s, having in mind the construction of a National Center for Art and Culture on the Right Bank, President Georges Pompidou wanted the center to open onto an esplanade that would evoke the one in front of Notre-Dame Cathedral. By so doing he was emphasizing the sacred nature of art, and his multidisciplinary home for it—the Centre Pompidou—would become a cathedral open to all forms of devotion.

on Rue de la Colombe, kitty-corner from Rue des Ursins. At number 19 Rue des Ursins is the Saint-Aignan chapel, which remains the last of the some twenty-three churches that once surrounded Notre-Dame. Then, moving in the direction of Rue Chanoinesse, at numbers 18 and 20 once stood two houses, one occupied by a barber and the other by a pastry chef. The barber cut the throats of students living in the dormitories of Notre-Dame and delivered their bodies to the pastry chef, who made pâté out of them, which in turn was then delivered to feed those living in the dormitories. These two accomplices were burned alive in 1387. In the garage of the motorcycle policemen who live in these locations today you will find another part of the Gallo-Roman rampart, dating from the fourth century: an odd projection of stone that has survived the centuries under the name Butcher's Stone, for it was there that the pastry chef received his sinister ingredients. At numbers 22 and 24 the quite beautiful houses that were once students' living quarters, dating from the sixteenth century, are still visible. If you make your way into number 26 you will see tombstones, which for several centuries have served as flagstones to keep feet dry in the event of floods. But this older Paris is more and more hidden, and the digital codes guarding the doors make it less and less accessible.

To find the heart of Frankish Paris, you have to go back through the centuries, back to the death of Clovis in 511.

When this Christian king died, the country was divided up between his four sons: Thierry inherited the eastern part; Clodomir, the region of the Loire; Clotaire, the northern part; and lastly, Childebert, who got Picardy, Normandy, Brittany, and especially the Île-de-France, with Paris, already a populous city of twenty thousand citizens.

The chronology that followed was somewhat complicated and sometimes confused. The sons of Clovis spent their time strangling their nephews, out of fear that they might claim a part of the succession; making war to enlarge their inheritances; and attempting to make peace with one another, under the insistent pressure from the good-hearted Clotilda, the grieving widow of the Frank king.

Then, because someone needed to be king, they would bump off neighboring monarchies with the intention of enlarging their inherited kingdoms. Hence Childebert and his brother Clodomir declared war on Sigismond, the king of the Burgundians—or more exactly the Burgundies, as they were then called. They laid siege to Autun, but on the field of battle Clodomir was recognized because of his long hair and the Burgundians cut off his head and stuck it on the tip of a pike. This incensed the Franks and spurred them on to victory. The triumph was celebrated by an all-out massacre of the defeated soldiers. Sigismond, his wife, and his children received a very particular kind of justice: they were thrown into a well.

The death of Clodomir worried his brothers. They feared that the dead man's sons would demand their part of the inheritance. Queen Clotilda wanted to avoid a family feud, and thought that she could prevent the worst by placing her three grandsons under her protection. Childebert brought his brother Clotaire to Paris and there dark plots were hatched in the palace of the Cité.

To ease people's alarm, Childebert and Clotaire spoke in reassuring tones. This meeting was nothing more than two kings gathering to help Clodomir's children inherit the throne of their father. Kindly Clotilda seemed relieved by this and leaned over her grandsons in a grandmotherly way and said, "I will no longer believe that I lost my son Clodomir if I can see you inherit his realm."

This turned out to be a false hope, for assassins were watching them. The Cité palace became the site of almost incredible violence. Clotaire seized the oldest son and without hesitating

Where did Saint-Cloud get its name?

Clodoald, Clodomir's third and youngest son, succeeded in avoiding his brothers' fates thanks to help from a few officers who took pity on him. The child had seen close up the horror of power and decided to cut off his long hair, a mark of his royalty, renounce the world, and devote himself to the adoration of God. He moved to a fishing village on the banks of the Seine, where he built a monastery. Clodoald today is better known by the name Saint Cloud, and the village that took him in perpetuates his name.

stabbed the boy in the throat. Horrified, the next oldest son threw himself at the feet of Childebert and cried out, "Help me, O pious Uncle! Keep me from perishing like my brother!"

Childebert hesitated. Was it really necessary to eliminate the entire household of the dead Clodomir? He turned to Clotaire.

"Please, sweet brother, show your generosity and spare the life of this boy."

This was strange. Spare the life of a child who could one day turn against his family? This was unthinkable. The entire race of Clodomir had to be wiped out.

"Give up!" roared Clotaire. "If you don't, you'll die in his place!"

Childebert was stunned by his brother's rage, and let the boy go. Clotaire immediately plunged his dagger into the boy and then finished his young victim off by slowly strangling him.

After the murder of Clodomir's two sons, Théodebert, Thierry's son, convinced now that his uncles were plotting his assassination, allied himself with Childebert to vanquish Clotaire. Alliances shifted. The two armed families were in full force, but the elderly Clotilda was still hanging around in an attempt to reconcile her descendants and to prevent future homicidal acts. She prayed so hard that a terrible storm broke over the field of battle. The combatants were impressed by the fury of the skies whose purpose was clearly intended to keep them apart. Perhaps they didn't really want to tear each other apart in the muck. The brothers and the nephews ceased hostilities and fell into each other's arms.

Still, the troops were so well armed and so ready to fight that it would have been a shame to waste them. They decided to march on Spain, where the Visigoths lived. Surely there would be a village or two to seize.

After occupying Pamplona, Childebert and Clotaire, the reconciled brothers, headed off to Saragossa, but the village resisted and the Frankish army was decimated. For Childebert, the moment had come to break camp and head back for Paris.

But, in this year of 542, the king did not return to his capital with his tail between his legs. From this militarily fruitless expedition he brought back two precious relics: a golden cross and a tunic that had once belonged to Saint Vincent, a Spanish martyr from the third century who has tortured to death during anti-Christian persecutions under the emperor Diocletian. Though a barbarian king and cruel by nature, Childebert nonetheless evinced a great respect for religion and vowed eternal friendship with the good abbot Germain, his counselor and protector of the poor.

Childebert never forgot the active role that the Church and Rome played in the growth and development of the Frankish realm. With the dissolution of the empire, the Church and its bishops had come to form Gaul's administrative and social infrastructure. The Franks relied upon its workings. Turning themselves into Christians was no big deal. Paris was worth saying a mass for.

Moreover, the order and organization of the Church had immediately appealed to the extremely disciplined Frankish tribes, who were less exalted than the other invaders, and who had been taken over by Arianism, an Eastern and heretical form of Christianity closer than not to the Platonic philosophy, against which Rome strongly fought.

In short, by general agreement, Rome was put in the hands of the Franks and Frankish Gaul became the elder daughter of the Church, benefiting from its influence over its people. This new Gaul was built upon religious fervor.

"Childebert, you must build an abbey in which to house the relics you have brought back from Saragossa," declared Abbot Germain.

Naturally, the abbey would be run by Germain himself, the first rung up the ladder that would transform this humble cleric first into a powerful bishop and later into a venerated saint. Slowly, the abbey-reliquary rose up outside the walls of Paris.

At the same time, the king interceded with the pope to get Germain ordained bishop of Paris. The good abbot, a modest and contrite man, tried to dissuade the king and pope from this. His life of contemplation and his love of the poor and the unqualified wisdom he could give to the mighty and powerful were enough to confer earthly happiness. But then the Holy Spirit visited him in a dream and revealed to him that the holy powers demanded of him—demanded!—that he accept the office. So he did, and was promoted to the head of the Parisian Church.

The Merovingian king, who still regarded himself as the secular arm of the Church, wanted his new prelate to have a cathedral worthy of the capital. To prove his devotion and submission, Childebert took charge of building a splendid edifice inspired by Saint Peter's in Rome.

On the easternmost point of Île de la Cité in Roman days stood a monument to Jupiter, the vestiges of which are kept today in the Musée de Cluny. Given the triumph of Christianity, it was right and good that the dilapidated old temple be replaced by the most beautiful of sanctuaries. Christian peace had replaced the *Pax Romana*, and thus the new structure would be, appropriately, built upon the ancient Roman ramparts. This new use for old walls would be the visible and tangible symbol of how Roman military might had been supplanted by an even more powerful spiritual power.

This was how the Saint-Étienne Basilica came into being. It was an impressive monument: five naves, 230 feet long and nearly 120 feet wide. It was the largest church in the realm. Those interested can find the drawings for it on informational signs in Notre-Dame's square. The foundations of the southern wall, built upon the Roman walls, can be found in the archaeological crypt.

In those days a cathedral was not an isolated edifice. Quite the opposite: it was the center of it all. A cathedral represented the meeting point of a number places of worship. Hence a baptistery was attached to Saint-Étienne, situated, logically enough, beneath the shrine to Saint John the Baptist, as well as a church already called Notre-Dame. This impressive cluster of ecclesiastical structures constituted Bishop Germain's new seat, his *cathedra*. If you believe the word of his followers, the prelate never stopped digging into the royal treasury to perform deeds of charity. He even took bread from the mouths of his monks and gave it to the poor. The brothers were furious but didn't dare confront a saint who was, after all, capable of performing miracles; it was said that Germain healed the sick and infirm, exorcised demons, and even raised the dead.

September 13, 558, stands as a great moment for Paris, its populace, and its clergy, for that was the day on which the church Saint-Vincent-Saint-Croix, located on the Left Bank, was completed, following more than ten years of construction. Everything was prepared for this monumental event, for which the elite of the Catholic

How did it come to pass that Notre-Dame replaced Saint-Étienne?

In 1160, Maurice de Sully, the bishop of Paris, decided to build a cathedral, one which would be even grander than Saint-Étienne and the older Notre-Dame combined. Saint-Étienne was as we've seen 230 feet in length; the new structure would be almost 400.

This was a gigantic project and took 107 years to complete, hence the expression (in French at least) "waiting a hundred and seven years" (and the printed page on which this sentence appears in the French edition of this book was, well, 107. Nice coincidence, don't you think?). It is said that a Parisian craftsman named Biscornet was put in charge of installing the panels on the iron doors as well as the locks. Faced with such a daunting task, he called upon the devil, and the Malevolent One gave him such effective assistance that it required holy water to make the keys work. But the metalwork was so particular that even today, it would seem, experts cannot explain how it could have been accomplished. Unfortunately, Biscornet died soon after completing his task and took his secrets with him to the grave.

Across the centuries, the cathedral was continuously worked
(Cont.)

on, and it's only by sheer luck that it still stands today, given all the events that threatened its survival. Condemned to be torn down during Revolution, it managed to escape. A little later, Napoleon's coronation took place in Notre-Dame, but it was necessary to hang tapestries in order to conceal the deplorable state of the walls.

In 1831, with his novel *The Hunchback of Notre-Dame*, Victor Hugo awakened the conscience of the government and of public opinion. From that point on, the whole world was in agreement that the cathedral must be saved. The architect Eugène Viollet-le-Duc, who specialized in reconstruction, was put in charge of the restoration. The work would take nearly twenty years and, for good or for ill, would involve an attempt to restore the cathedral to the way it looked in the Middle Ages.

In particular it was necessary to rebuild the Gallery of the Kings, which extends along the façade beneath the three main doors. Originally this consisted of twenty-eight statues of the kings of Judah and Israel, representing the traditional ancestors of Christ. During the Revolution, they were believed to resemble the kings of France and hacked to bits with iron bars. Viollet-le-Duc put his own statues into the empty niches in order to give the wall its original *(Cont.)*

hierarchy and the cream of the nobility would all gather. Childebert was expected and, indeed, this would be his hour of glory, during which, all at the same time, his military campaigns, his religious loyalty, and his successful governance of the realm would be celebrated. Germain was there as well, surrounded by six other bishops recruited for the occasion.

They awaited the arrival of the king. And they waited some more. No king. The king couldn't come because, as it turned out, the king was dead. Suddenly and without warning, he had chosen the moment of his triumph in his city to give up the ghost. A sad fate, and yet also one conferring glory.

The question was, what to do? Germain was unsure, as were the prelates. Should they postpone the ceremony and throw themselves into grief? Germain revealed his gift for using symbols and his mastery of communications by deciding to proceed with the ceremony, and then, that very day, to conduct the royal funeral. He would do both.

With a red cape draped over his shoulders, surrounded by his priests and disciples, Germain daubed holy oil on the basilica's twelve pillars, representing Christ's twelve apostles, and then he poured the liquid onto the altar, the church's sacred core, the meeting place between heaven and earth.

appearance. In 1977 came some welcome news: a few pieces of the ancient figures had survived destruction and were found during construction along Rue de la Chausée-d'Antin. They are on display in the Musée de Cluny.

In a strong and steady voice, the bishop recalled the prophesy of Saint John:

"I saw the Holy City, the new Jerusalem, coming down out of heaven from God, prepared as a bride beautifully dressed for her husband. And I heard a loud voice from the throne saying, 'Look! God's dwelling place is now among the people, and he will dwell with them. They will be his people, and God himself will be with be with them and be their God.'"

Gloria in excelsis Deo: glory to God in his heaven, incanted the assembled, and Germain blessed the water in which those present would be dipped soon afterward, bonding the faithful to the holy mysticism of this sacred place.

The ceremony finished, the remains of King Childebert were taken down to the crypt that awaited him, and which he himself had designed only a short time before.

Barely had Childebert been laid to rest than it became necessary to face the somewhat delicate issue of his succession. His widow had only given birth to girls. There was no law preventing a female from being crowned, but the issue didn't even come up. No one thought even for an instant that it would be possible for a Frankish kingdom to be ruled over by a woman. What was required was a vigorous male, handy with the sword, ready to have at the enemy, a rough-and-tumble kind of guy who wasn't afraid to slay a few Visigoths.

Of Clovis's four sons only Clotaire, the nephew killer, was still alive, and thus it was to him that the mantle was passed. He succeeded in reuniting the four states of his deceased brothers. Now he was the sole inheritor of the immense legacy of his father,

meaning all of Gaul, augmented by the region of Thüringen, located on the other side of the Rhine; Burgundy; and several provinces in the Midi, or southern France. And what was the first
thing that this all-powerful king, whose realm now extended
across a good part of Europe, did? He left his residence in Soissons—
for he lived there as well—and headed for Paris. The master of
such an empire could only govern it from the banks of the Seine.
No strategic thinking went into the decision. He was following no
rule and adhering to no tradition: it was simply that Paris, inevitably, had come to seem the capital of the great realm taking shape.

Clotaire, however, was no longer a young man. He was past
sixty, and worn down by the numerous military campaigns as
well as the six wives whom he married either successively or
simultaneously—marriage not yet being considered a sacrament
by the Church. Clotaire could quite happily do what he liked
and polygamy was a well-established tradition among the royal
families. Clotaire ruled only three years until his death in 561,
when he was somewhat stupefied to learn that God had apparently
refused immortality even to a monarch as considerable as he.

"Alas! Who is then this king of the Heavens who would allow
one of the most powerful kings on Earth to die?" he asked before
closing his eyes for the last time.

While the monarch's body was being carried to Soissons, Chilperic, the youngest of his four sons, tried to seize control of the
kingdom for himself. He took command of the paternal treasury
and ran to the Cité palace to distribute gold coins to the ministers
and administrators. Blinded by such largesse, the court immediately celebrated him as the legitimate king.

When one knows the twisted mind-set and unbridled ferocity
of the Merovingians, one can easily imagine that the three other
brothers were not simply going to stand by and let this gold-
distributing usurper triumph. They marched on Paris with their
soldiers and rapidly put this self-proclaimed sovereign in his place.
After several debates and not a few shouting matches, the four
brothers got things worked out. Guntram would take over Burgundy and Orléans; Sigebert would have Austrasia all the way to

the Rhine; Chilperic would have Neustria with its capital of Soissons. And Charibert would inherit Paris and with it Western Gaul.

In Charibert Paris had a king who was peaceful and moderate, a friend of the arts, and a defender of justice. His personal habits tended toward the dissolute end of the spectrum, perhaps, but he was nonetheless respected by one and all. In this year of 561, the capital of the kingdom had not much changed over the course of two centuries. On the Left Bank, a network of interlacing streets led to the forum, to the thermal baths, and to the arena, which, no longer in use, had slowly disintegrated before yielding to fire and to neglect. In fact, what had really changed in Paris were the numerous churches, cathedrals, monasteries, oratories, and sanctuaries that had been raised on the Île de la Cité and on both sides of the river. They were everywhere. Some of these sacred spots had been built hurriedly, consisting merely of a few planks of wood, but most rose up to heaven with their proud stone towers. And the palace of the bishop, the seat of the Church's authority, was still on the island, surrounded by Saint-Étienne. Paris was ostentatiously Christian.

The builders of these sacred places could construct them at their leisure: under the authority of Charibert, there were no military misadventures and fewer plots were hatched. It was a peaceful period. After all, how could a king find the time to go to war? He was distracting himself with any woman who came close. In the end, however, it was deemed better to live under a king who chased skirts than one who chased armies.

This kingly appetite for women of Paris was not, of course, to the clergy's liking. The prelates got together and furiously reproached the king for his concubines, and particularly for having married the sister of one of his wives, which canon law regarded as incest. An epidemic that decimated the population of Paris demonstrated celestial wrath, and Germain, still the bishop of Paris, threatened the king with the ultimate punishment of excommunication.

Charibert pacified his holy brethren by renouncing his wife's sister. He then married a saintly lady who was widely admired. This marriage represented more than a mere moment of sobriety for the king. Charibert had fathered only daughters up to now and needed to sire a boy, a future king to rule over Paris.

He was disappointed in this. He rendered his soul unto God in the year 567 near Bordeaux, during the course of one of his periodic visits to his southern holdings.

And so it started all over again. His three brothers—Chilperic, Sigebert, and Guntram—fought each other like wolves over the inheritance until finally agreeing upon a more or less equitable division. That left the crucial question of what to do about Paris, which each brother felt he deserved. Ah, Paris, the true capital of the Frankish kingdom. Whoever possessed it would be more kingly than the others. None of the brothers wanted to give it up, and so instead they agreed upon a form of joint ownership: the revenue raised there would be divided into thirds, and none of the brothers could enter the city without the agreement of the two others. A triple and solemn sermon, preached over the relics of Saint Martin, Saint Hilary, and Polyeuctus confirmed this arrangement. Paris had three kings.

For seventeen years, no one knew exactly who ruled the city, but its inhabitants did well by this arrangement. All the fratricidal bloodletting was taking place elsewhere. Thus, when Sigebert was busy pushing the barbarians of the east, Chilperic took advantage by wresting Reims from his absent brother. Once he returned to his estates, Sigebert took back his city and, in revenge, wrested Soissons away. A new invasion by the barbarians took Sigebert beyond the Rhine but this time the king was taken prisoner, and only released after a substantial ransom had been paid. This process emboldened his perfidious brother Chilperic, who picked up the war against his brother. Surrounded in Tournai, Chilperic was defeated, and his only way out lay in a rout of the enemy troops. To pull this off, he would have to kill his brother

The Pillar of the Boatmen.

The Cluny Baths.

Since St. Denis was the first bishop of Paris, the underground church in which he was catechized was indeed Paris's first cathedral.

The City Walls. With barbarians threatening, it was decided that the city of Parisii, concentrated by the end of the third century on the Île de la Cité and already protected by the river, would be even more secure if surrounded by a fortified wall. From then on, at the first sign of suspicious activity, Lutecia was ready to defend himself. A trace shows us the thickness of the wall at 6 Rue de la Colombe.

The Tomb of Saint Geneviève, which held the body of the saint, was spared by the Revolutionary fury. Rediscovered in 1802, it was transferred to the Church of Saint-Etienne-du-Mont (Place Sainte-Geneviève). Today, the tomb is partially covered with elaborate gold plating.

The front courtyard of Notre-Dame, viewed from a tower of the cathedral. In the foreground, note the rounded outline that indicates the entrance of the old basilica of Saint-Étienne.

The Throne of Dagobert, who reigned over the Francs from 629 to 639. His beloved minister, Saint Eloi, a master goldsmith, carved the good king's throne, which is now preserved in the cabinet of medals at the National Library, 58 Rue de Richelieu.

The burial site at the Basilica of Saint Denis.

The Prison of the Petit Châtelet. If you really want to get a sense of what the insides of Châtelet looked like, cross the Seine and visit number 42 Rue Galande, and the Grotto of the Oubliettes (literally "forgotten places" or dungeons). Downstairs you will find ancient graffiti of former prisoners: "I'm done for" and "Death to Marat."

Rue du Faubourg-Saint-Denis. At the end of the tenth century, the Right Bank's main axis shifted from the Rue St. Martin to the Rue Saint-Denis, which ended in the faubourg, thus creating the new major road of Paris.

Sigebert, which might instill panic in the ranks of his soldiers. In short, Chilperic hoped through trickery and crime to gain the victory denied him by means of arms.

In the month of December 575, two henchmen surprised Sigebert in Vitry-en-Artois and planted their scramsaxes—small swords whose right edge was soaked in poison, the weapon of choice of the Merovingians and their bodyguards—in Sigebert's chest.

"Here is what the Lord said through the mouth of Solomon: he who digs a ditch in his brother will suffer the same fate," pronounced Germain with a groan.

Indeed, nearly ten years later, Chilperic himself was assassinated, stabbed during a hunting party by an unknown assailant who managed to escape.

Guntram, the last of the brothers, became the sole king of the Franks in 584, and was a figure in keeping with the times: unctuous and violent, wily and brutal. He was fiercely religious, indeed as devout as one could have wished. The people attributed to him miraculous cures and the bishops called him Saint Guntram, which was the very height of toadying.

Still, Guntram did rule with intelligence. To avoid being disemboweled by his nephews, and to prevent his family from being liquidated, he convoked in Paris a Gathering of the Great. He managed to turn the family tendency for aggression toward a common enemy: the Visigoths. The war against this people who ruled over Languedoc in the south of France turned out to be fruitless, but it really didn't matter, for it temporarily preserved the Merovingian dynasty from assassination plots.

Unlike so many others in his family, Guntram died peacefully in his bed in 593 at the age of sixty-eight. He left behind a daughter, who quickly became a nun, and thus the realm was divided between Sigebert's son, Childebert II, the king of Austrasia in the east, and the son of Chilperic, Clotaire II, who was nine years old and the king of Neustria in the west.

In 613, murder and disease had reorganized the family ranks in such a way that Clotaire II was able to unify the Frankish kingdom under his sole authority, though it was a kingdom torn between Neustria, Austrasia, and Burgundy. Perhaps it was for that reason that he chose not to live in Paris but in his palace at Clichy, located northwest of the Île de la Cité.

In any case, it was in Paris that he convoked a grand council whose purpose was to revamp the kingdom's clergy. In October of 614, seventy bishops and everyone whom the country deemed its officers and noblemen gathered around the tomb of Clovis in Saint-Pierre-et-Saint-Paul. Clotaire II made a push to preserve his royal authority and the unity of his estates.

After a week of debate, an edict was announced. The council granted to the clergy the power to judge the righteousness of its decisions, which henceforth would have by royal proclamation the power of law. In exchange, the council promised the nobility certain reparations for the damages caused by the years of war and internecine struggle. Thus a kind of order was established over the kingdom. In fact, with impressive diplomatic skill, Clotaire II had established the groundwork for centralized monarchic power.

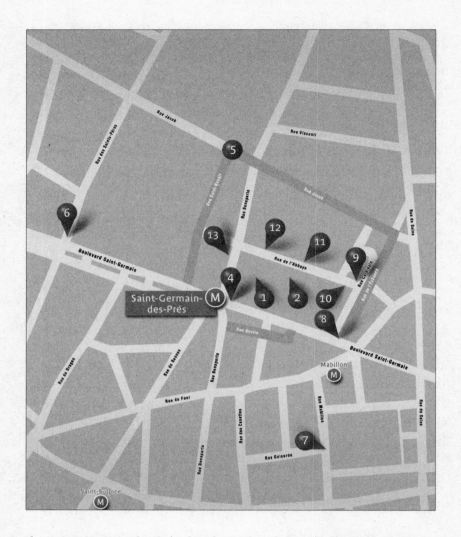

1. The Saint-Germain-des-Prés church. Its foundations, still visible in the Saint-Symphorian chapel, go back about 1,500 years. **2.** The one remaining clock tower of Saint-Germain-des-Prés. **4.** Walk along the right side of the church and follow along the Boulevard Saint-Germain, and you will notice the sharp edge of a wall jutting out into it. Baron Haussmann and his demolition crew cut straight through here to create Boulevard Saint-Germain. **5.** The former boundaries of the Saint-Germain courtyard. **6.** Remains of the Saint-Pierre church, located at what is today 51 Rue Saint-Pères. **7.** Vestiges of the Saint-Germain Fair on Rue Mabillon. **8.** Rue de L'Échaudé. **9.** Home of the bailiff. **10.** Home of the cardinal, at 3 and 5 Rue de l'Abbaye. **11.** Chapel of the virgin, at 6, 8, and 10 Rue de l'Abbaye. **12.** Remains of the monks' dormitory, at 14–16 Rue de l'Abbaye. **13.** Looking right from 16 Rue de l'Abbaye, an angel statue stands in front of a round tower (accessible by going into 15 Rue Saint-Benoît), the last vestige of the abbey's defensive wall.

Seventh Century

Saint-Germain-des-Prés

From One Abbey Emerges Another

Arriving at the Saint-Germain-des-Prés Métro station, the first things that come to mind are Existentialism, jazz clubs, writers huddled for warmth at tables near the stovetops of the Deux Magots, and of course lovers embracing at the Café de Flore. These shadows have never entirely vanished from our minds. This is all an illusion, of course, for Jean-Paul Sartre and Simone de Beauvoir, just like Boris Vian, Jacques Prévert, and all the others are long gone. In his or her quest for them, the literary tourist will find only a somewhat pathetic sign stuck on a post at the edge of the sidewalk. PLACE SARTRE-BEAUVOIR, it proclaims. The city elders clearly believed it necessary to offer at least a small nod to touristic nostalgia and came up with this dual attribution, posted in a noisy and busy intersection facing the Rue de Rennes and right at the spot where it plunges into Boulevard Saint-German.

The stones of the Romanesque clock tower are more than a thousand years old, and the foundations, still visible in the Saint-Symphorian chapel, date from the same Merovingian period, meaning they go back about fifteen hundred years. The steeple rises up over the neighborhood, somewhat desultorily witness to the sad truth that high-fashion clothing stores have replaced the bookstores to which, not so long ago, students came seeking intellectual nourishment.

Walk along the right side of the church and follow along the boulevard. You will be stopped short by the sharp edge of the wall jutting out into it. It is as if some power could still cut straight through the jumble of buildings, a power that, once upon a time, must have been far greater than today. And indeed this stony interruption was formed by the remains of an ancient and powerful abbey. It juts into the street because during the Second Empire, Baron Haussmann and his demolition crew cut straight through here to create Boulevard Saint-Germain.

The construction nonetheless allowed the archaeologist Théodore Vacquer to undertake digs along the edges of the new construction sites, and to find one of the richest collections of Merovingian artifacts, which today are conserved in the Musée Carnavalet.

Farther along is a delightful Renaissance particularity: the southern door of the abbey, which was covered up at the end of the sixteenth century. Here one would have had a view of three ancient clock towers, of which only one survived the Revolution. The other two were so badly damaged that they had to be taken down. In fact, during the Revolution, the church was turned into a saltpeter storehouse, saltpeter being used in the manufacture of gunpowder for cannons, and this caused the ancient walls to blister. By introducing this destructive substance into this place of worship, the *sans-culottes* (as French revolutionaries were known) were intentionally rotting out this religious edifice from within. It is a miracle that the church of Saint-Germain-des-Prés managed to survive in one piece.

Everything here and in the adjoining streets evokes the history of the Saint-Germain-des-Prés abbey, so named to distinguish it from the Saint-Germain-l'Auxerrois and because it was surrounded by large fields (a *pré* is a meadow) of which it was the proprietor. Indeed, once upon a time, the church possessed the entirety of what are today the Sixth and Seventh Arrondissements.

The Benedictines were the masters of this prosperous terrain, with its orchards and vineyards, bringing in considerable revenue. This didn't prevent them from also requiring payment for the right to fish in the branch of the Seine which they had formed by diverting the river in order to obtain an ample source of water. Until the seventeenth century, what are currently the Rues Gozlin and Bonaparte were submerged.

A township gradually developed up around the abbey, to the point that its inhabitants demanded to have their own parish: the Saint-Pierre church located in what is today Rue des Saint-Pères (a corruption of "Saint-Pierre"). By this point you could clearly see the outlines of a village that once was. It went from Boulevard Saint-Michel all the way to Rue des Saint-Pères, and from Rue Saint-Sulpice to the Seine.

The meditations of the monks of Saint-Germain-des-Prés began to be disrupted by the rowdy students from the Latin Quarter who liked to walk on their property. These students were particularly numerous during the Saint-Germain Fair, which took place at Easter around the abbey. Actually, the monks put up pretty well with these disruptions to their routine, for they benefited handsomely by collecting taxes from the merchants and their clientele. A place for shopping and strolling, the fair drew the rich and poor alike, the great and the modest, all of whom came to see actors, jugglers, and animals. Gaming took place here. Henri IV lost somewhere close to three thousand silver écus at the fair.

Quarrels, fights, and petty thievery were common fair occurrences, until the day, at the end of the eighth century, when the students started an outright riot. In order to preserve the peace Philippe IV—known as Philippe the Fair—took over management of the fair. This was a grievous loss to the abbey, given all the extra income that it had generated for the friars. The fair and its beneficiaries, meaning the Benedictines, eventually got it back two centuries later, at which point they again profited from it, an arrangement that lasted until 1762. One night in March of that year a fire destroyed the fairgrounds. Everything was reconstructed, but it wasn't the same. Finally it was closed down completely during the Revolution.

The area was brought back into the jurisdiction of the City of Paris, which constructed the current Saint-Germain Market. At first glance, all that seems to remain of this place are the fairly common-looking buildings constructed at the end of the nineteenth century. But if you look more closely you can still find vestiges of earlier days: in the slope of the little streets, or the playgrounds of the Rue Mabillon, or the cobblestones of the ancient fair down below. A stone stairway still leads down to the ancient level of the street and treading upon this little paved irregularity can still bring back echoes from the past—the cries of the fair vendors and the roughhousing students.

One can also still do the tour of the Saint-Germain courtyard, which now extends across four streets but whose trace can yet be seen: the Rue de l'Échaudé to the east; Rue Gozlin to the south; rue Saint-Benoît to the west; and Rue Jacob to the north.

The first of these is quite curious. A medieval holdover, the Rue de l'Échaudé has a central channel right down the middle that once was used to wash away whatever the denizens of the street at the time threw into it from their windows. Better ways of taking away garbage have since been found, but the little street is still very quaint. Walking it you have that feeling that each section of it doesn't belong to the same street, as if an imaginary wall separated one side of the street from the other, whose building styles are representative of different periods. Actually, there was once a wall there—that of the original abbey.

During the time of the Hundred Years War, a tight triangle was formed between the fortress wall later built by Philippe Auguste, a few dozen feet of the Rues de l'Odéon and Dauphine, and the inner court of the abbey. This constituted a no-construction zone, given that even the smallest structure would have enabled a potential assailant to get over the abbey wall. When this danger receded, this little zone of protection lost its purpose; buildings began timidly poking their nose into it, adapting to the tight angles that now were open to construction. The Rue de l'Échaudé has a pointed nose, and now you know why.

At the end of Rue de l'Échaudé, at the corner of the Rue de l'Abbaye, is a very old house dating back six hundred years and characteristic of buildings of the fifteenth century, meaning narrower at the ground level than on the floors above, to permit the passage of carriages. This building belonged to the bailiff, the officer who decided the fate of prisoners detained by the abbey. There was no recourse for them to appeal to the king or the Paris council: until Louis XIV, Saint-Germain-des-Prés was a separate state within the city and had its own administration for justice, its own court, and even its own prison. Today, to the right of the church on Boulevard Saint-Germain, a bronze statue of the enlightenment philosopher Denis Diderot, watches over the place where the jail once stood.

> **But what was "scalded" (échaudé)?**
>
> The "scalding" of the street's names referred not to boiling water, but to a kind of pastry that was and is still a favorite in the Aveyron regions. The échaudé was a cone-shaped pastry that had been boiled. It was because of the triangular conical shape of the houses along the street, which used to be called the "path through the ditches of the abbey," that the street took the name of this delicacy, whose recipe dates from the Middle Ages.

The abbey possessed a head abbot, a cardinal whose palace at the end of the sixteenth century, located at number 3 and number 5 Rue de l'Abbaye, was long considered one of the most beautiful residences in all of Paris. It remained a testament of Renaissance architecture and an example of religious opulence.

There are other vestiges at numbers 6, 8, and 10 along the same street, which were still in the heart of the former courtyard of Saint-Germain-des-Prés: the remains of the Chapel of the Virgin and its adjacent properties, and the buildings in which the monks lived their lives. Even if fragmented, disjointed, and ruined, the remains speak to the splendor of an age—the thirteenth century—when people came to Paris from distant regions to find intellectual stimulation and relief from petty cares, which they thought studying with the Benedictine monks would provide. The architect of Sainte-Chapelle, Pierre de Montreuil, designed the stone lacework of the Chapel of the Virgin. Several pieces of it can be seen in the small northern square of the church: the ornate curvature of delicate rosework that you would think came from Notre-Dame, or some tombstone, and the remains of wells. The great master builder has been buried here since 1264, contained within the fragments of his work whose foundation stones now comprise the interior walls of boutiques on the Rue de l'Abbaye. Incorporated into contemporary life, these vestiges nonetheless allow us to look back centuries. Even if they cannot speak, the stones convey sensation, color, and light to anyone willing to look and listen.

If you want to see them for yourself, go to 14–16 Rue de l'Abbaye. You won't regret it. This modern building contains a section of the abbey's past. Once the door has been closed behind you, in the silence and the kind of reception appropriate to such a place, you will discover to your right the remains of the monks' dormitory. On the adjoining wall, separating the refectory of the house from the guesthouses of the abbey, the stone moldings remind you of windows. If you lift your head to admire them, your line of sight will take you to vestiges half enfolded into the wall. Imagine monks coming and going beneath the vaults whose majestic height was such that they remained untouched by the Revolution. Here you find a perfect example of the modern assimilation of medieval remains, because the combination of the chalky purity of the renovated stones, artfully illuminated by both natural lighting and spotlights, seems like the creation of some fantasist playing with time and styles.

From 16 Rue de l'Abbaye look over to the right. You will see an angel over the building facing the church. And behind it, a round tower, accessible by going into 15 Rue Saint-Benoît. This tower is the last vestige of the abbey's defensive wall, constructed in the fourteenth century, shortly before the Hundred Years War.

In the seventh century, of course, this whole neighborhood hadn't even started to form . . .

The centralized power imagined by Clotaire II was shaped by Paris, subject to the endless comings and goings of important figures from all the regions of the country. The king himself left less often, and sent only the occasional emissary out to his states, but he received at the Palace of the Cité the sons of the nobles and members of the clergy who came to solicit something or bring him news of their distant provinces. Little by little, the king abandoned his villa in Clichy and settled in Paris, the center for decision-making.

Beginning in this period one "climbed up" to Paris, as believers in the word of the Bible "climbed up" to Jerusalem. The Parisian population thought itself rather superior to all the other cities in the kingdom. Had not King Clotaire walked its muddy streets with his queen and his son, Prince Dagobert? This proximity to royal grandeur swelled the heads of the city's inhabitants slightly, or so some would have us believe.

In any case, the other regions of the realm grew envious; they, too, wanted to have a king living among them. Hence Clotaire sent his son Dagobert to Austrasia. For a number of years, this young man of twenty-three had studied the affairs of state and proven an effective counselor to his father. But now all that was changed. He had to leave Paris and head to Metz, to administer the lands of the east. For seven years Dagobert played the role of assistant king, until his father died at the age of forty-five, in October of 629. As soon as his death was announced, Dagobert left Metz to attend the royal funeral in the Saint-Vincent-Sainte-Croix Basilica, which is also where both King Childebert, Clotaire's great-grand-uncle, and Clotaire's father, Chilperic, were interred.

In the choir of the church were numerous Gothic effigies of the kings of the seventh century. That of Childebert, which was discovered in excellent state and represents the oldest tomb effigy in France, was put in Saint-Denis.

Dagobert was never to return to Austrasia. He moved into the Cité Palace and quite naturally it was he who was given the Frank-ish crown—a crown slightly gnawed at around the edges, for Dago-bert had a half brother named Charibert II, a slightly deranged lad, though such a handicap did not stop the Merovingian family from being once again divided in its succession. Brodulf, Chari-bert's maternal uncle, and an ambitious and sly individual, de-manded for his dear nephew half of his inheritance. Moreover, he claimed that this was what the deceased Clotaire had wanted. Everyone had some difficulty believing that the former king would have wanted to cede a part of his kingdom to the family simpleton, so Brodulf produced witnesses. Former counselors maintained that not long ago they had heard their master ex-press edifying thoughts about Charibert II's virtues. Interro-gated harder, they started to waffle. Then they threw in the towel altogether. Actually, no, they knew nothing and had re-ceived no special confidence, and did not know the former king's true intentions.

His ploy uncovered, Brodulf took flight to Burgundy and the banks of the Saône River, where his wife was mobilizing a few allies. Would the debate over the inheritance of Clotaire go on forever? As it turned out, it didn't, because good King Dagobert had the evil Brodulf assassinated, putting an immediate end to all machinations.

Given that Charibert was, after all, of royal blood, it was nec-essary to offer him some kind of consolation prize. He was given the kingdom of Aquitaine, with its capital, Toulouse. His kingly title was a fiction, in fact, because the shy Charibert was entirely under the thumb of his half brother. After three years, he had the good sense to die, disappearing from the pages of history. But he left a son. And on it would go, for one day this child would de-mand his part of the kingdom. As the adage has it, governing means foreseeing. In the name of the unity of the Frankish kingdom, the infant was promptly suffocated in his crib. And that's how the business was handled. Dagobert was not the sort to let himself be thwarted by a baby.

From that point on, Dagobert ruled as absolute master. The Cité palace became, more than ever before, the center of power. From Metz, Limoges, Rouen, Lyon, or Bordeaux the prominent and wellborn sent their children, both boys and girls, to take the air of the Parisian court. They came to Paris in the way that French kids today do internships in London or New York: to learn and to make useful connections. Where else could you network with young people from Neustria, Austrasia, and Burgundy? Where else could you meet young people who had come to learn good manners in the Frankish capital? Thus did King Edwin, the sovereign of North Umbria (in the northeast of England) have his two sons educated in Paris, convinced that they would find in King Dagobert the model for a powerful and respected monarch.

In Paris, the nobles from the provinces were initiated into all the necessary arts. A wellborn boy needed to learn how to use weapons, as well as rhetoric and law. Young noblemen were prepared to become both good soldiers and perfect administrators.

Paris was also the place for amorous adventures—whether passing fancies or promises exchanged for life, the pleasure of one night or a definitive engagement. The young discovered love on the Île de la Cité, and in the process brought about the union of families from different regions, regions that were sometimes in conflict, but which suddenly found the advantages of peaceful coexistence, particularly if one had royal ambition. People came to study, or to use a sword, or to marry if necessary, but intrigue and interests always lurked. The families watched over their offspring and counted on them to draw substantial benefit from their loyalty to the court. These benefits could take various forms—influence, territory, gold coins, or titles. For example, a certain Saigrius left Paris with the title of count; a Radulf was sent as a duke into the border regions of the north; a Desiderius made the contacts that later proved indispensable for getting himself named bishop of Cahors.

Why did Dagobert wear his underwear backward?

According to a French children's verse, good saint Éloi once remarked to good king Dagobert that he was wearing his underwear backward. A bit of an anachronism, because said underwear is actually a *culotte*—puffy shorts that went down to the knees—which would be re-created by inspired fashion designers about a thousand years later. French Revolutionaries came up with this old rhyme to make fun of all the kings and all the saints. The radicals ridiculed royal pretension or, in one of the bawdier versions of the song, poked fun at the supposed love between King Dagobert and Saint Éloi. This was love in the wrong direction, exactly like the king's culottes. Finally, as His Royal Majesty hurriedly "put them straight," morality was preserved.

Conscious of status, Dagobert had his throne installed in the great hall of the palace, a seat fashioned by Eligius, his personal goldsmith, and a man in whom he placed so much confidence that Eligius would be appointed silversmith of the realm, and then a bishop, and even eventually be canonized, entering history under the name of Saint Éloi.

However, the future saint wasn't yet the skilled artisan he would later become. The throne, with its rustic leather slats, was not all that comfortable. Still the frame shone with gold-ornamented bronze and was intended to make an impression, with its armrests thickening out to turn into the heads of lions with open jaws. Dagobert's throne today is kept in the Medal Room of the Bibliothèque Nationale.

As a mark of his absolute power, Dagobert needed symbols such as this throne. But they weren't enough; he also needed to inscribe his greatness into stone. Paris already had its abbey, and so he turned his eyes to the sancuary of Saint-Denis. Here he would construct the greatest of his monuments.

Profoundly religious and quite superstitious, Dagobert was persuaded that Saint Denis watched over him from on high. He could feel it, for once, long ago, when he had seen the sepulcher of the decapitated saint, Denis appeared to him in a dream in which the saint promised him protection, on the condition that once he had become king, Dagobert would build him the most sumptuous of all tombs.

Saint-Denis Church had been founded earlier by Saint Geneviève, of course, but in the century and a half that had passed since then, the place had become slightly dilapidated. In fact it was hardly more than a ramshackle little sanctuary located north of Paris; few pilgrims ventured in. About a dozen years before, a Benedictine monastery grew up adjacent to the holy place, and a small community had grown up around the monastery, consisting of a few farmers and artisans who made a modest living by serving the needs of the monks. But it was all a little sad and pathetic. Dagobert was determined to please his patron saint and to enlarge and beautify his resting place.

What Saint Denis required was a mausoleum as legendary as his story, and therefore a basilica would replace the rundown little church. Éloi was ordered to produce a reliquary appropriate to Saint Denis. Éloi fulfilled his mission, creating a first-class piece of work made of gold and precious stones with balustrades inlaid with gold, silver doors, and a marble roof. Denis's disciples had to have been pleased: the remains of the miracle-working saint were finally housed in a sepulchre worthy of him. Éloi went further and exceeded the royal command: to receive the offerings from the faithful, he made a throne out of silver, and to exalt the faith of the believer, he created an enormous gold cross studded with garnets and other precious stones.

Dagobert was also thinking of the spiritual health of women. He founded a nunnery on the Île de la Cité, authority over which would lie outside the jurisdiction of the bishop of Paris. Aure, the first abbess, received the order directly from the hands of Éloi, and hence it was decided that it would be called Saint-Éloi. Before long, three hundred sisters were crowded within its walls. For their benefit two churches were constructed, one dedicated to Saint Martial, which is where the sisters would go to chant the service; the other was consecrated to Saint Paul, and into this church they retreated from the world. For those who enjoy looking through keyholes, we should note that these women, agitated by the military garrison that was given the responsibility of maintaining the security of the nearby royal palace, were so seduced by these handsome soldiers that eventually the community would be dissolved on orders from the pope. But that occurred five centuries later, enough time for several generations of good sisters to accommodate in their inimitable way both the sword and the holy-water sprinkler.

After that, Dagobert showered his favors upon the Saint-Vincent-Sainte-Croix Abbey. Naturally, the king's pious generosity when it came to abbeys and convents was not without political subtext. The monarch was perfectly aware of the benefits he would gain by association with martyrs and saints. Religion was the guarantor of the realm's unity; it could do what neither language, nor nationalism, nor tribalism could accomplish with a kingdom as spread out and diverse as Dagobert's estates. Catholicism, with its procession of saints, its accumulation of relics, and its opulent churches and powerful abbeys, offered a means to unify in spiritual fervor the various parts of the Frankish kingdom.

Nonetheless, in order to confirm his authority, the king sometimes needed to collect money. To do this, he felt no compunction about turning to certain religious orders, whose riches were somewhat astounding. The palace constantly needed to fill its coffers to keep Paris, whose population was constantly growing, running, as well as to wage war against the Gascons and the Bretons, who were calling out for independence, or against the Slavs, who were threatening the borders. In order to pay for all this, Dagobert confiscated a number of lands that had belonged to the Church. The question was whether the monks would go along with this. As it turned out, they did, as the king played them off skillfully: he received the prelates and used his loyal follower Desiderius, the bishop of Cahors, to intercede on his behalf.

"When one has had the honor of working directly under the orders of Your Sublime Majesty," pronounced the good bishop, "one knows that he is incapable of bullying the Church, and that only his sense of justice and his appreciation for what is necessary and right can lead for him to make such decisions."

Following this episcopal declaration, the king made it known that this confiscating was not a matter of personal enrichment, but of maintaining security and unifying the realm. There was nothing to be said against this, and the bishops submitted to being stripped of riches without too much recrimination.

At the end of the year 638, Dagobert, though only thirty-five years of age, looked like an old man. His puffy trousers and the toga that he draped over himself couldn't hide the fact that the king had lost a great deal of weight. His thick beard had gone gray and his beautiful hair now hung down limply. He suffered increasingly from inflammation of the intestines, and his hemorrhoids had become so bad that he was bleeding profusely. The doctors believed in bleeding patients, but this only succeeded in making him even weaker.

In the month of October, Dagobert asked to be taken to Saint-Denis. There was some question whether he would even survive the journey. To avoid being bumped around, he was conveyed in a wagon drawn by two oxen, which took small steps. Finally he reached his beloved abbey. After several prayers, Dagobert was taken to his villa in Épinay, where he had been born. Here he was not far from Saint-Denis and it was there that he had decided he would be buried. He had hesitated over this. Three years earlier he had asked to be buried in Paris, in Saint-Vincent-Sainte-Croix, next to his father. He modified his will, wishing to lie alongside the tomb of the holy martyr.

From Épinay, Dagobert ran the affairs of the realm, but when it was suggested that his son Clovis (the future Clovis II) be brought to him, a boy of only four, the king cried out, "The sight of a dying man is not fit for a child. I would prefer that he retain a better memory of his father."

On January 19, 639, the king was found dead in his bed. The

What's on Dagobert's tomb?

In the thirteenth century, the monks of Saint-Denis wanted to pay homage to King Dagobert by building a unique tomb for his remains. But the king's sulfurous reputation worried them greatly. They therefore came up with a somewhat ambiguous stone sculpture that looks something like a cartoon. The soul of the king, pictured as a naked child with a crown, is carried off to hell in the clutches of demons. Happily, Saint Denis, Saint Martin, and Saint Maurice succeed in delivering his soul, take him to heaven, and gain him admission into paradise. The message is clear: Dagobert deserved to go to hell and only the intercession of the saints miraculously prevented this. This rather peculiar tomb is still visible in Saint-Denis, near the main altar.

abbot of Saint-Denis planned an opulent funeral, but such was resisted, for it was pointed out that Dagobert's private life had not been above reproach. He had had three wives—Gomentrude, Nanthilde, and Wulfegunde—as well as two known mistresses—Ragnetrude and Berthilde—and this didn't include innumerable dalliances with servants, slaves, and the ladies of the palace. The abbot would brook no resistance, however. He could do no less than to have the man to whom the abbey owed its very existence buried with pomp.

In Épinay, the king's body was boiled in heavily salted water, a rudimentary method of embalming, and then his body was carried to his tomb in Saint-Denis. There were gathered all the great figures from all the regions of the kingdom. The palanquin bearing the king was brought in; he was dressed in the red coat of royalty, his hands joined together piously in prayer.

After Dagobert's death, the Frankish kingdom was, once again, divided up, this time between two royal children: Sigebert III, who was but ten years old, and to whom was given Austrasia in the east; and Clovis II, a child of four, as we've seen, to whom was given Neustria in the north, as well as Burgundy. From this moment on and for quite some time, true power was held by the palace's mayors, who acted as prime ministers and made all the decisions.

Clovis II would leave Paris and establish himself in Clichy. The

Cité palace became an empty shell, which was occasionally re-animated, such as when an ambassador was being greeted or for grand convocations. Poor Clovis therefore took his place on the throne, his crown placed upon his long hair, like a true Merovingian. This poor pale-faced child, whose name was too much of a burden for him, simply watched events without saying a word, his great and innocent eyes opened wide.

The citizens of Paris were actually somewhat surprised when he came to town. He didn't traverse the city on horse, as kings until then had generally done. Instead, he was carried in a wagon drawn by four oxen. The young king was perpetually ill and not strong enough to ride a horse; this was the most he could manage. The locals made fun of him for this, and soon enough had come up with what they deemed an appropriate nickname: the Lazy King. It stuck—both to him and to all of his descendants.

Nonetheless, on one occasion Clovis II displayed royal determination. When a famine was decimating Paris, he decided to take back a silver vessel that his father had given to the monks at Saint-Denis. He sold it and with the money bought wheat that he had delivered to the city. The abbot of Saint-Denis was outraged by this. Taking any of the abbey's riches was a sin.

It would seem that the king looked with some disfavor on Saint-Denis and its riches. One day, deciding that he needed for his personal oratory in Clichy a holy relic powerful enough to ward off the devil, he went to Saint-Denis, and coolly ordered that the tomb of the saint be opened. Then, with a swipe of his sword he hacked off one of the martyr's arms. After which, he left cheerfully, carrying the martyr's arm under his.

Several months later, at the age of only twenty-two, Clovis II fell victim to a mysterious lethargy and the monks of Saint-Denis, who hoped to get their martyr's arm back, made it known that the king had died young and in lunacy because he was being punished for his terrible sacrilege. The arm was returned to the crypt in the abbey and Clovis II was buried near his father.

From this second half of the seventh century, Saint-Denis saw its influence grow to the point of becoming an increasingly serious competitor to Saint-Germain-des-Prés, which, as we've seen, had been the necropolis of choice for the Merovingian kings.

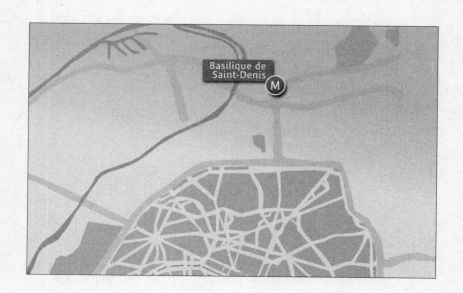

The Final Splendor of Kings

Sometimes the subway affords shortcuts, which allow us to move away from the heart of Paris and inspire us to go outside the city limits—into a suburb, or a new neighborhood, or the Paris of to-morrow. The project of Greater Paris is already in the works; with the help of the Métro it has been realized. It can be found in one of the major new pillars of this Paris: the Stadium of France with its seats for eighty thousand spectators—me among them—who were there when the French national team won the World Cup in 1998.

The true pillar of our history can be found a little farther off: in the basilica in the very heart of the abbey of Saint-Denis. When you approach the church, the Gothic style of the façade can seem a little heavy and massive, nearly Romanesque. This is probably because before you stands the first Gothic church in France, constructed in 1136. Extensively restored in the nineteenth century, it nonetheless retains the appearance desired by its creator, Abbot Suger.

Within the church, on the other hand, one finds a more en-chanting prospect, with the columns rising up in airy elegance. The windows allow in rays of brilliant light that play with the lines and lighten them. Here the Gothic has the upper hand, in its radiating phase. In this, again, Saint-Denis was a pioneer, the

Where did the royal bodies go?

In 1793, the Convention decided to "destroy the sumptuous mausoleums of the monarchy in Saint-Denis." Under the direction of a commissary and wearing black clothing and a tricolor pointed hat, a group of workers carrying picks broke into the cavern of the Bourbons. Three heavy stones blocked the entrance; the picks went at the thick walls, which resisted for a number of hours. Finally they gave way and the workers made their way into the long crypt in which reposed fifty-four oak coffins. They were opened systematically. Louis XIII's moustache caused a sensation, the face of Louis XIV was strangely black, and the body of Louis XV gave off a horrendous odor.

Soon there was the eerier face-to-face confrontation between the incorruptible Robespierre—the commissary in black—and the good king Henri IV, assassinated one hundred and eighty-three years earlier. Time had barely altered the monarch's features, though his neat beard had become bushy, gray, and stiff. The body bound by strips of cloth was leaned, upright and stiff, against a pillar of the church. Robespierre, cinched up in his suit with its long folded collar, his hair powdered and set in perfect white curls, examined *(Cont.)*

term "radiating" deriving from the rosette designs that adorn the transept.

Here in the half-shadows of the interior, the history of France awaits us. Here is where the ancient kings can be found. Most of them, anyway. The actual mortal remains of these rulers have long disappeared, but here at any rate is the mausoleum constructed for the purpose of celebrating the grandeur of the monarchy across the centuries. How can one not be awed by this dazzling domain of effigies, by these centuries of royalty immortalized in limestone and marble? You can see them, talk to them, and touch them, proudly laid out for eternity. Here is Dagobert, who founded the necropolis, as well as Pepin the Short, Robert the Pious, Louis X, Charles V, François I, and on and on. There are more than seventy of them with their frozen stares. The tombs were profaned during the Revolution—emptied of their occupants—but most of the tombs themselves were miraculously preserved.

The crypt of the basilica also stands as wonderful witness to the deep past. The mausoleum of Saint-Denis, the first to inhabit the setting, was removed. All that remains is the empty spot where his tomb once was. Around him are the remains of the eighth-century crypt belonging to Fulrad, the abbot of Saint-Denis, with its little niches in which sit candles lit to his memory. A little farther off is the ninth-century crypt in which were placed the coffins of Louis XVI and Marie-Antoinette, having been retrieved from the common pit on Rue d'Anjou in which they had been thrown after their execution. For me this is history's most symbolic setting.

One afternoon in November of the year 751 a delegation of nobles and bishops respectfully presented themselves before King Childeric III and to his stunned amazement announced, "The Frankish nation has brought the reign of Your Sublimeness and the continuity of your dynasty to an end."

Childeric opened his eyes wide in surprise but before he had time to react a strong arm seized the frail man, forced him into a low chair while other men, armed with

closely the royal face whose eyes remained obstinately closed. What did Robespierre, this instigator of revolutionary terror, hope to find in this time-defying meeting?

Suddenly, driven by some irresistible force, Robespierre raised his hand toward the beard of the desiccated corpse and, with a sharp gesture, pulled out two hairs. He carefully placed these royal relics into a small wallet that he had pressed close in his suit.

Others there had their way with the corpse. An amateur collector of souvenirs pulled out two teeth, and took them away, a soldier cut off a large portion of the beard with his sword. Finally the body of the Vert-Galant, as Henri IV, or Henri de Navarre, was called, was thrown along with all the others into a common pit located north of the church, near what is today the garden Pierre-de-Montreuil.

Exhumed during the Restoration, the remains of the royals, mainly destroyed by quicklime, were piously replaced in an ossuary of the crypt.

scissors, went at cutting off his long hair, the symbol of his royal authority. The strands of blond hair fell silently to the cold floor and marked the end of the Merovingian reign.

His hair cut short, Childeric was lifted into a litter carried by two horses, which, with a flick of the whip, took off at a gallop toward the north, all the way to the Saint-Bertin Abbey, built on a small island in the Aa River. For the last of the Merovingians, the monastery represented a golden retreat; the community was prosperous and capable of doing honor to a deposed king. Despite it all, the thick walls were a reminder to the former king that he would never leave.

The idea for this coup, which destroyed the royal line, was not arrived at suddenly. Fulrad, the abbot of Saint-Denis, had gone to Rome to see Pope Zacharias, a gentle man, fair and good, but also expert at politics; his advice was sought after in difficult situations. Who should be the king of France—the listless Childeric or Duke Pepin, who had effectively been leading the country for ten years?

"To whom is it right to give the name of king? To him who has no more royal authority than that conferred by a name, or to him who has possessed it completely without a name?" asked Fulrad.

His Eminence slowly stroked his gray beard, and after a long silence responded in a grave and measured voice. "It is reasonable and just that whoever truly exercises royal authority should be given the title of king."

The pope had given his blessing to Pepin, who would ascend to the throne of the Franks. This showed fairly stunning ingratitude to the Merovingians, who had imposed Christianity onto their kingdom. Thus was poor Childeric deposed.

A new day was dawning. Pepin, called "the Short" because of his diminutive stature, was a hyperactive man who micromanaged and had an insatiable appetite for glory, honor, and power.

Rome had given benediction to his ambitions, but he needed still greater legitimacy than that conferred in a few words spoken by an aging pope behind closed doors. Bishop Boniface, an able diplomatic adviser to the new king, thought up a coronation service that exceeded Pepin's imagination. He took his inspiration from the Bible, specifically the Book of Samuel, with its use of oil on the kings of Israel: "Samuel took a flask of oil and poured it on the head of Saul." (1 Sam. 10:1.) Then he looked across the Channel at what the Britons did on their great island. The kings of Scotland were blessed and ordained by the highest ecclesiastical authority. Boniface concocted a mixture of traditions and came up with a coronation that artfully combined the authority of God and the faith of men.

The ceremony took place in the cathedral at Soissons. With his long hair, his full beard, and the purple robes draped across his shoulders, the king repeated the words Boniface whispered to him.

"I do solemnly swear to preserve in peace the Church of God and all the Christian people under my governance, to fight injustice, whatever its source, and to combine justice and mercy in all of my judgments."

After this, Boniface solemnly poured the holy oil—a mixture of olive oil and perfume—on Pepin's face. It would instill in him the Holy Spirit. He then conferred the emblems of authority, placing the crown on the king's head and the scepter in his hands.

"May he be always victorious and magnanimous. And may all of his judgments be fair and wise. And may his reign be a peaceful one."

The nobles and the clerics who were gathered together under the vaulted ceiling of the cathedral responded by chanting three times:

"Vivat Rex in aeternum!"

In an instant the king of France became a monarch by holy right, unifying in his person both God and the nation.

Three and a half centuries later, Hincmar, the archbishop of Reims and a man with more imagination than scholarly rigor, would write that Clovis had been anointed by God. Indeed, a dove had carried in its beak the holy oil used in the ceremony. Actually, this never happened. First of all, the ceremony had not yet been instituted. And secondly, Clovis was not Christian when he was crowned. Still, this holy myth permitted the kings of France to believe that they were part of a line of kings whose power had been consecrated by God Himself.

The benediction of Pepin the Short was not necessarily good news for Paris. The new king had shown only scant interest in settling in the Merovingian capital. Moreover, he apparently saw no need to install his court and his authority in any particular location. He would turn out be an itinerant king, who went from his palace in Cologne to his palace in Thionville to his villa in Worms and to the one in Compiègne. The Frankish nobility followed him around during this constant shuffling, more a result of royal whim than kingly necessity.

A little after his coronation, while Pepin was back on the road, the good pope Zacharias, whose approval had led to the deposition of the Merovingians, took his place in paradise. Stephen II replaced him on the throne of Saint Peter. Now it was he whom it was necessary to placate in order to remain in the good graces of the Church. This changed everything. Zacharias had been a capable politician; Stephen was a priest of faith and charity who spent his life visiting the poor and having hospitals built for the sick. While His Holiness as yet knew nothing about diplomacy, events would very quickly force him to catch on.

Aistulf, the king of the Lombards, wanted to extend his power across all of Italy. He demanded a sizable tribute from the pope and threatened to march upon Rome. The natural protector of the Church was Constantine V, the emperor of the Eastern Roman Empire who ruled from Constantinople; Constantine believed that he had more important things to worry about than saving the Eternal City. He was attempting to consolidate his empire, having invaded Syria, and planned on retaking Cyprus. He was entirely indifferent to the danger in which Rome and its inhabitants found themselves.

Stephen II no longer knew to which saint he should appeal. Who would protect him from the Lombards? That's when he thought of Pepin, who, after all, was king thanks to the good grace of his predecessor. He would prove himself an ingrate if he did not now come to the aid of Zacharias's successor. His Holiness immediately gave a letter to a Frankish nobleman who was then doing his pilgrimage to Rome. In this missive the pope asked the king to send an ambassador to Neustria. This invitation, to which the Lombards were of course opposed, permitted the pope to set a trap.

Pepin immediately saw the benefits of the situation. If he acted carefully, he could align himself with the Holy See forever. A second ambassador was thus immediately dispatched to Rome and the pope departed from the City of Seven Hills—to the great surprise of its population, who were therefore delivered up to their enemies the Lombards. Leaving Rome at this moment seemed the height of folly. No one could think of a precedent for this.

In the month of December in 753, Stephen II arrived in the Aosta Valley, crossed the Alps, and stopped at the monastery of Great Saint-Bernard, a vast building lost in the immense whiteness of the landscape. Soon a Frankish delegation, led by Abbot Fulrad, joined the pope there. Fulrad and the others kneeled respectfully before Stephen, who was somewhat surprised to find his authority so respected and piously celebrated.

The pope and his escort continued on their way while Pepin and his queen, Berthe, moved toward them from the opposite direction. They met just south of Champagne. Pepin galloped toward the pontifical procession, got off his horse, prostrated himself and begged for the pontiff's blessing. This made for a good start: the pope was happy to recognize him as king of the Franks.

The next day, discussions began within the walls of the royal villa at Ponthion. Now the tone had changed: it was Stephen who was forced to kneel before the king and make his plea.

"Give us your help to put an end to this oppression by the Lombards, and save Rome from the tribute that Aistulf wants to impose upon us."

Pepin was rather flattered by the pope's earnestness. In effect, the pontiff was choosing him rather than the emperor of Byzantium to come to his aid. From now on it would be the king of France who would guarantee the continuance of the Roman Catholic Church.

Pepin was prepared to negotiate the departure of the Lombards from Rome, and even wished that the Holy See would henceforth benefit from greater territory to protect itself from further predations. Would a few royal declarations do the trick with the Lombards? Probably not, and hence the king of the Franks declared himself prepared to raise an army and lead a military expedition.

Stephen was appeased by this and indeed thrilled, for his

What became of the treasure of Saint-Denis?

As we've seen, the abbey was gutted during the Revolution, but the pillagers were disappointed by what they found there—a few measly pieces of gold and silver. Nonetheless, during an inventory that was done in 1634, there were documented 455 objects considered of great value. These consisted of the weapons of ancient kings, jewel-encrusted crowns, holy relics kept in precious chests, illustrated manuscripts—all these were listed.

There were those who wanted to believe that the treasure of Saint-Denis had been hidden somewhere. In 1939, one particular gentleman by the name of Leclerc bought the property of La Dimeresse, near Messy, located twenty or so miles from Saint-Denis. The new owner found in the papers discovered in the house a deed of sale that proved that the land had once belonged to the monks at the abbey. This was enough to persuade that man that the mythical treasure was buried beneath his feet. A dowser by training, he called upon his colleagues to help. They all came and brought their divining pendulums and declared that there were underground passages and detected deep within them the presence of precious metals.

(Cont.)

pontifical throne and his city were saved. Pepin demanded something in return: a new coronation ceremony led in person by His Holiness. The ceremony would settle definitively, and before all Christendom, that the king and his sons would be uncontested in their rights, sanctified by the Holy See, thus instituting forever the line of Pepin. The pope agreed. He didn't really have much choice.

While waiting to perform this second coronation, Stephen II determined not to return to Rome, not out of some political calculation but because he wanted to spare himself the rigors of a new voyage in the middle of winter.

Therefore the pope spent several months in Saint-Denis. Dagobert's abbey had become rich and powerful, and the abbot fought hard to gain fiscal privileges, as well as lands that extended all the way to Pantin and La Villette. Out of esteem for his dear friend Abbot Fulrad, Pepin was magnanimous toward Saint-Denis and refused those cranky lords who wanted to stem the abbey's territorial expansion.

Naturally the new consecration of Pepin would take place within the walls of Saint-Denis. But before then, the pope had a holy mission to accomplish: the solemn transfer of the remains of Saint Germain. The good bishop of Paris was canonized for curing the sick, exorcising demons, fighting against slavery and paganism, and in general living a life of boundless charity. Nonetheless his remains had spent the previous 177 years in a modest chapel at the entrance to the Saint-Vincent-Sainte Croix Basilica. This was not a resting place worthy of a venerated saint, and it was past time to place the body in a more appropriate spot: in the choir, just behind the main altar.

Everyone was reunited in Paris for the ceremony: Stephen II, King Pepin, Queen Berthe, their son Charles, the future Charlemagne. Once again the city was witness to the kind of grandeur that it had once known. For one moment it refound its place as the capital of the Frankish kingdom.

Leclerc leaped into action and started digging. In 1954, the excavations discovered a series of steps that led down into the ground. Getting wind of this, the newspapers announced the imminent discovery of the treasure of Saint-Denis. But alas the small passage they discovered was unsafe, so they retreated in a hurry. It is said that when he was dying in 1961 Commander Leclerc asked that one last hole be dug on his property. His final hope was that his dream would be realized, a dream in which he had invested all of his money and his time. As with the others, alas, the digging produced nothing of interest.

Before the kneeling crowd, the crypt was opened and the coffin of Saint Germain was carried into the chancel. During the entirety of the following day and night, he remained there, subject to the veneration of the faithful.

The next morning, in the presence of Pepin and his son Charles, the sarcophagus was to be transferred to the place chosen for its burial. The trouble was that it couldn't be moved. Levers and ropes and pulleys did no good; the thing simply wouldn't budge. Was this a sign that the saint refused to be taken from the choir in which he was placed? The bishops who were witness to this offered an explanation.

"Glorious king," they said to Pepin, "Your Highness knows well that blesséd Germain was a bishop. It therefore seems appropriate that his precious relics be borne by the bishops. That is perhaps what the saint wants to tell us."

The gathered prelates tried to lift the coffin by means of levers. No luck.

"Most pious king, is it possible that only the blessed monks of the monastery have been accorded the honor of moving the holy relics?"

The monks took the place of the bishops and tried to move the coffin by the same means, and they as well couldn't move it an inch. Tears poured down Pepin's face. He wondered whether he had committed a terrible sacrilege in taking the saint far from the place that he himself had designated as the spot at which he would await the Resurrection.

At that moment an unknown man came forward from the gathering of faithful. Through a remarkable feat of intuition, he had finally solved the mystery.

"If His Most Mild Majesty Our King would deign to listen to the word of the humblest of his servants, I believe I have found the true cause of this unfortunate resistance. Not far from the royal villa at Palaseau, the monastery possesses a number of out-buildings. The treasury agents, emboldened by the power of Your Greatness, exert in this place a tyrannous and intolerable oppression. They have killed the inhabitants, destroyed the vines and the harvest, the fields and woods, and seized the animals and in general inflicted upon this land great terror. That, I believe, is the injustice that the Venerable Germain wants to make us aware of today."

That was the reason. The miracle manifesting itself here was not a call for human nature to change, or to bring a bit of goodness to the earth, or to relieve the misery of the human condition. No, it really was all about some overzealous tax agents and adjoining new land to the benefit of the monastery.

The monks of the abbey must have dreamed all this up to obtain a few extra land grants. In any case, the trick worked perfectly and Pepin consented to what the Venerable Germain was demanding of him from beyond the grave: he offered the monks his beautiful villa at Palaiseau along with several extra farms.

"I ask in return the power to transport your sacred body," begged the king to the spirit of the saint.

And it came to pass that the blessed spirit of Germain was appeased, for the coffin now was lifted with disconcerting ease and taken down into the new crypt. Those there remembered smelling a sweet perfume waft through the basilica; the most fervent among them saw an angel descend from heaven to carry the body of the saint. Young prince Charles was so joyful of the happy solution to the business that he jumped into the crypt to observe the miracle from close up. He didn't meet any seraphim, but during the fall he did lose his first baby tooth.

A little later, a chiseled stele would confirm the royal gift. One couldn't be too careful and it seemed like a good idea to set in stone the king's generous bequest. "On this spot where lay Saint Germain the day of his transference, King Pepin gave to him the treasury of Palaiseau."

And to mark the greatness of the event, the abbey Saint-Vincent-Sainte-Croix was henceforth to be called Saint-Germain-des-Prés.

You have to have an ability to see beyond what's there now to imagine the dimensions that this abbey and the neighborhood assumed in the days following this. Its adjacent lands spread far and wide and added to them were the fiefdoms of Issy, Vaugirard, Châtillon, and Thiais, comprising lands that went all the way to Montereau and Saint-Cloud, and to Palaiseau, of course. It was roughly the equivalent of what is today called a *département* in France—a small state. The congregation's prestige included learned Benedictine monks, who were friends of the arts, sciences, and letters and who gathered here to reflect, work, and write. The *quartier* already had its identity, and the number of intellectuals would grow. Today when a writer sits at a table at one of the famous cafés there, or feverishly composes on her laptop, I would like to think that she still is inspired by the spirit of intellectual curiosity that took root here so long ago.

———

Pope Stephen now devoted his attention to the ceremony for Pepin, but there was a problem. Queen Berthe informed His Holiness that her husband was living in a state of sin. Though Pepin's legitimate wife, she was condemned to solitude in the palace while the king frolicked, spending his nights with a pretty Saxon girl. The pope was horrified. The heavens would punish this adulterer. Stephen met with the king in Saint-Denis.

"We cannot proceed with a ceremony for a king who is living in a state of sin. Not only is he not in a state of grace, he shames those around him and sullies the throne of the Franks to which all of Christendom has turned its gaze."

What a lot of to-do over nothing, thought Pepin. He immediately placated the pope and had the pretty Saxon girl locked up in an abbey in the diocese of Langres, praying firmly that she never be allowed to leave and do penitence for the rest of her life.

Finally, at the end of July 754, nothing stood in the way of the consecration of the king of the Franks by the Vicar of Christ. All was in readiness. Two days before the ceremony was to take place, however, Pope Stephen became deathly ill. The pontiff requested that he immediately be taken to Saint-Denis Church, near to the tomb of the blessed martyr. While His Holiness lay in a comatose sleep and approached death, the apostles Peter and Paul, accompanied by Saint Denis himself, visited him.

"Our brother is asking for his health," said Peter.

"He shall have it immediately," added Paul.

And then Denis, holding an incense thurible in his hand, turned to the dying pope.

"Peace be upon thee, brother. Rise up, for you are cured."

And that is what the pope did, apparently no longer debilitated by whatever it was that had laid him low. In gratitude, he conferred gifts upon the abbey: exemption from episcopal jurisdiction, new lands and buildings for the monastery, and favors galore to Abbott Fulrad.

Stephen II proceeded to the ceremony with King Pepin the

Short, which took place on July 28 in Saint-Denis. This was not a complicated affair involving holy unguents or anointing oil. Stephen was not the kind of pope for such grandiosity; his approach was more sober and direct. He did exactly what was expected of him, which was to consecrate Pepin and his two sons, Charles and Carloman, in the name of the Holy Trinity. Then Queen Berthe was clothed in royal insignias and blessed by the Holy Father in the name of the Seven Virtues of the Holy Spirit.

Afterward, the pope turned to the princes and nobles gathered to witness the ceremony. He blessed them and then spoke.

"We order you upon pain of excommunication never to choose any other king than those descended of Pepin, to keep the scepter in this family that Divine Mercy has deigned to choose, and which the Holy Apostles have confirmed and consecrated by the hands of the Pontiff, their chosen Vicar."

Pope Stephen had done everything in his power to ensure the grandeur of the Frankish realm and of Saint-Denis. In the three years that followed, and until 758, King Pepin repaid his debt. He undertook three successful military campaigns against the Lombards and gave their lands to the pope—adding up to no fewer than twenty-two towns, including Ravenna and Perugia. From the collection of conquered provinces would emerge the notion of the pontifical states, whose power, riches, and extent would henceforth protect the pope from unwarranted invasion.

By 768, Pepin, a man of fifty-four, was worn out. During a visit to Poitou he was suddenly gripped by a high fever; he was dying and he knew it. Expiring in Poitiers didn't seem an enviable fate—he thought the town unworthy to receive his final wishes—so he asked to be taken away immediately. He made it to Saint-Martin Abbey in Tours, whose treasury he had mercilessly drained to make charitable gifts. He then asked to be taken straight to Saint-Denis.

Within the abbey's vaults, before the great and grand of the kingdom, he divided his estates between his two sons and died on September 24. His request was that his remains be placed in the most modest section of the abbey, under the outer porch, facing the earth, as a symbol of the expiation of his sins.

Two weeks later, Charles was consecrated king of the Franks in Noyon. His younger brother Carloman took the title of King of Austrasia in Soissons, the capital of his realm. Paris disappeared from the royal chronicle. And when, three years later, Carloman died prematurely, he was buried in Saint-Remi Church in Reims. For his part, Charlemagne had slowly been accumulating territories that would lead to his assuming the crown of Emperor of the West. He eventually chose Aix-la-Chapelle (Aachen) as his capital.

This was a tough blow to Paris, which now was little more than a small port on the Seine, its population reduced to a few thousand inhabitants, perhaps five or so.

Charlemagne did not completely ignore the ancient capital. In 779, during a trip back from Rome, he came up with the idea to found schools that would instruct young men who desired instruction in the human sciences. By his command several centers of study were established in Paris: in the palace of the bishop, in Sainte-Geneviève Abbey, and in the abbey at Saint-Germain-des-Prés. One could learn about things in Paris, even if the grand march of history no longer passed by the Cité palace, which was abandoned to the four winds.

Also abandoned were the plans for a Carolingian necropolis whose a idea was essentially initiated by Pepin the Short. This was not permanent, of course, because the heroes of Paris in the coming centuries, such as Count Eudes, soon to be king of the West Frankish kingdom, and the first of the Capetians, Hugh Capet, would be buried there, sure signs of the abbey's prominence. But it would only truly be under Saint Louis in the thirteenth century that Saint-Denis would officially become the "cemetery to the kings," the royal necropolis where nearly all the great rulers and central figures of royal power would be gathered together.

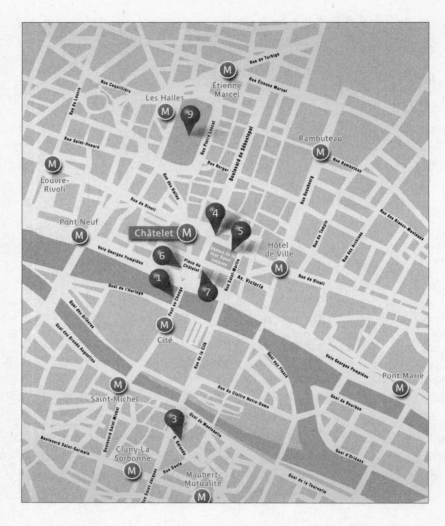

1. The creation of the Pont-au-Change. **3.** The Petit Châtelet, at 52 Rue Galande. **4.** The Place du Châtelet, located in the heart of Paris, became the center section of a gigantic north-south and east-west cross during Baron Haussmann's renovations. **5.** The Saint-Jacques-de-la-Boucherie church, built in 1509, was the parish of the Grande Boucherie (*boucherie* meaning "butcher"), where cattle were slaughtered. **6.** The Châtelet fountain was built to celebrate the campaigns of Napoleon, and was moved twelve meters to the west by Baron Haussmann, fifty years later. **7.** Remains of the Sarah Bernhardt Theater at 2 Place du Chatelet. **9.** Les Halles.

Ninth Century

Châtelet-Les-Halles

The Hour of the Counts

The RER station—RER standing for Réseau Express Régional, Regional Express Network, connecting Paris to its burbs—of Châtelet-Les-Halles, along with the Métro stations Châtelet and Les Halles, form an enormous network through which half a million *Franciliens*—meaning inhabitants of the Île-de-France, the country's wealthiest and most populous region—commute to work each day. Welcome to the largest subterranean railway station in the world. If you want to avoid the truly hideous Forum des Halles, which though only thirty years old is already falling apart at the seams, get out at Châtelet. You will head down endless corridors by means of moving walkways and hear the grating guitar played by musicians licensed by the RATP, the organization that runs the Métro system, and you will pass a number of vendors of knick-knacks and Parisian memorabilia until finally you emerge before a fountain constructed in 1808 to celebrate Napoleon's victories in Italy and Egypt.

This, dear readers, is the Place du Châtelet, located in the very heart of Paris and which, thanks to the efforts of Baron Haussmann, became the center section of a gigantic north-south and east-west cross, designed to make Paris more fluid and accessible. Hence why Boulevard Sébastopol on the Right Bank was pushed north, and extended south into the Left Bank by the Boulevard Saint-Michel, while the Rue de Rivoli ran east-west.

This new outline brought with it the displacement of the Châtelet fountain and its column, which got pushed about forty feet to the west, a feat completed in thirty minutes thanks to some rails on which the blocks of stone were raised up.

With the good baron and his new Paris, the last of the twisting and inconvenient streets of the *quartier* disappeared, replaced by roads that were far larger. This in turn gave rise to two great theaters: on the left is le Châtelet, in which operettas were the dominant form; and on the right the Sarah Bernhardt, which was managed for a period by the great tragedienne herself. Today all that remains of the immortal heroine of *L'Aiglon* is the name of the café on the opposite corner, because the hall, for various reasons, became the Théâtre de la Ville. Nonetheless, on the inside, taking the metallic stairway to Level 3, on the odd side, you will discover hidden away the dressing room of the Divine, as Bernhardt was known. Her bathroom, sink, folding screen, posters, photos, are all there, looking as if she might return at any moment.

If you look hard you'll also see it's not what it once was. In fact, it's kind of sad. Outside the theater runs the Rue de la Vieille-Lanterne, the dark alley in which, on January 26, 1855, the poet Gérard de Nerval hanged himself from the bars of an iron grill, on "the most sordid corner that he could find," as his friend Charles Baudelaire would say. Legend has it that the spot where Nerval put the rope is on a direct line with the prompt box under the stage.

By the beginning of the ninth century, Europe's civilizations and empires had forgotten about Paris. In the year 820, one might even say that the city was in its death throes. Every possible kind of misery was visited upon the banks of the Seine: famine, floods, and epidemics. Bread was hard to find because of poor harvests, and the river rose, flooding the Île de la Cité; the only way of getting around was by boat. Everyone seemed to be dying. Bloated cadavers floated on the waters or piled up against the shores of the Left Bank, which was untouched by the water. Had they drowned, or died of hunger, or been struck down by some disease? No one could say. All they could say was that Paris had become a place to die.

Soon, however, a tremor of hope went through the city. The waters of the Seine had miraculously spared the bed in which Saint Geneviève rendered her pure soul to the Lord nearly three centuries earlier. This sacred relic was conserved in a monastery located near the baptism basin of Saint-Jean-Baptiste, on the Île de la Cité. Arresting the flow of the water with her bed, Paris's guardian angel had revealed yet again her love for the city and its inhabitants. Parisians came to see Geneviève's bed, forming a long procession around it, begging to be spared. At that moment, the river, which had until then risen inexorably, began to recede. In effect it left the bed of the blessed saint and returned to its own.

Geneviève's spirit seemed to be the only one to take an interest in Paris. Well, perhaps not the only one. Away to the north of Europe a group of people were outfitting their boats and, by sailing down the Baltic Sea to the Channel and then up the Seine, were preparing to show that they were interested as well.

The insatiable appetite of the Nordic nations was whetted by the funk in which the states of Charlemagne had fallen after his death. His son Louis the Pious inherited the empire. Louis's three sons overthrew their father in November of 833 and divided up the spoils. Intrigue and rivalry tore at the hearts of these rebel princes, and the empire began to crumble.

This was exactly what the mighty warriors from the Scandinavian peninsula were waiting for. At first they had not ventured very far from their homes, content to pillage the Isle of Sheppey in greater England, the port town of Dorstadt at the mouth of the Rhine, and Anvers (Antwerp), a small town on the Escaut River (known as the Scheldt by the Dutch). The populations terrorized by these attackers called them *Normands,* meaning "people of the north." Soon it was learned what they called themselves: Vikings.

Louis the Pious's sons finally came to an agreement, signed near Verdun in 843, according to the terms of which the empire would be divided into three strips of what henceforth would be called "Francia": eastern Francia went to Louis II, "the German"; Middle Francia was given to Lothair I with the title of emperor; and western Francia was given to Charles II (the Bald), Louis the Pious's youngest son by a second marriage, instead of Pepin of Aquitain, who died in 838. From eastern Francia would be born Germany, and from western Francia would emerge France. As to middle Francia, extending from Flanders to Italy, it would become chipped away at by its two powerful neighbors, though one could say that present-day Italy is the true inheritor.

Charles the Bald was a zealous servant of the Lord who owed his name to the large tonsure he had shaved in his head as a sign of his submission to the Church. He was pious, without question, but he was also extremely combative, and when he learned that the Vikings were making their way up the Seine, he sent some troops to meet them while he himself took refuge behind the walls of Saint-Denis. He hoped that he would not be too inconvenienced by this barbarian invasion.

The Frankish soldiers who moved down the Seine, meanwhile, were completely taken aback by the vision that greeted them: an endless line of boats slowly advancing up the river to the regular rhythm of arms, the heads of colorful dragons set on their prows. Most terrifying of all was the grim determination of these pitiless warriors. No point in hanging around; the only safe maneuver was a retreat. The soldiers of Charles the Bald immediately opted for exactly that.

On March 29, 845, Easter Day, terror gripped Paris. No defense had been established and nothing was organized, and the city's crumbling old ramparts would not keep the Vikings from gaining entry. It was time to get out. Everyone took what they could—a few heads of cattle, jewels, a little butter—and hurriedly made their way into the interior of the country. The monks abandoned their monasteries, taking with them the Church's ornaments and sacred vessels, and most especially its most precious possessions: the relics of Saint Germain and Saint Geneviève. This was a useless precaution, for the Vikings were fiercely pagan in their beliefs. They had no intention whatever of making off with a few bones. What they craved were riches—any kind of riches, as long as they were eye-catching: pieces of gold, precious stones, jewelry. They also had no intention to occupy the land and were not looking to impose their power. This expedition was not designed to extend their influence. This was a smash and grab.

They took over the little port on Île de la Cité, disembarked, slew whomever they came across, and then systematically began to pillage the mostly deserted city. The monasteries and abbeys were the places they found the baubles they were looking for. They felt no compunction about pillaging the treasures of a religion about which they knew nothing. The cottages and the farms held nothing of interest for them and they simply burned them. And when they came across a pretty virgin or young lord, they enslaved them. They might make something by ransoming them.

The Vikings proved insatiable. They prepared to attack Saint-Denis, convinced that an enormous treasure must be contained within. Charles the Bald mobilized his knights.

"Now it is upon you, my brave soldiers, to go and defend the tomb of Saint Denis, our holy martyr!"

But the Frankish combatants balked. This wasn't the right season for fighting, they argued. It was early spring and the grass hadn't grown back; the horses would be hungry and there would be nothing upon which to feed them. Really, it would be best to launch the assault later, when the grasses were high and the weather was a little more pleasant.

What's more, given an enemy craving only gold, why not just give them what they want? Seven thousand livres of silver (a "livre" was roughly a pound) was the amount that Charles the

Bald proposed to Ragnar, the Viking chief. They had a deal. The pillagers left for home, their ships filled with silver.

Meanwhile in the extreme north of Europe, other war chiefs also planned to come and raid the riches of vulnerable France. They had been told stories about the marvels to be found in the realm of Charles the Bald. A certain Godfred took his turn and made his way toward Paris with his flotilla. A few soldiers gathered on Montagne Sainte-Geneviève and a new financial transaction proved sufficient to make the invaders go away. Then another one named Sidroc came and by this point the realm's coffers were becoming dangerously empty. Sidroc couldn't be bought off. So the Viking took his revenge and pillaged from Paris what there was left to be pillaged, and burned what was still left to be burned. "What afflictions!" wrote Aimon, the chronicler of Saint-Germain-des-Prés. "The Franks took flight without a fight, and turned tail before the first arrow was let loose, and before the first shield was struck. The Normans knew that the Frankish lords no longer had any courage."

Several years later the Vikings found a new way of getting silver out of Charles the Bald: they kidnapped Louis, the abbot of Saint-Denis, and his brother Gozlin, the bishop of Paris, both grandsons of Charlemagne (illegitimate, it's true, but still). The raiders evidently demanded an outrageously high ransom to return these two pillars of the Church. This time the king of Francia couldn't claim that his treasury was empty; he had to pay up. "For this ransom, much of the treasuries of the churches of the realm of Charles were emptied upon his orders," wrote Prudence, the bishop of Troyes, in his *Annals of Saint-Bertin*.

Exasperated by these endless invasions, Charles the Bald finally got the idea of building protective works. First he reconstructed Paris's two bridges, which, until recently, had connected Île de la Cité to the Right and Left Banks. Then, to better protect the bridge spanning a large branch of the Seine a few hundred feet downstream he put up pillars of stones on which was set a wooden sign that read PATHWAY OF CHARLES THE BALD. The Pont-au-Change, as it was called, ultimately would change the shape of the city. Then, to ensure that this barricade across the Seine could not be breached, Charles built a massive tower at the far end, on the Right Bank. On the Left Bank, the Petit Pont was guarded by a massive wood and stone tower surrounded by a deep moat.

So two enormous towers, two stone edifices, formed what were effectively the gates of Paris, designed to protect the Île de la Cité: the Grand Châtelet, located at the end of the new bridge built by Charles the Bald, and the Petit Châtelet, located at the end of the Petit Pont.

In 885, a dozen years after the construction of the two Châtelets, very little had changed: the Vikings were still threatening Paris. By this point Charles the Bald had died and been buried in Saint-Denis. A statue in the Louvre, said to be of Charlemagne and which dates from the ninth century, actually represents Charles the Bald, to whom Parisians owe a great part of their history.

What became of Châtelet?

In the twelfth century, Philippe Auguste's wall was built around the city to protect it. The Grand Châtelet, rendered useless, thereafter became the police headquarters of Paris. The building was bisected by a vaulted passageway: the little street Saint-l'Euffroy or Lieuffroy, meaning, roughly, "fearful place." The name was well chosen, for the Grand Châtelet was a truly dark, sinister place: a prison, a morgue, and a torture chamber—the most feared corner of Paris, apart, that is, from Gibbet of Montfaucon, the main place of execution located near what is today Place du Colonel Fabien.

The square was not as large as it is today; it consisted of a maze of small twisty streets, dark and unwelcoming. To complete the picture, not far away was a large slaughter yard, used as such since the tenth century. The cries of animals whose throats were being cut mixed with the cries of the tortured, and the groans of prisoners, the acrid smell of the morgue, all held together by the stench of coagulated blood. And looming over this scene of horror was the terrifying outline of Châtelet. In short it was one of the most nightmarish of all places. The Saint-Jacques tower of the

(Cont.)

slaughterhouse, which dates from 1509, and the nearby Quai de la Mégisserie—the dock of the tanning of skins—preserves a memory of ancient times.

The Grand Châtelet was demolished in 1894. One can easily see why. It was a place with grim memories However, if you really want to get a sense of what the inner parts of Châtelet looked like, all you have to do is cross the Seine and visit number 42 Rue Galande, and the Grotto of the Oubliettes (literally "forgotten places" or dungeons). Go downstairs and you will find waiting for you the ancient graffiti of former prisoners—"I'm done for"; "Death to Marat." Here, also, are conserved the cells and other dark keeps of the Petit Châtelet, the Left Bank prison of the Grand Châtelet.

After the death of the king, the realm of western Francia was confided to Charles III, called "the Fat." Charles the Fat was also the king of eastern Francia, and crowned Holy Roman Emperor. The former empire of Charlemagne was momentarily reconstituted.

Given the danger from the Vikings, Francia's leaders hoped that their forces, united under one kingly command, would allow them to push back the barbarians of the north. They were mistaken in this. Charles the Fat preferred negotiating to fighting. He bought peace for the price of two thousand eight hundred livres of silver. To maintain peace, he was prepared to make any financial sacrifice. Not enough money? To flatter the enemy and to offer him something more than money, he named the Viking Godfred the Duke of Frisia, a province located in the north of the Low Countries. Godfred wanted more. He claimed several territories on the borders of the Rhine. Now he was asking for too much; the greedy Viking had succeeded in exasperating even the good-natured Charles the Fat.

The emperor had no intention of giving Godfred these territories but during negotiations he appeared to go along with the demand. A meeting took place on a small island called Herispich, where the Waal River empties into the Rhine. The Viking, eager and cocky, arrived with only a small escort. It was a trap: Charles's men came out of their hiding places and massacred Godfred and his lieutenants.

"Godfred has been murdered! To arms!"

This was the cry that echoed across Scandinavia.

The flotillas from the north descended upon Francia. At the end of the fall of 885, the Vikings were determined to attack Paris, which guarded the gates of Burgundy and then all of the country.

The Seine was covered with ships, all crowded together. Seven hundred of them proceeded in a leisurely fashion upriver, each with its square sail attached to the mast, its figures from Norse mythology sculpted upon the prow. It was as if a gigantic herd of brightly colored mythical creatures were silently and steadily advancing. So completely was it covered in boats that you could no longer see the river. A long and supple ribbon was moving around river bends and spreading up the canals in a slow procession toward Paris.

Parisians knew perfectly well that Charles the Fat wouldn't lift a finger for them. The cowardly king was counting his pennies and meticulously preparing the new chests that he would deliver up to appease the Vikings. He was a lost cause. From then on, the people and their leaders would rely on themselves. Paris was resolved and this time the population stayed put. The Parisians had been expecting this invasion for a very long time. This time they wouldn't give in.

On November 25, the enormous flotilla from the north stopped before Île de la Cité. Without having to strike a blow, the Vikings occupied the Left Bank, going after the riches in Saint-Germain-des Prés, forcing Abbot Ebles and many of the monks to take refuge on the Île.

Sigefroi, the leader of the Vikings, rendered smug and satisfied by the cowardice of Charles the Fat, asked to speak with the leader of the Parisians. He hoped to start negotiations that would prevent his having to fight.

Gozlin, the bishop of Paris, was sent to meet him. He had left behind his miter and his aube and had prepared himself for battle. He held himself rigidly in his armor of gray metal. Sigefroi had a long braided beard and was wearing a long-haired fur coat, a two-headed axe cinched into his belt. He reassured Gozlin that he wished only to occupy the Île de la Cité, to dock his flotilla under the bridges, and head off to pillage the territories of Francia farther upriver.

"Emperor Charles, who after God dictates the laws of the world, gave us this city not to bring down the realm, but to protect it and assure enduring peace," replied the indignant Gozlin. "If the defense of these walls had been confided to you, would you think it just that we permit what you ask of us?"

The honor of the Viking was touched by this.

"If I did," exclaimed Sigefroi, "may my head be cut off and fed to the dogs.

"You refuse me entry into your city," continued the Viking, "and my sword will cut a path. We will see if your towers can withstand my engines of war and the bravery of my soldiers. Tomorrow at first light, the arrows will rain down upon you, and they will not cease until day is done. The battle will continue for each and every day, and continue for years if necessary."

And indeed, the following morning, waves of Vikings disembarked from their boats and occupied the space around the Grand Châtelet. They let forth clouds of arrows and struck down some of the defenders. Bishop Gozlin himself was struck in one arm by an arrow; it was pulled out and a temporary bandage applied, after which the bishop returned to the fight. The entire Parisian population joined in the battle; the women shredded cloths to make bandages for wounds; the men struggled to carry the heavy stones that were hurled at the attackers. New abilities were discovered: Abbott Ebles, who had fled Saint-Germain-des-Prés, stretched his soutane across some brambles to make himself a shield. The abbot revealed himself to be an archer of the first order: he was said to have hit six Vikings with a single arrow.

The Vikings were not about to give up. From their ships they brought out machines made of wood planks, wheels, and ropes. Once constructed, these infernal things that looked like crouching monsters released a shower of heavy stones upon the Grand Châtelet. The tower held firm. A boat approached the Grand Pont; a rolling tower was unloaded and attached to the wall of the Grand

Châtelet; a drawbridge came crashing down. The Frankish soldiers realized the danger and rushed at the men emerging from it, swords drawn. The attackers were pushed back. Sigefroi was stunned by the Franks' fighting spirit and completely taken aback by their determination to resist; he ordered a retreat and quit the field, leaving behind a good number of dead and dying.

Night fell. Parisians prepared for the fresh assaults which they were sure would follow the next day. During the course of this first day's battle, a man emerged who was more resolute and fearless than the others. This was Eudes, the Count of Paris. He would henceforth be in charge of the defense. Since the eighth century, Paris had become a countship. The first holder of the title was Grifon, a son of Charles Martel. The title then fell to various dynastic families, depending on their influence and the nature of their coalitions.

For the moment the most urgent matter was to bolster the damaged tower of the Grand Châtelet. They needed its full height. Positioned too low down, the defenders would be vulnerable to Viking arrows. Rebuilding it with stones and bricks would take too much time. It was therefore decided to use wood as a quick fix. All of Paris was busy that night; everyone wanted to contribute his or her efforts to the cause: some hunted for wood, others sawed and nailed, and still others made beams and supports. The frenetic work paid off. When morning broke, Sigefroi was stunned to discover that the tower had somehow grown back during the night.

Determined to destroy the Grand Châtelet, a troop of Vikings swam across the moat that surrounded it. With picks and hatchets they tried to chip away at the tower's base. From above, on the wooden platform, Count Eudes had oil heated in giant vats and poured it down on them, followed by flaming arrows. The results were horrific: men were turned into living torches. They tried to douse the flames by jumping into the Seine, but the oil continued to burn and soon incandescent corpses floated on the river.

It almost seemed that at a certain point the tower would give way. Throughout Paris, church bells rang out the alarm. The Vikings seemed to come in endless waves, fresh troops replacing those lost in the fight. They worked at enlarging that opening at the base of the Grand Châtelet tower and eventually they succeeded in opening a breach and poured in. Facing them were Eudes and his men, swords in hand. A fierce and bloody melee followed. The Frankish soldiers knew that if they gave ground all of Paris would fall, and after Paris the entire Frankish kingdom. They held their ground until at last the Vikings abandoned their positions, setting up camp on the Right Bank near Saint-Germain-l'Auxerrois Abbey.

There the Vikings prepared new attacks with cautious deliberation, feeding themselves by pillaging the surrounding countryside. Between raids they constructed new siege towers and plotted their next attack. Meanwhile the Parisians reinforced the fortress walls and set a catapult at the top of them, one capable of hurling impressively large stones.

On January 31, 886, after two months of stalemate, two months during which both sides had dreamed up all sorts of new military maneuvers, the assault was renewed. In Paris, the blasts of a horn summoned the populace to mobilize.

The Vikings tried out their new tactics. One was to advance beneath a large covering made from the hides of beasts. These giant shields, which could protect several men at once, looked from above like monsters gliding across the bridges and under the tower. The Vikings filled the moat around the Châtelet with corpses and the bodies of animals slaughtered for the occasion, as well as those of Frankish prisoners. Crossing this corpse bridge, stepping on the putrefying mass of carcasses and bodies, they attempted yet another assault on the tower. Once again they were pushed back. Then they resorted to fire, approaching the tower in burning boats that bumped up against the pillars of the Grand Pont and bunched up on the water.

In the meantime a drama was taking place on the Petit Châtelet side. Waters that had risen due to the winter rains had carried off a part of the Petit Pont leading to the Left Bank. The tower was therefore isolated and vulnerable. A dozen brave Frankish soldiers were still resisting and try though they might the Vikings couldn't dislodge them. Enraged, the Vikings set fire to the tower; the Frankish defenders, overcome by smoke and exhausted, tried to take refuge in the part of the Petit Pont that remained standing. During the fight that followed they were surrounded and, one by one, perished. The last man standing, a handsome lad wearing an elegant uniform, was thought to be a lord. They tried to take him prisoner, thinking that he might be worth a ransom, but the young man continued to fight off his attackers; in the end he was killed. Stone by stone, the Vikings tore down the tower of the Petit Châtelet.

The futile but heroic last stand of the Petit Châtelet became legend, as did the names of its defenders: Ardrade, Arnold, Eriland, Ermenfride, Erwig, Eynard, Goswin, Gozbert, Guy, Ococre, Soties, and finally Hervé, whom the Vikings tried to take alive.

As spring approached, the combatants were losing steam. The Vikings counted their dead and began to wonder whether Paris was worth such a high price. It was becoming increasingly urgent to find an honorable end to the siege, when Count Eudes, who was proving as capable at politics and diplomacy as he was at military matters, sent a messenger to Sigefroi to propose a meeting. The two leaders and their senior officers met on the Grand Pont. The count proposed to give the Viking sixty silver livres. May they take the money and leave them in peace. This was a pitiful amount but Eudes couldn't offer more than that. Paris had been impoverished by the battle, which by this point had lasted for several months. Had Eudes offered more, he would have offended the Franks, who were prickly about slights upon their honor or courage.

Sixty livres of silver was just large enough a sum for Sigefroi to lift the siege without losing face. The other Viking chiefs, on the other hand, protested the deal. They wanted to keep fighting, or seek a greater sum for agreeing not to. They attacked Eudes on the bridge and tried to take him prisoner. But the count kept them at bay and managed to make his way back to Île de la Cité. Independent of Sigefroi, the Viking leaders tried to take the Grand Châtelet; these undermanned attacks were easily repulsed.

Finally, blessedly, the Vikings gave up. Not knowing exactly where to go, they left their camp on the Right Bank and settled themselves on the Left Bank, near Saint-Germain-des-Prés.

In Paris, there was little time to rejoice. A new calamity had struck the city: the decaying bodies in the moat of the Grand Châtelet had started an outbreak of the plague. Bodies ravaged by the disease were thrown in with men killed in the fighting. When the disease finally receded, famine became widespread; the city's resources had been exhausted by the siege. During the night shadowy figures could be seen slipping out from Île de la Cité and into the Viking encampment, where they stole a few head of cattle, which they managed to get back across the Grand Pont to feed the famished inhabitants.

The whole situation was a little odd: the Parisians didn't dare to leave their island, and the Vikings were camped out on the banks, not daring to invade it. Was this or was this not a siege? To clarify matters, Charles the Fat would need to get involved. Eudes and several other stouthearted men made their way to Metz to convince the ruler to send enough troops to chase the Vikings from Paris. Charles was weary of all these problems. All he really wanted was to be left alone. Why were they always pestering him?

In the end, Eudes was so insistent that Charles finally agreed to send a few troops to Paris. They would be led by Duke Henri de Saxe. The emperor himself would follow along later. Perhaps, anyway. He would have to see.

Eudes hurried back to Paris to deliver the good news to his fellow citizens. In the bright June sunshine the count appeared on the heights of Montmartre; the entire city held its breath. As for the Vikings, they were certain that all this agitation did not augur well for them and tried to prevent Eudes from getting back into the city. But there was no resisting a man like Eudes. His sword above his head, he galloped through the Viking ranks and reached the city's main square, where he was cheered by one and all.

The troops of Henri de Saxe arrived not long afterward and attacked the Vikings, who retreated. The Frankish nobles saw this as a chance to defeat their foes once and for all. To do that, however, they needed reinforcements, and the emperor himself to lead them. News came that he was on his way, at the head of a large army. He was near Montmartre! He would vanquish the enemy! Finally the nightmare would be over!

Only, big surprise, Charles equivocated. Charlemagne's great-grandson was unquestionably a shrewd negotiator and a clever man but he was clearly no warrior. So what if the Vikings wanted to head back down the Seine? Well, by all means he would let them. In fact to help them on their way he would offer them a few hundred more silver livres. The Frankish nobles were outraged by this act of cowardice. In truth, however, the emperor was more concerned by what was going on in Germany, otherwise known as eastern Francia, and preferred a temporary alliance with the Nordic chiefs to dealing with western Francia, even if it did comprise the heart of his estates.

The Frankish aristocracy nonetheless could never forgive this perfidy. Henceforth Paris no longer felt bound to agreements undertaken by the emperor. When Sigefroi attempted to send his fleet under the Grand Pont and head deeper into Francia, as Charles had been prepared to allow him to do, the city rallied to stop him. From the top of Grand Châtelet's tower, Ebles, the abbot-archer, took aim at the pilot of the first boat and sent an arrow flying straight into his chest. The Vikings knew better than to push matters. Parisians were then treated to what was a truly extraordinary sight: that of these intrepid men of the north dragging their boats across land and through the woods and fields around Paris. Swallowing their pride, the Vikings put their boats into the water farther downriver and, following the course of the Yonne, proceeded with their invasion. They attacked Sens, which they didn't manage to take, and hence turned on Meaux, which was less well defended. They pillaged the town and kidnapped the bishop, hoping to exchange him for a few pieces of gold.

By November of 887, a year or so later, discontentment had spread throughout the empire. To make peace with the Frankish nobility, Charles the Fat was compelled to convoke a diet at Trebur, near Mayence (Mainz). He attempted to justify his actions, or inactions, but few were interested in hearing his excuses. They had had enough of Charles. His titles were stripped from him. Charles the Fat was no longer the Western Emperor, or king of Italy, or king of eastern Francia. He was, in fact, lord of nothing. His nephew, Duke Arnulf, was proclaimed king of Germania. The throne of Francia, on the other hand, remained empty.

The following February, Frankish leaders met in Compiègne and proclaimed Eudes, Count of Paris, king of western Francia. So as not to lose time—and from fear that other pretenders might soon rise up—the coronation took place right there and then in Compiègne. They rushed through the mass, performed a quick unction, and presto! *Vive le Roi!*

"You, men of the Church and secular lords," declared the new monarch, "be faithful to me and offer your counsel and your strength. With God's help and your good faith, I will reform what needs to be reformed and restore justice, justice as it existed in former times."

These were pretty promises, and before he could make good on them King Eudes had to pick up the fight against the Vikings, who had returned in even greater numbers.

Eventually the Vikings definitively renounced capturing Paris, but by then the city was in rough shape. The invasions had decimated a number of buildings. All that remained of Saint-Germain-des-Prés Abbey was the lower part of the square tower. Sainte-Geneviève, Saint-Julien-le-Pauvre, Saint-Marcel, Saint-

Germain-l'Auxerrois, and a number of other churches had been sacked and burned.

Paris, nonetheless, had grown, at least in stature. Because of their ferocity, the Scandinavian pillagers had demonstrated to all that anyone who wanted to hold Francia would first have to take Paris. By their stubborn defense, the Parisians had distinguished themselves from the rest of the realm, and even if, at his death, Eudes gave back his crown to the direct descendants of Charlemagne, it was the Parisians who henceforth would make history, as well as kings.

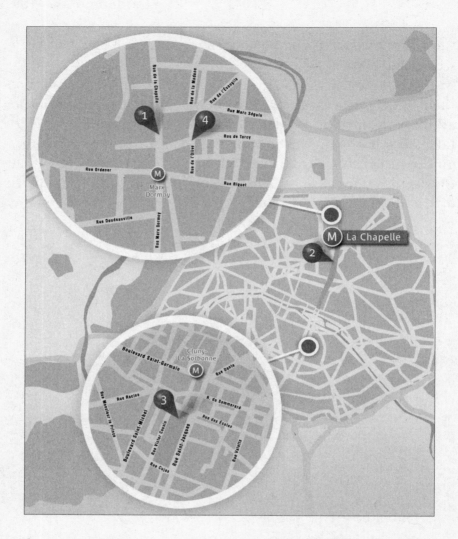

1. The church at 16 Rue de la Chapelle, where, among others, Saint Geneviève and Joan of Arc are said to have prayed. **2.** Rue du Faubourg-Saint-Denis, the new major road of Paris at the end of the tenth century. **3.** The Lendit Fair. **4.** In La Chappelle, only the Olive Market (on Rue de l'Olive), which opened in 1885, offers a distant echo of the fair.

———•———•———•———

Triumph of the Capetians

"Nameless miracle at the stop Chapelle / Is the Paris Métro coming out of its tun-nel," the French crooner Charles Trenet would sing one day. And indeed here the subway train comes out into the open, as if coming up for air. At the end of the platform you can see the white dome of the Sacré-Coeur on Montmartre. But the line and the station were built on far older remains: the fields and pastures that, amazingly, would survive until the end of the eighteenth century.

I love wandering this northern *quartier*, with its smells of spices; it has become a sort of Indiatown that beckons, offering up all kinds of discoveries. A few steps away can be found the Théâtre des Bouffes du Nord, a little off the general register of most great Parisian theaters, perhaps. It managed to escape a premature death thanks to the talent of the English director Peter Brook, who turned it into a living laboratory of innovative theater—sometimes strange, sometimes audacious, always passionate. But let's turn back to History.

Between Montmartre and Belleville, the village of La Chapelle grew up around the oratory, the chapel in which Saint Geneviève prayed, and then, as it became part of the lands attached to the Saint-Denis Abbey, it came to be called La Chapelle-Saint-Denis,

Where does the name "La Chapelle" come from?

From Charlemagne, who was an emperor devoted to relics of every kind. To feed his appetite for them he regularly sent knights off into Palestine to bring him back the last remnants of Christ's Passion or the remains of the first Christian martyrs. His envoys returned from these long voyages to the ends of faith laden down with bits of wood, cloth, and various bones in beautifully engraved chests. Transformed by the magic of dogma, these became holy relics that would be admired by crowds lost in veneration.

One of the most beautiful pieces of his collection was Saint Martin's cape, half of it, anyway, since the young man had of course cut it in half to give to the beggar. For this glorified piece of fabric, Charlemagne had constructed in the heart of his palace in Aix a place of devotion—a chapel, a term that derives from the Latin *cappa*, or cape.

The word entered into common use. In Paris, it was notably attributed to a small oratory where, it was said, Saint Geneviève had once stopped to pray on the road taking her to Saint Denis's sepulchre.

before its annexation by Paris in 1860, when it became part of the Eighteenth Arrondissement.

The church located at number 16 Rue de la Chapelle sits on the spot of the ancient oratory, and which some believe was once the tomb of Saint Denis.

After Saint Geneviève, another celebrated penitent once came to this place: Joan of Arc. A statue recalls that *la Pucelle* came here to pray on September 7, 1429, hoping to free Paris from the English and their allies the Burgundians. On this occasion she wasn't successful; she was wounded in the thigh during combat.

The current church dates mainly to the eighteenth century. The only parts of the original church of 1204—at which Joan had prayed—are the first four bays, separated from the others by round pillars.

The old village was located behind the Métro station at the level of Place Paul-Éluard, at the end of Avenue Marx-Dormoy. It was a small village—the buildings were huddled close to the road and not very large to begin with—but a prestigious address.

In the tenth century, the great fair of Lendit left Saint-Denis and moved closer to Paris, relocating in La Chapelle, between the town and the abbey, where today the La Chapelle traffic circle can be found.

Lendit—derived from the Latin *inductum*, from *indicere*, "to proclaim"—lasted for two weeks every June, drawing thousands of merchants from across Francia, as well as from Provence, Lombardia, Spain, and even Constantinople, who would gather to exchange and sell cloth, sheep, herbs, spices, perfumes, and—most rare and valuable of all—parchment. As soon as it had opened, the masters arrived. These were the teachers in black robes who dispensed their wisdom in the open schools within the monasteries, as well as in the institutions on Mount Saint-Geneviève, despite the bishop of Paris's strong disapproval. At the heart of the debate was what should be taught, by whom, and how. That debate had already begun, but in any case everyone needed the invaluable parchment imported from the east, and elbowed each other at the Lendit Fair to purchase it.

The La Chapelle fair attracted both those seeking supplies and those who came simply to admire the wares being hawked in the stalls, which were sometimes elegantly appointed and therefore very unlike the drab rooms in which they lived and worked in Paris. Coming to the fair was like going to the theater—a chance to see what the world could put on display. Among the scents and colors came a whiff of elsewhere, and in addition to the rich silks there were tightrope walkers, fire-eaters, dancers, and fife players. And in the middle, in a stall made of wood, was the abbot of Saint-Denis—stiff and serious-looking, a sour expression on his face. He was there to settle claims and disputes, of the sort that inevitably arose between merchants and their customers.

Here came Paris's wealthy—wearing gold-embroidered shoes, their legs wrapped in bright cloth, sporting a sheepskin or brightly colored linen vest, a two-edged sword stuck in their belt and a cane in their hand, and short blue or green jacket. They came with their ladies, who wore their boots to protect them from the mud and grime of the streets, and generally two mauve or violet gold-embroidered tunics—a shorter and longer one. As was the fashion, they wore their hair under a small scarf. Compared to

What became of the Lendit Fair?

With the development of the Parisian university in the eighth century, the Lendit Fair—and its parchment market—became a festival for teachers and their students. Starting at dawn on the first day, students came to gather on Montagne Sainte-Geneviève. They formed groups and marched in step to the sound of fifes, horns, and drums, and then headed toward La Chapelle. The procession formed a pretty display and was visible from the courtyard at the Sorbonne.

In 1444, the fair returned to Saint-Denis due to disruptions created by the students. Later, the Lendit became an animal auction, and then in the nineteenth century it became a summer festival. In La Chappelle, only the Olive Market (on the Rue de l'Olive), which opened in 1885, offers a distant echo of what once was.

the colorful vestments worn by these Parisians of ease and wealth, the farmers and craftsmen seemed a little drab in their gray, beige, or brown clothes; they couldn't compete with these lords and ladies.

In 978, the Count of Paris called himself Hugh Capet, to distinguish himself from his father, Hugh the Great, who had held the title before him. In truth, no one knows why he decided upon "Capet." Perhaps it was because he had a large head—in Latin, *caput,* or "head"—set on a somewhat frail body. Perhaps it was because he always wore a hood, hence from *capuchin.* Perhaps it stemmed from the fact that he possessed several abbeys and therefore was a *chappet,* meaning "one who wore a cape." He was the laic abbot of Saint-Martin de Tours Abbey, and the name may have been an allusion to the cloak that was cut in half by the martyr. When he rode with his troops into battle he always carried Martin's relic for protection.

As the Count of Paris, Hugh's responsibility was to defend the city and keep it running. The question was, which Paris? The areas around the riverbanks had been ravaged by the Vikings, and nothing was done to revive these precincts. The abbeys there lay in ruins. People became accustomed to living and praying among crumbled walls, half caved-in churches, and sacked abbeys.

On the Île de la Cité, the scene was hardly more joyful. Most of the houses, which were made of wood, had been burned or damaged by flaming projectiles and then repaired in a hurry. Everything seemed askew; walls leaned together and seemed ready to topple on top of one another. On the ground floor of these shacks were small shops that opened out to the street, but they were dark and moldy and smelled rancid; little surprise that most transactions took place in the streets and from carts. Everyone was in the street. The bootmaker carts made their rounds, with poles and strings from which hung shoes on offer; the wine dealers had their carts; the fruit merchants' carts featured canopies; and the dealers in trinkets and knickknacks dragged around a large sack over their shoulders. Everyone was advertising their goods at the top of their lungs, trying as best they could to be heard over the others.

Though the city had lost its prosperous environs, and though Lothair, the grandson of Charlemagne and the king of Francia, preferred his residence in Laon, Paris was still lively. It was still a desirable address. Desired by whom? By Otto II, emperor of the Germanic tribes, for one.

In this year, 978, palpable tension existed between Francia and Germania. Lothair accused the Germanic emperor of stealing Lorraine, an ancient part of Middle Francia—and a part of the world that would change sides until the middle of the twentieth century.

Lothair decided to punish the arrogant Otto, and gathered together all the great men of his kingdom in Laon. He asked whether they would support a military campaign against the Germanic tribes. Hugh Capet and the other feudal lords voiced their support, and were quick to add their money and manpower to support such an expedition.

Thus it was that at the start of summer a Frankish army of twenty thousand men marched on Aix-la-Chapelle. Everyone thought this was the right thing to do. The lords hoped that their obeisance to Lothair would gain them something in return; and the men were only too happy to be out pillaging. The only unhappy ones were the peasants whose fields were trampled by soldiers. But, in the end, if all you had to worry about was a band of thieves, how bad could it be?

Lothair's army advanced, crossed the Meuse River, and reached the palace in Aix. The most battle-tested of his soldiers led the attack against the palace only to find that it was . . . deserted. The emperor and his family had left the palace only moments before. The food on the tables was still warm. After feasting, the soldiers proceeded to ransack armoires and chests—from which were taken gold dishes and imperial jewels. Satisfied that they had found everything of value, the soldiers and their leader returned contentedly to Francia. Lothair was delighted to return to the tranquility of Laon and disbanded his army. War would be continued at some later point.

In the meantime, Otto returned to Aix and, outraged to find what had been done to his royal residence, vowed revenge. The emperor immediately raised an army of thirty thousand men. In the month of October, Germanic soldiers invaded Francia. They had come to devastate the place and this is exactly what they did. The royal palaces in Attigny and Compiègne were sacked, and the fields around Soissons and Laon were burned. Still, that wasn't revenge enough for Otto, who wanted to take Paris. *That* alone would match the humiliation inflicted upon him by the raid on Aix-la-Chapelle.

Lothair had fled Laon and in cowardly fashion taken refuge in Étampes. His only hope was that Hugh Capet would somehow manage to defend his city. There was no time to mobilize an army. Once again, Paris was on its own. The Germans arrived; one could see the movement of knights creating clouds at the top of Montmartre. The enemy army set up tents but at least for the moment maintained its distance. Otto was in fact hesitant to attack Paris. He was well aware that the city had survived the siege of the Vikings. How could he do better than those barbarians from the north?

One of the emperor's nephews, a proud and intemperate young man, demanded the right to be the first to attack. Otto consented, thinking, *Let this hothead find out how he stacks up against the Pari-*

sians. The very minute that the small attacking force reached the gates, Capet's men came pouring out, surrounded the brave band, and proceeded to massacre the whole lot of them, not even sparing the nephew.

This hardly emboldened Otto to try his luck. Still, he also knew that he couldn't simply retreat. To establish the Germanic presence and to test the nerves of the Parisians, he sent a giant of a soldier to stand in front of the Grand Châtelet, the very symbol of Parisian resistance, and in a deep voice shout out insults to Paris and all of Francia.

This continued until Hugh decided that he had had enough. This provocation could not stand. On the other hand, sending out his entire army seemed like a waste. He had a better idea.

The gates of the city opened and out emerged Francia's champion, a knight named Ives, astride his horse. Ives and the Germanic giant prepared to joust while their supporters urged them on furiously. The German's lance shattered Ives's shield and lodged deep into his chest. The champion of Paris fell from his horse. The giant ran to his adversary to finish him off; the Parisians gave a collective groan. Just as the German reached his wounded adversary, however, Ives opened his eyes and, raising his lance, shoved it through a chink in the giant's armor—the spot between his stomach and where the leather was attached to the metal armor. The German keeled over. The Parisians let out a whoop of joy. In the space of a second they seemed to have won the war.

By November 30, after a siege of two months, a siege which had started to take on the quality of a neighborly visit, Otto unpitched his tents. It was growing cold; mud was everywhere. The tents were taken down and the German army began to abandon the heights of Montmartre. Near Soissons they were set upon by Lothair's battle-hardened troops and defeated.

His victory at the gates of Paris—a victory in which only one blow was struck—enabled Hugh Capet to consider himself first lord of the Frankish realm and the most powerful figure after the king. The Auvergnian Gerbert d'Aurillac, who would become pope under the name Sylvester II, would later write: "King

What is the truth behind the German giant?

From the memorable joust between Ives the Frank and the colossal German was born the legend of the giant Isoré. The David-and-Goliath story would be picked up in the twelfth century in the *Chansons de Geste,* intended to galvanize French resistance to outside invasions. The giant would become a Saracen and the hero would take on some of the characteristics of William of Orange, a knight of Charlemagne, defender of Christianity. In Paris, Rue de la Tombe-Issoire took its name from being the spot where the fallen enemy was buried.

Lothair was first lord of the realm in title only. Hugh was, not only by reason of his title, but by his deeds and accomplishments."

In the years that followed, Hugh Capet thought more about his personal ambitions than he did about the city of Paris. His position was a complex one; he had to learn how to oppose his king while also remaining a loyal vassal to him. He went to Rome to meet with the pope, fought against the dukes of Lorraine, and even sought an alliance with the Germans, before finally returning to serve Lothair. During this long period he did very little for Paris. This was too bad, for the city was in dire need of a face-lift. Saving it from Otto was enough glory for Hugh Capet.

And then circumstances permitted him even greater glory. In 986, Lothair died and the crown passed to his son Louis V, who had just turned twenty. The following year fate struck again and the young king died after a fall from a horse. Following the funeral rites, an assembly of the nobility took place in Senlis and by acclamation they offered the throne to Hugh Capet. The whole business was quickly concluded in Noyon, where, on July 3, 987, Hugh received the insignia of royal power. Kneeling, the king of the Franks pronounced his solemn vows.

"I, Hugh, soon to be made by God's grace the king of the Franks promise before God and before His saints, on this day of my coronation, to preserve to each his canonical privilege, the law that governs it, and the jurisdiction which it exercises and from which it emerges. I swear that with God's help, and to the best of my abilities, I will assure complete security as must a king do to every bishop and to every church. Finally, I swear to govern the people in my care according to the laws and to their rights."

Hugh received holy ointment and was pronounced "King of the Franks, the Bretons, the Danes, the Aquitaines, the Goths, the Spaniards, and the Vascones." It was a resounding title that hid a rather less splendid reality. The Danes were really only the Normans of Neustria; and the Goths, the Spaniards, and the Vascones represented only a few inhabitants of the south. Moreover, the king's direct possessions were limited to a modest domain in Île-de-France, between Compiègne and Orléans, and Paris, which he would make into his capital.

Over the rest of Francia, royal authority was distant, diffused, and theoretical. The king was still the king, of course, but he had almost no way of imposing his authority over powerful vassals. All he had was a limited military force and unimpressive financial resources. On the other hand, King Hugh was fortunate enough to benefit from the network of abbeys, which represented the true economic and strategic power in the land. These included Saint-Germain-des-Prés and Saint-Denis.

Hugh Capet depended on this network. A charter deeding lands

Where was the first stock exchange in Paris?

To find it you have to ask yourself how people traversed Paris in the Middle Ages. It was doubtless to Hugh's son, Robert the Pious, that we owe the reconstruction of the "Charles the Bald Way" at the end of the tenth century. A bridge was constructed to restore the ancient Roman original, which was a wreck, and which had been progressively abandoned. Thus for nearly five hundred years, the only axis for crossing Paris was not a straight line but more like a broken arc.

The principal axis of the Right Bank would be moved from Rue Saint-Martin to the Rue Saint-Denis, in front of the new street that would connect the Cité palace to the prestigious Abbey of Kings.

This great bridge would take the name Pont-au-Change—Bridge of the Exchange—starting in the twelfth century, when the *courratiers*—runners of a sort—moved in to exchange debts and claims of the various agricultural communities of the realm for private financiers. It was therefore on this Pont-au-Change that the first stock exchange in Paris appeared.

As for the "Paris crossing," if you head up Rue Saint-Denis, you'll find at the end of the great

(Cont.)

boulevards the magnificent Saint-Denis Gate that Louis XIV had built in 1672, on the spot where an ancient rampart had once stood. The comparison with the modest Saint-Martin Gate, which rises at the same height, 650 or so feet to the east, reveals how this medieval axis replaced the older one.

It's somewhat amazing to consider that for five hundred years Paris had only two bridges, one for each bank, and that one wasn't even the extension of the other. It would take until the fifteenth century to create an additional bridge over the Seine via the Île de la Cité.

Today the city's bridges are all nineteenth-century constructions, aside from the Pont Neuf—the "new bridge," though "neuf" means both "new" and "nine"—which was built in 1607, and is therefore the oldest bridge and not the newest. It was also not the ninth bridge across the Seine but in fact the fifth. Confusing, no?

to the Saint-Maur-des-Fossés Abbey, preserved in the National Archives, offers magnificent testimony to the year 989 and to the Church's strategic leverage. In effect, the king needed ecclesiastical power, as from a purely political point of view he was in danger of seeming weak. Hugh acted cautiously. He was not a sovereign seeking great change, nor was he interested in grandiose projects. His main preoccupation was preserving his kingship, and establishing a line that would replace the supplanted Carolingians. Soon his efforts would pay off: only six months after his coronation, he gained the right to pass the throne along to his only son, Robert, who was consecrated in Orléans.

Hugh Capet's efforts to form a future for his descendants were triumphant. The Capetian dynasty would last from 987 to 1328, and then distant branches of it would rule from 1328 to 1848, with interruptions caused by the Revolution and the Napoleonic period. Hugh may not have transformed Paris, but his successors would turn it into the City of Light.

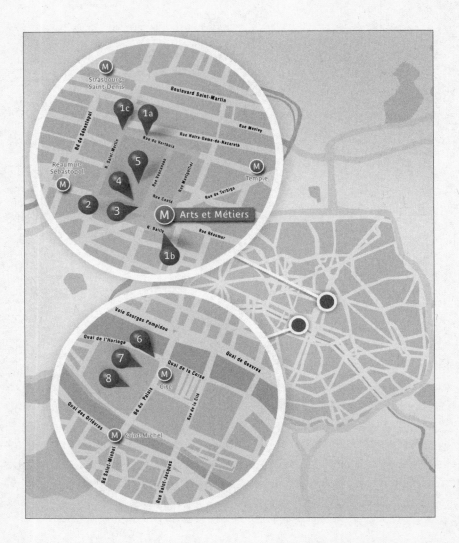

1a. Of the ancient grounds of the Saint-Martin-des-Champs, a turret and courtyard remain partially restored on the Rue du Vertbois. **1b.** The bend in Rue Bailly retains the southeast border of the enclosure, whose corner tower is visible in the stairway cage of number 7. **1c.** The Vertbois tower, about which Victor Hugo wrote to an architect who had suggested the demolition: "Demolish the tower? No. Demolish the architect? Yes." **2.** The boundaries of the priory. **3.** During the Revolution, the priory was turned into the Conservatoire National des Arts et Métiers, which you can still find at 292 Rue Saint Martin. **4.** Inside and outside the conservatory: Cluny's Romanesque design. **5.** The refectory of the monks. **6.** Vestiges of the Cité palace. **7.** The staircase of the condemned in front of the Palais de Justice. **8.** The Sainte-Chapelle chapel.

●———————●———————●

The Millennium Myth

The Arts et Métiers Métro stop is very handsome indeed. In fact it looks like it figures in a Jules Verne story, the Art Nouveau copperwork making it seem like something a mad scientist might come up with—a vessel to take us on a long voyage not only to some other place, but to some other time.

This is all a daydream, of course, because this ship doesn't actually move; to get anywhere on it you have to get on the antique wood escalator, heading down one side and coming up the other, then repeating the operation. You will find yourself going round and round the Conservatoire National des arts et métiers on Rue Saint-Martin.

Until the Revolution, this stop is where the Saint-Martin-des-Champs priory had stood, a small oratory that had been constructed on the very spot where Saint Martin had kissed and cured a leper. The chapel was torn down in the eleventh century and replaced by a large monastery, which could be found on what are today the streets Saint-Martin, Vertbois, Montgolfier, and Bailly.

But let us return to the year 1000. It is an imposingly round number, to be sure. Nonetheless, millennialism did not seem greatly to disturb the thoughts of the realm's inhabitants, although in certain Parisian churches somber-faced abbots proclaimed the imminent arrival of the Antichrist. These men were opposed by clear-thinking theologians who denounced such superstitious beliefs and assured their flocks that no one on earth could predict the end of the world.

In short, the year 1000 was not a doom-and-gloom moment. The notion of the medieval millennium was popularized in the nineteenth century by romantics and historians such as Jules Michelet, who viewed Christianity in the Middle Ages as a time of fervor and passion, a seething caldron of emotion.

With or without fear of the Apocalypse, the year 1000 was nonetheless part of a period dominated by the Church. Supported by the faith of its adherents, the pontifical seat gained enough momentum to reform practices that it deemed unworthy. Until then, it must be said, the Church had been completely integrated into the feudal system: the sacred and the profane intermixed; the preoccupations of the bishop were the same as those of the aristocracy, at least in terms of the governance of the land, the system of earnings, and the collection of taxes and duties. At bottom the spiritual and the temporal were one and the same. A more serious problem from the Church's viewpoint was that some ecclesiastical functions were being monopolized by aristocrats, who didn't necessarily have the ecumenical training but who nonetheless considered religious titles hereditary, to be handed down father to (eldest) son.

For Rome and all true Christians, the time had come to purge the Church of its abuses and rediscover the way to God. Rome would not be the plaything of barons and lords. Render unto the Lord what is the Lord's.

This renewal started at Cluny, the Benedictine abbey in Burgundy that sought to release itself of all temporal domination and be placed under the sole authority of the pope. The two monks leading this fight for spiritual purity were Raoul Glaber and Adémar de Chabannes. They had endured years of war and invasions, and began convincing the people of Francia that if they, too, wanted peace and prosperity they needed to place themselves in God's hands.

The Holy Father, for his part, was happy to inspire the faithful and in the process to enrich these new monasteries, refuges of the Truth Faith that came to flourish nearly everywhere in Francia and elsewhere in Europe.

The rules instituted at Cluny and its dependencies were those of Saint Benedict, and, apart from manual labor, which was essential to cultivate humility, occupations other than spiritual were considered secondary to prayer, writing, chanting, and copying manuscripts. Cluny became a temple of knowledge and intelligence.

The influence of this powerful congregation, which sought to take in hand man's spiritual destiny, would reach Paris later. The Saint-Martin-des-Champs monastery would be brought into the Cluny orbit in 1079. Here, in the glory of God, the lights of Cluny illuminated Paris and its pious parishioners.

But before this "taking in hand" of religious matters by the Church, some seriously contentious issues faced the Church, starting with the son and successor of Hugh Capet, Robert II, who brought down upon himself the fury of the Holy See for having a somewhat turbulent private life. It had all started for purely political reasons, when, on the orders of his father, the sixteen-year-old Prince Robert married Rozala, an elderly woman of thirty-three, the widow of the Count of Flanders and the daughter of the king of Italy. The reason was her dowry, which consisted of the countship of Ponthieu, which henceforth became part of the royal properties.

After a fairly grim conjugal life (which nonetheless lasted for a dozen years), Robert met the woman of his dreams. Her name was Berthe and she was thirty-two. She dazzled the still-young prince. Berthe was the daughter of the king of Burgundy and Provence, which somewhat complicated the situation, because her mother was the sister of King Lothair, the last of the Carolingians. Therefore, in the play of relations and unions, she was the great-grandcousin of the smitten Robert. The Church made no exceptions when it came to consanguinity, however distant and tortuous. Robert didn't care. Shortly after he had ascended to the throne, he repudiated Rozala and found a bishop willing to bless his relationship with his beloved Berthe.

The young Pope Gregory V was outraged by this. With this illicit marriage, the king of the Franks was defying not only papal authority but the holy laws of the saints. To prove his submission and to calm the waters, Robert sent an ambassador to the pontiff with a clear purpose: "We have certain matters in litigation with the Holy See. Assure Gregory that I will concede on them all if he lets me have my wife."

The pope was in a real bind. Robert would agree to everything except the one thing that was being asked of him. Gregory refused to budge in the matter and ordered that the lovers part.

The ambassador returned sheepishly to Paris, bearing a message of intransigence.

"He will never make me part from my wife!" the king exploded. "She is dearer to me than anything in the world and I want the world to know this."

In reply, the pope convened a synod in Pavia, and from the assembly of prelates came this declaration: "King Robert, against direct apostolic orders, has married his kin, and must deliver himself to us so that the matter can be rectified. Should he refuse to come, he will be denied communion." They were delivering the ultimate threat: excommunication.

Robert was more than happy to respond to the summons, which obviously did nothing to restore his relations with the Holy See. So the pope convened another synod, this time in Rome. A ruling emerged from the debates, one that was canonically rigid and clear: "King Robert will leave Berthe, his kin, whom he has married against the laws. He will do seven years' penance, as demanded by the Church in matters of incest. Should he refuse to submit, may he be excommunicated."

At first Robert did not submit, and therefore was expelled by the Church and banned from the community of the faithful. The Cité palace emptied out. Terrified by the excommunication, courtiers, counselors, and clerics all departed, one after the other. Between the pope, who promised paradise, and the king, who could promise only earthly goods, lay no real choice. The last remaining servants purified the king's plate by fire and prayer after each use, for fear of being contaminated by this terrible sentence upon him and because they believed that mere physical contact with the condemned man would lead to their own eternal damnation.

And it was thus that the king and the queen spent the year 1000 living in sin. On the Île de la Cité this absurd state of affairs endured, transforming the sovereigns into virtual prisoners in their own palace. Finally, Berthe was the first to crack. She had never wanted that badly to be queen of the Franks, and the idea of being forced to remain forever behind the palace's walls horrified her.

In 1001, after four years of communal life, Berthe and Robert agreed to part, a separation that took place with tears of contrition but also in a somewhat noisy display of sentiment and regret. Berthe climbed aboard a carriage led by four horses, crossed the Grand Pont, went through the Left Bank, climbed up the long Saint-Jacques Passage, went over Mount Sainte-Geneviève, and headed south, toward Vienna, on the banks of the Rhone, where she would rejoin her father's court.

Robert played up his show of repentance to the maximum. He wept, he lamented, he visited Parisian churches on each and every day, he sang the service louder than all the others, and he spent entire holy nights in prayer, prostrate.

And yet all this was still not enough. So he founded monasteries. In Paris he had Saint-Germain-l'Auxerrois reconstructed, and Saint-Germain-des-Prés as well; both had been treated rudely by the Vikings. To get on God's good side, Robert had a chapel built in his palace and dedicated to Saint Nicholas; a century and a half later it would become Sainte-Chapelle.

Robert considered the state of his soul, of course, but not at the cost of ignoring personal comfort as well. He also restored the Cité palace, enlarged it by adding the Conciergerie, the residence of the palace concierge. "Concierge" is today not a prestigious title—designating as it does a building supervisor-cum-janitor—but

What was the fate of the Conciergerie?

Along with its clock tower and Sainte-Chapelle, the kitchens, the guardroom, and the chamber housing the gendarmes of the Conciergerie are the sole vestiges of the medieval palace. The rest of what is there dates only back to Haussmann and looks lke something worthy of the Musée Grévin, a wax museum. The somewhat tacky results, which you now can visit, strives to re-create the prison that occupied the premises in 1392, after Charles V and his successors had abandoned the palace, until it was closed in 1914. The cells took up the ground floor of the building, which borders the Quai de l'Horloge.

What does remain takes us to the eighteenth century and the revolutionary period, a period quite rich in the number of those detained.

First of all, the women's courtyard with its fountains where prisoners were forced to do their laundry and the iron grill that separates it from the men's side. Here can be found the Chapelle des Girondins, in remembrance of those who spent their final hours here on the night of the twenty-ninth and thirtieth of October, and the Chapelle Marie-Antoinette built under Louis XVIII to commemorate *(Cont.)*

in Robert's day it meant something quite different. The concierge levied taxes, enforcing them by means of the bailiffs of the lower and middle justice courts. This was a position of real privilege and power. The concierge had the right to levy a tax on every barrel of wine and every bushel of oats. And despite the popular myth that "concierge" was a shortened form of "count of the *cierges*" (candles), hence presumably whoever was in charge of lighting, the term actually derives from the Latin *conservius*, "slavery companion," and designated someone who worked at the pleasure of the palace.

By restoring the Cité palace, King Robert restored to Paris its role as a capital, a role that the Carolingian kings had somewhat neglected. Nonetheless, the status of this agglomeration of neighborhoods was still a little vague. Things simplified when the countship of Paris was finally attached to the crown. But what was Paris aside an island bordered by high walls? On the Right Bank, expansion was limited by the *marais*—or swamp. The Left Bank was principally home to the abbeys, churches, and their orchards.

In the year 1003, Robert's efforts paid off: his wife—his first wife, Rozala—died in Flanders, where she had lived in seclusion. According to canon law, Robert was now free to remarry, which he did immediately, as he needed an heir. He wed Constance d'Arles, who was all of seventeen years old and neither a widow nor a matron.

The king was thirty-one and as far as his wife was concerned he was a grizzled old man. She therefore brought to the palace a host of young people. The old guard found these young pups alarming, in part because they wore their hair short, were clean-shaven, and dressed ex-

the cell in which the queen had spent her last moments in 1793.

The room located between the two chapels was the one in which Robespierre, his head bandaged, waited to lose it entirely.

Stand in front of the eighteenth-century façade of the Palais de Justice and look for the small stairway on the right that leads to the bar. This is the staircase the condemned used when they were taken to the scaffold. This is the most moving and yet the most mute reminder of this terrible place.

travagantly. Their boots were ridiculous, for starters, since they had curled toes. If one wasn't careful, all the youth of Francia might be taken in by these grotesque affectations. The pious abbots who surrounded the king tut-tutted and grumbled that the court wasn't what it once was, that the youth of today seemed to think only of pleasure and debauchery. In short, Paris was going to the dogs.

Robert himself could have cared less about the boots his wife and her friends wore. He had done his conjugal duty to bring an heir to the throne; he had been quite assiduous, in fact, as pretty Constance gave him seven children. But his happiness was still elsewhere. His beloved Berthe had returned to the palace. Discreetly, of course. Happily, the royal residence was large enough to prevent unintended confrontations.

In any case, Constance did not really want to remain in Paris. The clerics and counselors looked askance at her, reproaching her for her arrogant youth, her escapades, and her joie de vivre. But there was more: every time she went through the passages of the palace she came across beggars whom her pious husband had sought out in order to feed and offer them a few coins. She wanted to lose herself in carefree frolics, and here she was forced to confront misery and unhappiness. On some days as many as a thousand beggars would clutter the palace, each one more filthy and foul-smelling than the next.

The worst was just before Easter. On Holy Thursday, some three hundred poor people made their way into the palace, settling down noisily at their tables. The king himself joined his valets in serving food to these miserable creatures. After dinner, in a well-planned ceremony, His Royal Highness cleansed the feet of several of them while a deacon sang the story from the Book of John in which Christ washed the feet of his disciples: ". . . so he got up from the meal, took off his outer clothing, and wrapped a towel around his waist. After that, he poured water into a basin and began to wash his disciples' feet, drying them with the towel that was wrapped around him."

Had it only been beggars, Constance might have resigned herself, but there were also lepers. Robert adored lepers, for they allowed him to show how deep his devotion and boundless his charity. He received them in the palace and kissed their disease-ravaged hands. Some of the lords were surprised by such excessive goodness.

"Jesus Christ took the form of a leper," the king reminded them in a sententious voice.

According to Scripture, Christ cured the lepers; the king, in his noisy humility, would do no less. A few miracles were indeed attributed to him: he had made the sign of the cross over one poor sufferer and the man's leprosy cleared up. The people believed, or pretended to believe, in these stories. Beginning with Robert and continuing until Louis XVI, kings were believed to have the power to cure scrofula.

Surrounded by his beggars and scrofulous subjects, Robert was as happy as he could be. In fact the longer he lived in sin with Berthe the more he made himself into a good Christian, modest and observant. Finally, Constance had had enough of the hypocrisy. She left Paris, leaving Robert to his beggars and his lepers and his mistress, and went off to Étampes, where her château quite comfortably housed her courtiers and her children.

In 1031, Robert the Pious—there was nothing else to call him—was fifty-nine, a formidable age for the period. He seemed in good health. On June 29 an eclipse of the sun took place and this aroused his religious fervor, convincing him that it foretold his death. And indeed soon enough the king was struck down by a fever. Three weeks later, he was gone. From Melun, where the king had taken sick, the king's body was taken to Saint-Denis, where it was placed next to that of his father, Hugh Capet.

The monks of Saint-Denis were so grateful for all the generosity the late king had shown them that in their writings they ascribed to his death all sorts of extraordinary and cataclysmic phenomena: a comet that streaked across the sky; rivers that overflowed their banks, taking houses and drowning children. Heaven itself wept at the death of the pious king.

His piety had restored Paris. For the first time since the Viking invasions, a sovereign had cared enough to rebuild the city. It is true that Robert's munificence had been lavished mainly on monasteries, abbeys, churches—in addition to his own palace, of course—but it was a start.

Henri I, son of Robert the Pious, succeeded his father, and his reign marked the dawn of a difficult period: shortages, epidemics, and fires visited one after the other. And Parisians were divided. Some supported the new King Henry; others thought that the crown should have been offered to his younger brother, Robert. Henry thought it prudent to leave town and took refuge in Fécamp, with his ally the Duke of Normandy.

He was wise to leave Paris, for there was nothing left to eat in the city. In the markets vendors were selling dog meat or mice, and even, it was said, meat taken from the bodies of the recently deceased, all of which had to be thoroughly cooked of course. The miserable and starving crowded into the churches, hoping to find some kind of help or simply an easy death—anything to end their suffering. Everything was going wrong. In 1034, a fire that was more destructive than any before destroyed the huts in which a small crowd had sought shelter. In 1035, famine accompanied a new kind of plague, one even more deadly than the famine.

King Henri meanwhile chased after rebels who were contesting his throne. This meant that he had almost no chance to come to Paris.

The moment had come for the Church to establish its authority and put an end to this chaos. In 1049, the newly elected Alsatian pope Leon IX was determined to eradicate the corruption that was plaguing the clergy. In Francia as a whole and in Paris in particular, the titleholders of the bishoprics and abbeys were not always the most devout or the most deserving. They had, after all, purchased their titles. This practice suited the ambitious wealthy, of course, as well as the king, who received a nonnegotiable fee from the sale of ecclesiastical positions. Moreover, the high clergy, beholden to the monarch, could not refuse him when he needed money to raise an army in the event of war.

Henri wondered why the pope chose to meddle in all this. Aiming to put an end to the worst practices, the Holy See was trying as well to extend its influence across all the Christian countries, which was unacceptable to the secular rulers. No bishop of Francia was permitted to accept the invitation by Leon IX to attend a council on the touchy topic of clerical simony.

Moreover, the pope was constantly trying to pick a fight with the king of the Franks. During a stay in Ratisbonne, His Holiness visited the abbey of Saint-Emmeran in which was housed a chest said to contain the body of Saint Denis. Saint Denis reposed near Paris; everyone knew that. Actually, not so, responded the pontiff, who declared that the true remains of the saint were secure in the care of the Germanic Empire.

Henri refused to accept this. Solemnly and before a large crowd of Parisians, he had the sarcophagus in the Saint-Denis Abbey opened. The odor that emanated from it was so sweet that everyone knew at once that they had to have been produced by the remains of a saint. Somewhat bitterly, they continued to pray to Denis at his church.

Henri did more than that to weaken papal influence and control. He constructed a sumptuous abbey of which he would remain master, despite all kinds of protests from Rome. At the site of the chapel dedicated to Saint Martin, Henri founded the Saint-Martin-des-Champs monastery, protected behind thick walls, and gave it money and lands, as well as income, rights, privileges, and exemption from taxes. This undertaking was so enormous that it was only finished by Henri's son, Philippe I. At the moment of its dedication in 1067, Saint-Martin-des-Champs boasted a huge wall with crenellations, eighteen bartizans, and four very solid guard towers.

In 1079 this monastery was given to the order of Cluny. The deacons who had occupied the place were immediately replaced by seventy Benedictine monks. Saint-Martin-des-Champs became a priory—"the fourth daughter of Cluny," as a

What does all this have to do with Arts et Métiers?

The kings of France who followed made sizable donations to Saint-Martin-des-Champs. And the post of prior was much sought after: it brought with it 45,000 livres in annual income.

The priory also ran the jails, and in the sixteenth century the cloister would become the royal prison of Saint-Martin. Inside were imprisoned prostitutes arrested in public places. One can only imagine how the ladies of limited virtue and the austere monks got along.

Starting in 1702, the old cloister was razed and reconstructed. The main building featured thirty crosses facing each other and the vestibule measured thirty "king's feet" (nearly a hundred feet) by thirty-six (about 120 feet). Nonetheless, it soon became apparent that the building material had been shoddy; the monks had been ripped off. One mason had used earth and gravel; a carpenter had used old wood. The carpenter, for one, regretted what he had done and, fearing for his soul, confessed to his sin. He offered a small reduction of 25,000 livres to cover all of the construction.

The monks used this money to construct large and beautiful houses along Rue Saint-Martin, building a fountain at the corner
(Cont.)

of Rue du Vertbois and opening a public market.

Situated outside of Paris, the cloister had its own boundaries, as we've seen; those we can see today date from 1273. The town that developed around it was annexed by Paris in the fourteenth century and integrated behind a new wall built by Charles V.

During the Revolution the priory was turned into the Conservatoire National des Arts et Métiers, which visitors can still find at 292 Rue Saint-Martin. The Musée des Arts et Techniques within remains, just as it was during the days of the Cluny monks, a refuge from the march of human progress.

The outside of the conservatory is also worth a side trip: Cluny's Romanesque design remains an example of the kind of architecture emanating from Rome in the year 1100. The base of the southern clock tower, with its two-toned tiled roof, and the supporting apses that take the form of halos are handsome vestiges of the eleventh century. Inside the church one can still see the choir, whose foundations date back to 1067, and whose appearance actually dates from the beginning of the twelfth century, a period during which the Gothic style had begun to make an appearance: the fullness of Romanesque arches are intermixed with ribbed vaults, symbols of Gothic art.

(Cont.)

phrase from the period put it. This abbey possessed other abbeys, not only in Francia but in Spain and in England as well.

By means of this monastery Philippe very clearly intended to extract concessions from the Holy See and to get under the pope's skin just a little bit. He had resigned himself to being forced to negotiate between two widely disseminated bans.

And so the century ended as it had begun: with illicit love. In 1092, Philippe fell hopelessly in love with a young woman named Bertrade, who was engaged to the Comte d'Anjou, an elderly man. The king repudiated his wife and had her locked up in the château at Montreuil-sur-Mer. In the meantime, unfortunately, Bertrade had married the count. Philippe was not about to let that stand in his way. Otherwise, what was the point of being king? He spirited Bertrade away, which didn't prove all that hard to do given that the young woman was quite willing. She gave herself passionately to the king, who was nearly thirty years older, happy to parade around the Cité palace as if she were queen of the Franks.

The Parisians accepted her and greeted her as their queen when she came out of the palace. The king had the right to some happiness, thought some. Others held a somewhat different opinion.

Pope Urban II, for one, was outraged. "Such an event reveals the decadence of the entire kingdom and presages the ruin of your churches," he wrote. Later, because he couldn't make the lovers see reason and part, he excommunicated them for good. From then on the king and his lady could not attend church, and the gates of monasteries were closed to them. In fact, however, a number of them—in opposition to the pope—remained loyal to the king.

This lasted for twelve years:

The grandeur of the priory's past can be found in the refectory of the monks, which has been turned into a library and remains a sublime example of twelfth century Gothic. A small courtyard and a partially restored turret can be found on Rue du Vertbois.

The bend in Rue Bailly retains the southeast border of the enclosure whose corner tower- is visible in the stairway cage of number 7.

Finally, at the level of the intersection of Vertbois and Saint-Martin, rises up the tower of Vertbois, about which Victor Hugo wrote to an architect who had suggested its demolition, "Demolish the tower? No. Demolish the architect? Yes."

twelve years of councils, negotiations, broken promises; and twelve years during which the Cité palace was home to scandalous passion. In 1104, Bertrade rediscovered her faith. Her state of sin had become too much for her to bear, and she wanted to do penitence and thought only of putting on rags and retiring to a hut in Poitou.

As we might expect, Philippe was flabbergasted. Nonetheless he had no choice but to accede to Bertrade's wishes. During a council meeting in Paris the king arrived in bare feet and wearing a simple habit, to swear that he had renounced the woman whom he had already lost. The king returned alone to his palace. Bertrade went off to her little hovel in Poitou. The bull of excommunication was lifted, and the world turned again.

Remnants of the Right Bank wall: **1**. Rue de l'Oratoire. **2**. 148 and 150 Rue Saint-Honoré. **3**. 11 Rue du Louvre. **4**. 9 Rue du Jour. **5**. Jean the Fearless (Jean-sans-Peur) Tower at 20 Rue Etienne-Marcel **6**. 55–57 Rue des Francs-Bourgeois. **7**. Charles-Victor-Langlois square. **8**. Rue des Jardins-Saint-Paul. **The Left Bank wall**: **1**. 1 Quai de la Tournelle. **2**. 7 Rue des Chantiers. **3**. Rue des Écoles. **4**. Rue du Cardinal-Lemoine. **5**. 9–11 Rue Arras. **6**. 60–64 and 68 Rue du Cardinal-Lemoine. **7**. 4 and 6 Rue Thouin. **8**. 1 and 7 Rue Clovis. **9**. 47 Rue Descartes. **10**. Rue Monsieur-le-Prince. **11**. The Maison de Catalogne, on the corner of Rue Saint-André and Rue de l'Ancienne-Comédie. **12**. 27 and 35 Rue Mazarine. **13**. 13 Passage Dauphine. **14**. Rue Mazarine and Rue de Nevers. **15**. 29 Rue Guénégaud. **16**. Institute de France, Quai de Conti.

Paris, Capital of France

When you emerge from the Philippe Auguste Métro station, which is a short walk from Nation, you are well outside the walls of Paris, such as they were in the twelfth century. The *quartier* still evokes something of this king's era: there is the avenue bearing his name; the Avenue de Bouvines, a memorial to Philippe Auguste's victory over the Germanic emperor; and most especially the thirteen-foot-high statue of him atop one of the columns of the Trône, raised in 1843 in the Place de la Nation. Still, this little nonconcentric detour offers an occasion to ruminate on the limits that the king wanted to set on his capital.

Paris bears the imprint of Philippe Auguste, a conquering and combative king, who established his sovereignty through war.

First he had to defend his capital, which he did by constructing a thick wall around it. Philippe Auguste's wall measured nearly ten feet in width and thirty feet high, and was punctuated by towers, some of which rose up as high as eighty-five feet. These formidable ramparts would establish the boundaries of Paris for nearly two centuries, and pieces of them are still visible today.

If you want to find them, you have to move farther away, starting with the outer boundary on the Right Bank, where the wall was begun, as that is where the most imminent attack would have taken place—from the north.

To the west, the Seine was blocked off by heavy chains and bordered on one side by the citadel of the Louvre, which went the length of the river. Philippe Auguste would establish an anchorage around which soon enough the city's defenses revolved, the spot that protected the entire kingdom.

First, to crown this mighty edifice, it was necessary to build a strong keep, nearly one hundred feet high. In a radical departure from typical military architecture, the keep was not rectangular in shape, as was usually the case, but circular, which made attacking it more difficult, since it reduced the targets for projectiles, and simplified the watch, facilitating surveillance.

The building itself grew up around the keep, an enormous rectangular structure with thick walls. In the center of each wall was a tower, and there were other towers at each corner. The re-channeling of the Belleville and Ménilmontant creeks fed the water in the large moats that surrounded the structure. The main entryway, located on the east, was fairly narrow, and guarded over by two new towers. To get in, and to allow troops and carts to cross the moat, a drawbridge could be lowered and raised again fairly quickly, making the Louvre—for that is what this was— into an almost impregnable fortress, ready to defend Paris against possible invasion while at the same time offering a refuge for the king should a popular uprising take place. Moreover, the apartments designed for Philippe Auguste and his family were located in the keep, in the deepest and most fortified spot. Just in case of emergency.

The wall, whose height remained at the same level as the current Pont des Arts by the Tour du Coin, crossed the Louvre to pass the Rue de l'Oratoire, where one can still see a fragment of it in the sacristy of the reformed temple. Let's move on and cross into Rue Saint-Honoré, where chimneys on the houses at numbers 148 and 150 reveal that these structures once leaned on the outer walls (the building at 148 has the same width as the wall).

Here once stood the Saint-Honoré Gate. We are now on the

Rue du Louvre, on which number 11 preserves the base of another tower: the rounded forms of the adjoining buildings make it seem as if they are emerging from this stone mold. Past the Bourse du Commerce—the stock exchange—the wall follows the shape given to the Rue du Jour located on the path of its rounded interior: at number 9, a piece of the tower is still perfectly visible. We are hunting for the old Montmartre Gate, which a plaque at number 30 Rue Montmartre recalls for us, and we move on to Rue Étienne-Marcel, which also follows the shape of the original inside wall. We continue until we come to the Jean the Fearless (Jean-sans-Peur) Tower, a dungeon, a remnant of the palace that the dukes of Burgundy built in 1409 outside the abutting wall. At ground level you will see a rounded vestige of one of Philippe Auguste's towers. In other words there are two towers here: one located inside the other.

Let's move along to the Saint-Denis Gate, which can be found at 135 Rue Saint-Denis. From there the wall continues to the right of the Impasse des Peintres—roughly, "painter's dead end"—that went around the wall's exterior. From there we go to the Saint-Martin

Where are the remains of the Louvre fortress?

In the end, the fortress keep, called the Great Tower, never served as a royal residence, but, starting in 1295, as a prison and as a depository for the royal treasury. In 1527, François I had it demolished, and the medieval fortress was replaced by a Renaissance château.

During restoration work on the Louvre's Carrousel between 1984 and 1989, archaeologists came upon remains of the fortress Philippe Auguste had built beneath the Square Court. These impressive foundations are visible in the museum's archaeological crypt. Standing before those massive stones one senses the scope of the Louvre's defensive function at the time.

The magnificent Saint-Louis room remains the last vestige of the medieval interior of Philippe Auguste's castle. Where the keep once was are the remains of a well and a moat, remnants of the original fortress.

Not until Charles V in 1360 would the Louvre become a royal residence. From then on every king, or nearly every one, would alter the palace in his own way. Napoleon III, who did major construction on the site beginning in 1854, called for the destruction of the huts that until then had prevented the expansion of the palace. The *(Cont.)*

appearance of the Louvre that we know today is due in large part to him. There was one last transformation: the pyramid built during François Mitterrand's presidency by the architect I. M. Pei, which offers an entry worthy of one of the world's great museums.

Gate, at number 199 Rue Saint-Martin. From here the wall turns off in a southeastward direction, following the angle of the Impasse Beaubourg toward the Sainte-Avoie Alley. This leads to Rue des Archives and thence to Rue des Francs-Bourgeois, which in great part joins up with the circular path that went along the outside of the fortress walls. At numbers 55–57, Rue des Francs-Bourgeois, one can find the base of a tower somewhat awkwardly enhanced by a more modern building. The pavement reveals the outline of the curtain wall. We follow the trace that goes along the wall to number 10 Rue des Hospitalières-Saint-Gervais, then the one along Rue des Rosiers, where, in the courtyard of number 10, you can still find a tower. The wall was raised up along this axis to Rue de Sévigné, where it starts heading south, past the Baudet Gate and all the way to the intersection of Rue Saint-Antoine, then went along to the right of the church, in which the double thickness of the walls are clearly visible in the Charlemagne Passage. We have arrived at the most beautiful part of the fortress wall still standing: the part that goes along the Lycée Charlemagne located on Rue des Jardins-Saint-Paul, more than two hundred feet of wall that included the Montgomery Tower—which got its name from a Scottish guard who was imprisoned there after having wounded Henri II during a tournament in 1559. On another tower, in the gardens of the Hôtel des Tournelles, we discover the *marques de tâcherons*, the signatures (*marques*) of those drudges (*tâcherons*) who worked on the stones. The fortress wall ends with the Seine at 30–32 Quai des Célestins.

To get to the Left Bank, we have to move in the direction of the Rue Poulletier on Île Saint-Louis, which at the time was deserted and made up of two small islands separated at this very spot. At the time of the fortress wall, a heavy chain was raised from here at night to prevent traffic on the Seine.

Once we're on the Left Bank the wall picks up at number 1 Quai de la Tournelle, which took its name from the tower located on this corner. The narrow little building at number 7a Boulevard Saint-Germain retains the footprint of the wall, which passed through here. We find vestiges of it in the courtyard of number 7 Rue des Chantiers, as the foyer preserves traces of one of the lookout points. From here we follow the pieces of the ancient wall all the way to Rue des Écoles, where, beneath the post office, an arch breached the rampart in order to accommodate the flow of the Bièvre River, which winds through here.

If we follow along the Rue du Cardinal-Lemoine, starting at the Rue des Écoles, we can find part of the moat that lay outside of the wall: a portion adjoins the firehouse at 48–50 and another is found in the garden at number 9–11 Rue Arras. Some large segments are also visible in a number of spots: at 60–64 and 68 Rue du Cardinal-Lemoine; at numbers 4 and 6 Rue Thouin; at numbers 1 and 7 Rue Clovis; and most especially at number 47 Rue Descartes where, if we are prepared to be patient and make our way through three separate doors, each with its own Digicode keypad, we can climb up the rampart's ridgepole. Finding this charming passage, so jealously protected, was the most rewarding of all my quests. It is a magical place.

At number 50 on this same Rue Descartes we can see a map of the Bordelle Gate, or Saint-Marcel Gate. We are on Rue des Fossés-Saint-Jacques, still located on the other side of the wall, and arrive at number 151 Rue Saint-Jacques, the location of the Saint-Jacques Gate, the most important of all the gates on the Left Bank. The wall descends from here down Rue Soufflot until it reaches Rue Victor-Cousin.

The Saint-Michel Gate can be found at number 56 Boulevard Saint-Michel, since the wall extended along the right-hand side of Rue Monsieur-le-Prince; there a commemorative plaque at number 40 reads, ANCIENNE RUE DES FOSSÉS—since formerly it was known as "street of the moats." There's a Chinese restaurant here called

La Grande Muraille, or "Great Wall." Obviously it refers to the Great Wall of China, but it seems to give a nod to Philippe Auguste's magnificent construction. The walls at the back of the restaurant, as well as those that go all the way to Rue Racine, are made of the original fortress wall itself.

The wall is cut off by Boulevard Saint-Germain, then picks up on the other side. A tower can still be found in the Maison de Catalogne, on the corner of Rue Saint-André and Rue de l'Ancienne-Comédie.

The Rue Mazarine, right up to the Seine, contains a trace of the exterior moat of the wall, of which we can also find several remnants in the parking garage at number 27 and in the small garden at number 35. At number 13 Dauphine Passageway, climb up to the first floor of the language school and you will find that the terrace offers an exquisite view from the top of one of the towers.

Farther along, Rue Mazarine joins up with Rue de Nevers, but a wall brings the street to a dead end. That wall is *the* wall. Back on Rue Mazarine, take a left onto Rue Guénégaud. At number 29, duck into the entrance of the Éditions du Seuil publishing house, and at the back of the courtyard you will find a tower from the wall.

Paris's protective wall ended in the Seine, next to the celebrated Tour de Nesle, which once stood on the spot now occupied by the Institut de France, Quai de Conti (a plaque on the left wing of the institute reminds us of this).

Other pieces of the great wall can doubtless be found in private homes and in the foundations of buildings. There are people for whom finding remains of the wall is a passion akin to embarking on a treasure hunt.

Finding Philippe Auguste's wall was my first quest. If I have gone on for a bit too long about it all, it is simply to show the challenges that need to be overcome to find its traces. For those who know a little of its history, Paris is a charming puzzle.

———

Like his great wall, Philippe Auguste was also quite compelling. He did nearly everything, imagined everything, invented everything. He secured royal authority, enlarged the country, and renovated Paris.

When he had ascended to the throne in 1179, Philippe II, as he was called, was but fifteen—an immature nobody ruling the Franks from the Île-de-France. Fate would transform him into a somebody. He made himself king of France by force of arms and will, giving coherence to his territories and offering to them a history as well, a language, a common sense of purpose. With him Paris started to take on the appearance of a city worthy of being the capital of a growing kingdom. Philippe II turned into Philippe Auguste, a title reminiscent of imperial Rome—and yet it was one that priests conferred on him in their sermons and scribes in their manuscripts.

Naturally the king's methods were expedient. They were, to be honest, more than crude; they were abominable. For example, pressed by a need for money from the moment he sat on the throne, he decided to ransom the entire Jewish community. One Saturday morning in the year 1181, he threw all the Jews of Paris into prison. To secure their release, they had to transfer their worldly goods to the king. It didn't stop there. The following year, Philippe Auguste simply forgave all Christian debts to Jews. This worked out well for public financing, for the erstwhile debtors were forced to give a fifth of what they owed to the royal treasury instead.

On June 24, 1182, an edict of expulsion was declared and for the first time in history a Christian realm exiled the entire Jewish population by official decree. The synagogues of Paris—one could be found under the shadow of the cathedral on Île de la Cité and another on Rue de l'Attacherie (today Rue de la Tacherie) on the Left Bank—were turned into churches, and property owned by the Jews was auctioned off by royal authority. With the sums gained from all this, the king built a market on the former Jewish neighborhood of Champeaux, henceforth emptied of its inhabitants. He ordered the construction of two covered buildings surrounded by walls whose doors were closed at night. These

How did *Les Halles* disappear?

The market started by Philippe Auguste grew exponentially, and in the sixteenth century François I undertook a reorganization. He started by having very strange-looking structures built, the so-called *piliers des Halles*, on the ground floor of which were covered galleries that housed the shops; in the middle of these galleries of arcades was the *carreau*—the tile—where one came to buy bread and dairy products.

In the nineteenth century, the Halles posed a number of problems—hygiene among them—and needed to be restructured yet again. An architectural competition was held in 1848 and won by Victor Baltard, who between 1852 and 1870 constructed ten pavilions with glass roofs and stone floors, supported by cast-iron columns. Two other pavilions were added in 1936.

In the twentieth century, the old Halles simply had to go. The explosion of Paris's population and public health realities forced major changes; the market was moved elsewhere. In 1969, Les Halles packed up and moved to Rungis, in the suburbs.

During 1971 and 1973, stupidity, ignorance, the arrogance of urban renewal, and plain greed resulted in the razing of Bal-
(Cont.)

marketplaces were an improvement over the old system, for they permitted merchants to leave their merchandise in complete security, protected from rain and thieves. Very soon the *marché des Champeaux*, as it was called, would become the busiest and largest in all Paris. Nearly anything could be bought or sold there. Thus the king established the basis of what would become, for nearly eight hundred years, les Halles de Paris.

Philippe Auguste looked hard at Paris and saw that the city needed work. Near the Halles, the vast and very old graveyard Cimetière des Innocents offered an example. Between the stones and the large open common grave, all kinds of nasty things took place—pigs rustled around and prostitutes plied their commerce. Here was a place in need of walls. The whores were forced out and the pigs returned to their sties and garbage was removed. Henceforth the cemetery could only be visited during the day—for purposes of grave visitation or burial. At night, the gates were closed tight.

The king desired order and cleanliness, not a city that resembled an open cesspool. One day, when he went to the window of the

Cité palace to watch the boats along the Seine and movement of carts, he saw how mired everything was in mud. The horses chewed up the roads and deposited their manure, over which wheels skidded, sending shit flying. The putrid smell of rot and decay was everywhere.

The king wondered whether anything could be done to end this. In the old days the Romans had paved the streets with stones, but with time successive layers of garbage and filth had piled up so high that of the original road there was but the dimmest memory. Philippe Auguste convoked the burghers and the city administrator. Whatever the cost, the main roads of the city would all be paved with "strong and hard stones" on which carts could circulate without creating a nauseating cloud.

tard's structures. This truly was a sad period for the city from an architectural point of view: Les Halles was taken down and the Montparnasse Tower was put up. One of Baltard's pavilions survived, however, and was moved to Nogent-sur-Marne.

The current Forum des Halles is covered by the *Canopée*, a building made of earth and glass and designed by the architects Patrick Berger and Jacques Anziutti.

In 1187, Heraclius, the Latin patriarch of Jerusalem, arrived in Paris while the city was in full transformation. The prelate was the bearer of news that would tear at the heart of Christianity and cause all good Christians to lament: Saladin had taken Jerusalem and the Holy City was now in the hands of Saracens. Pope Urban III had died almost instantly upon learning of this grievous news. For Heraclius there was but one course of action: raising troops throughout France, England, and Germania and heading off to conquer Palestine. The patriarch had come to call for the Third Crusade, the object of which was to deliver Jerusalem.

Heraclius made his plea in the cathedral of Notre-Dame, which was under construction, for indeed the old church Saint-Étienne was too dilapidated and small for a city that was growing by such leaps and bounds; it had been torn down by order of the bishop,

Maurice de Sully. In its place a new basilica was under construction, one that would take twenty-five years.

The work was far from completed during Heraclius's visit, and he offered his sermon in what was essentially a holy construction site—a large open field of carved stones, ropes, pullies, ladders, and wooden mortar mixers, at the end of which was a half-built cathedral. This was the choir, which was already quite splendid and impressive. Four stories of it rose up to the sky, toward the vaults whose ribs descended from the heights and extended onto rounded pillars; all around a double walkway opened onto small chapels.

The stone cutters, carpenters, and roofers; the metal casters, masons, and carters—they all worked under the authority of a magistrate who had sketched out the plans on parchment. What was emerging was a church more vast than anyone could have imagined. Despite the bishop's impatience to finish the job, the work progressed with almost desperate slowness. In this month of October, as in every year at the same season, the work tapered off and entered a period of relative inaction. The impending frost would spoil the mortar, so the masons put down their trowels and covered the partially completed work with straw, leaving the worksite until spring, when they would return. As for the stone cutters, they continued their work in the cold weather, but more slowly, and working in the wood huts that were scattered on the worksite.

It was in this sublime but unfinished site that Heraclius sobbed, cried, harangued, and announced the arrival of the fire of the Apocalypse upon them all were Jerusalem not liberated; his words seemed to mount up to the very gates of heaven, amplified by the rolling echoes under the choir's vaulted spaces. His audience trembled at the message of this venerable patriarch; the powerful fretted and the humble shivered.

Philippe Auguste was pressured to take part in the deliverance of the Holy Land and the tomb of Christ. The mood in Europe had turned extraordinarily bellicose. In Paris and throughout the realm, and in England as well, aristocrats and landowners supported this holy quest. The king of France didn't have much choice; he must go. First, however, he would need to conclude a peace with Richard the Lionhearted, the English king, whom he would join on the expedition. The two sovereigns signed a treaty: "We will make this voyage to Jerusalem together, guided by the Lord. Each of us promises to hold and protect the other in good faith and friendship."

On March 15, 1190, Queen Isabelle died while giving birth to stillborn twins. The king wasn't yet twenty years of age. Philippe Auguste had married Isabelle de Hainaut, still but a child, ten years earlier for territorial reasons; her dowry was Artois. He had never much liked the frail and weepy young woman, but her death erased all that and he ordered that an extravagant funeral be held for her, and that it take place in the choir of the cathedral of Notre-Dame. Her body would be buried in a crypt dug for this occasion.

Before leaving on the Crusade, the king of France had other tasks to complete. He knew, for example, that Paris was a city almost without defenses. There were still the old walls around Île de la Cité, but for the most part they had been built only along the two riverbanks. There was little to stop an invading army, and both the Normans and the English had periodically threatened to invade. What was needed was a wall protecting the north, on the Right Bank.

Philippe Auguste had grand plans for his capital. He hoped that the security afforded by the new ramparts would bring even more people to the city, and indeed had in mind a veritable urbanization plan. Within the future wall, he imagined green spaces and gardens scattered among new construction that would be built to house the new population.

The king designated six prominent Parisian burghers to execute his plans during his absence, then went to Saint-Denis where he received the benediction of the "Holy Nail and Holy Cross" and took possession of a banner embroidered with a golden cross, his rallying symbol. Thus armed, Philippe headed off to conquer the Holy Land.

On July 4, 1190, the king of France and the king of England arrived in the Burgundian town of Vézelay. They traveled together down the length of the Rhone Valley, where enthusiastic crowds greeted the two monarchs who would crush the arrogant Saracens. Philippe embarked in Marseille; Richard continued toward Genoa.

Philippe Auguste was absent from Paris and his realm for nearly a year and a half. And very little was accomplished by it. The Crusade resumed after six months in Sicily, waiting for the waters of the Mediterranean to calm, and started off with a siege of the coastal city of Acre, which did not accomplish its purpose and roust out Saladin's soldiers. To complete this litany of woe, Philippe fell gravely ill with a high fever that caused him to lose his hair and his nails, and created an inflammation that struck one of his eyes and blinded it. The poor man wanted nothing more than to leave this wretched land and return to Paris. He sent emissaries to Richard, asking him to relieve him of his duties and allow him to depart immediately for France.

"If the king leaves without accomplishing his duty," declared the king of England, "dishonor will be upon him and shame for the kingdom of France. It is not my counsel that he do this. If he must choose between death and returning to his own country, let that be his decision."

Philippe had already decided. He embarked at Tyre, leaving the French crosses at Richard's disposition. When he arrived in Paris on December 27, 1191, he was but a shadow of the man who had left eighteen months before. Although twenty-six, he was nearly bald and half blind; he had seen death from close up and now was keenly aware of the passage of time. He wanted to build something that would last.

When Philippe Auguste had begun this disastrous expedition, construction of the wall on the Right Bank had already advanced some distance; the king began planning for its continuance on the Left Bank, and traced the borders the walls would encircle.

Meanwhile, Richard the Lionhearted persisted in the Holy Land. He occupied the port of Jaffa, reestablished the Latin kingdom of Jerusalem, but failed in his attempt to take the Holy City. Finally, to achieve closure to an adventure that had already gone on for too long, he negotiated a truce with Saladin. He left Palestine in October of 1192. Storms forced him to shelter on the island of Corfu, where he was taken prisoner by Henry IV, the Germanic emperor.

This turn of events delighted Philippe Auguste. He had no trouble controlling John, the imprisoned English king's younger brother. To take the crown from his brother, John was open to any alliance. He helped Philippe Auguste lay siege to the fortresses of Normandy, all English possessions, and permitted him to seize Gisor and other castles belonging to the Plantagenets, the royal family of England.

But all good things must come to an end, and Richard was finally released on February 2, 1194. War between Philippe and Richard erupted almost immediately. It was inevitable. The king of France wanted to expand his kingdom to his country's natural borders; the king of England wanted to retain control of his continental territories. Beyond this logical disagreement the two men simply hated one another. They were so different. Richard was a man of war and handy with the axe. Philippe, on the other hand, had fought because he had been forced, but he was born to administer his estates, improve the living standard of his contemporaries, and work for progress.

In any case, the French didn't offer the English armies great resistance. They retreated everywhere. There was really no battle to speak of, but rather a series of flights, retreats, skirmishes, burned villages, and castles taken and then abandoned.

On July 3, 1194, probably by accident, the two armies found themselves facing one another in the forest of Fréteval, near

Vendôme. Richard took the lead of his troops; the French beat a hasty retreat. In fact, they took off with such dispatch that Philippe Auguste had to leave behind his beautiful plates and his chests of silver. Perhaps even more seriously, he also left on the field of battle what he called his "archives," his accounts, which he took everywhere he went. He now realized that it had perhaps not been the wisest decision to take all this paper with him when he went to war. From then on, such papers would remain in the royal archives behind the thick walls of the Louvre. Thus, from necessity, and from the light of experience, Philippe Auguste created the earliest incarnation of the National Archives.

Richard the Lionhearted died in the only way he could have—in combat. On March 26, 1199, while laying siege to the château of Châlus in the Limousin, he was badly wounded by an arrow. Gangrene set in and eleven days later he was dead.

The hostilities continued, now against King John. The tide turned. Philippe won victory after victory, and depleted the realm of the Plantagenets on French soil and conquered Normandy, Maine, Touraine, and eventually even the cradle of the Plantagenets, Anjou and Poitou.

Finally, John Lackland, as he was known—Jean sans Terres—was definitively beaten by Philippe's son, the future Louis VIII, at La Roche-au-Moine on July 2, 1214. At the same time, the father defeated the Germanic emperor Otto IV at the Battle of Bouvines on July 27, 1214, and placed Capetian sovereignty over much of the weakened Germanic empire.

If Philippe Auguste had succeeded in defeating his principal adversaries—English, German, and also Spanish (at the Battle of Muret in 1213), he had also succeeded in building the Paris he wanted. Starting in the final years of the twelfth century, the city had expanded rapidly. Within a few decades, the population had doubled, and now reached nearly fifty thousand inhabitants. The

lines of communication had improved; commerce was flourish-
ing; the fairs and the Halles had expanded. Paris had been made
into one of the greatest cities in Europe, and the capital of the
most powerful kingdom of the West.

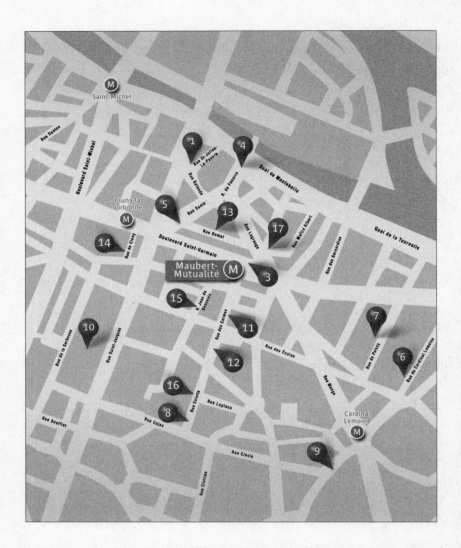

1. At 79 Rue Galande, a small twelfth-century church dedicated to Saint Julian the Poor, an example of the transition from Romanesque to Gothic art. **3.** The Place Maubert. **4.** The Rue du Fouarre. **5.** The Rue Dante. **6.** The oldest college (Cardinal Lemoine). **7.** And the most beautiful college (Bernardins). **8.** At 21 Rue Valette, a vestige of the Collège de Fortet. **9.** At 65 Rue Cardinal-Lemoine, a vestige of the Collège des Écossai. **10.** The Sorbonne. **11.** At 14 Rue des Carmes, a vestige of the Collège des Presles. **12.** At 17 Rue des Carmes, the remains of the chapel of the Collège des Lombards. **13.** The Collège de Cornouailles is hidden away in an alley that leads from the Rue Galende to number 12a Rue Domat. **14.** At 7 Rue de Cluny, a vestige of the thirteenth-century convent of Mathurins, installed in the annex of the Saint-Benoît-le-Bétourné church. **15.** At 9a Rue Jean-de-Beauvais, a seventeenth-century chapel surrounded by modern buildings, a remnant of the Collège de Dormans. **16.** At 4 Rue Valette, the Collège Saint-Barbe. **17.** At 29 Place Maubert, a plaque with Gothic letters shows the water level during a disastrous 1711 flood.

Thirteenth Century

Maubert-Mutualité

The University Takes Off

White letters set against a blue background: the Maubert-Mutualité Métro stop has the classic Parisian subway look. Were it not for the bright orange and very eighties-looking seats.

When you come up out of the subway you can either head toward the Palais de la Mutualité, whose subtle Art Deco façade masks contentious meetings of all kinds, or you can go in the other direction, toward Place Maubert, with its market and its streets teeming with history.

Before all the transformation wrought by Baron Haussmann during the Second Empire, this square was somewhat less grand than it appears today; it was more elongated, enclosed, and hard to access. The modest median strip with the fountain recalls this earlier shape, which was triangular and went north from Rue des Carmes until it hit the Rue Lagrange.

It was in this square that the University of Paris started—right out in the open—for on the Place Maubert, as well as on the Rue du Fouarre, students came to listen to words of the teachers.

Master Albert may have been a Dominican friar but he avoided teaching the lessons required by the Church. He kept his distance in both the literal and figurative sense. He left Notre-Dame to go and teach in the Dominican convent on Rue Saint-Jacques, whose

Rue du Fouarre, Place Maubert: What is the source of these names?

The word *fouarre* is from Old French and signifies *fourrage*, or "fodder." The reason is that young people with intellectual curiosity would sit here on the bales of hay just off-loaded from the boats that navigated on the Seine.

And why "Maubert"? This is a contraction of Magister Maubus, the Latin name of Albert von Bollstädt, a German Dominican monk who was made a Master of Theology at the University of Paris in 1245. Hence why nearby one can also find Rue Maître-Albert, a dogleg alley that existed in the eleventh century under the name Rue Perdue, or "lost street." Actually this street was not at all lost; it had been there for a thousand years and cut across all the construction sites and all the urban planning.

walls he soon found too confining, given the crowds of *escholiers,* or scholars, who squeezed into them. So he went off to teach in the mud on the Left Bank. Teaching out in the open required both faith and robust health; you were outside in sunshine or rain, or huddled during freezing weather in a simple wooden shack, while eager students sat on the bales of hay. Today students protest for better facilities, and they're right to do so. At the time, when a bad cold could kill you, their historical comrades ran the risk of picking up nasty illnesses—the flux, for example— simply by following their passion for learning.

Many came to Paris, attracted by the intellectual ferment. A young Florentine man with a thin face, for example, could soon be found sitting on the bales. This was Dante Alighieri, not yet the writer of *The Divine Comedy*. Hence why a few steps from the spot, the Rue Dante runs today. The poet knew the Rue du Fouarre when it was open-air and frequented by students night and day. Later, in 1358, all that changed. In order to prevent the scholars from coming and going with their drinking and prostitutes, authorities closed off the street by means of two wooden gates as soon as night fell.

The Place Maubert lay on an important axis of communication— the road connecting Paris, Lyon, and Rome via the Rue Galande and the Rue de la Montagne-Sainte-Geneviève, as well as the road that led to Saint-Jacques-de-Compostelle. In the twelfth century, a church dedicated to Saint-Julien-le-Pauvre, the patron saint of pilgrims and travelers, was built; small though it is, it remains a handsome example of the transition from Romanesque to Gothic styles. The current façade dates from the seventeenth century, but on the outside you can still see vestiges of the twelfth century, such as on the capitals and columns. On the inside the two bays in the nave are also twelfth century. When Paris as a place of instruction was recognized and restructured, its rector was based here, leaving the streets and squares to the colleges and schools that grew in such profusion on the Left Bank that the whole collection of them was simply called *l'Université*.

Once deprived of its students, Place Maubert became a dark and fearsome corner of Paris. Old engravings show it bristling with gallows and the "ladders of justice," with shackles in which blasphemers, bigamists, and perjurers were put on display, bearing the marks of their infamy. The square became a place of hangings and suffering. Moreover, given that the banks of the Seine were not very high and poorly buttressed, the square was often flooded. At number 29 Place Maubert, a plaque with Gothic letters, partly defaced, shows the water level during a disastrous flood in 1711.

In the twelfth century, knowledge and teaching were still firmly in the hands of the Church. Not just instruction in theology but also in science, grammar, rhetoric, and dialectics took place only within the monasteries. Students had to adhere to the episcopal school, and to submit to strict canon law as laid down by the authorities at Notre-Dame on Île de la Cité. Faced with such rigidly prescriptive interdictions, dissidents inevitably emerged. These were not dangerous rebels, nor even rogue humanists; they were simply clerics who dreamed of a little independence. To maintain some autonomy from the pope and the episcopal school—which alone was permitted to issue diplomas—they set up shop on the Left Bank, where the communities of masters and students gained greater stature by literally moving up the slopes of Mount Sainte-Geneviève.

All this was done in some confusion, with each master assuming that he could teach and each pupil believing that he could choose his professor. The bishop of Paris protested vehemently against these infringements on his authority.

In 1200, Philippe Auguste decided that he needed to restore some order. He regularized the relative freedom of the schools and conferred upon them letters of patent. Henceforth they would be collectively called *Universitas parisiensis magistrorum et scholarum*. Again the word *universitas* was being defined in its strictly Latin sense, which means "society," or "company." The term designated a collection of people engaged in the same activity. In any case, the king created a frame in which teaching could take place independent of the ecclesiastical yoke. The thirteenth century would be the century of the university.

The most illustrious teachers opened their courses on Mount Sainte-Geneviève and the students followed them in droves. These teachers sought to distance themselves from orthodoxy, meaning from *juste opinion,* or right-minded thinking, as imposed by the Church. They wanted to teach such things as medicine, a difficult task given that Pope Honorius III forbade instruction in it to the monks in 1219, fearing that instruction in such scientific nonsense would distract these servants of God from true scholarship. The works of Hippocrates and Galen were therefore studied more or less clandestinely—or in any case at the margins of the Church—and taught by independent-minded professors of various religious orders.

Soon enough, the Left Bank was teeming with colleges and schools that attracted not only students from the realm but from across Europe.

In his book *Western History,* Bishop Jacques de Vitry gives us a somewhat frightening picture of the Latin Quarter that was taking shape. He was of course a loyal cleric, and therefore horrified by what was happening there, as much on the intellectual plane as on the personal. Still, his account offers a view of medieval Paris.

For Jacques de Vitry, the city was "a scruffy goat" and the good bishop was shocked to find that prostitutes were everywhere. He described houses on the Left Bank in which there might be a school on the first floor and a bordello on the ground floor. Students could therefore pass seamlessly from the joys of learning to those of the flesh. And in this little world were gathered Frenchmen, Normans, Bretons, Burgundians, Germans, as well as Flemish, Sicilian, and Romans, all fighting each other under the smallest pretext, while the teachers, who seemed more preoccupied with coins than with pure science, tried to break up the fights. And in the meanwhile they were all engaging in useless and vain arguments, which, in the eyes of the good bishop, were simply wrongheaded, and based on considerations other than those of the well-being of the mortal soul and the inevitability of divine omnipotence.

To Jacques de Vitry's great displeasure, schools were proliferating on the Left Bank. Wealthy aristocrats, as well as a number of religious orders such as the Dominicans and the Franciscans, were financing operations in which students were fed and lodged and given instruction. Between Place Maubert and Mount Sainte-Geneviève, colleges were sprouting up everywhere. Some served only a small handful of students, and there were so many that they were constantly joining operations or getting swallowed up by one another. Hence for example the Collège des Irlandais—the college of the Irish—took over the Collège des Lombards, and the Collège du Danemark was sold to the Carmelite convent; the Collège de Presles became part of the Collège de Dormans-Beauvais, and the famous Collège de Coqueret was eclipsed by the Collège Sainte-Barbe. Forty-two thousand students, between the ages of fifteen and fifty, followed courses in some seventy-five institutions of higher learning. In the other European capitals schools were rare and few. Paris had unquestionably become the intellectual center of the world.

Where have all the colleges gone?

One of the oldest schools carried the name of its founder, Cardinal Lemoine. This college was to have been completely razed at the end of the seventeenth century, or so the history books tell us. Here again my insatiable appetite for going after lost stones came to the fore. Historians of Paris such as Jacques Hillairet quite often mention Le Paradis Latin, a large amusement hall constructed on the remains of the college and which features a mysterious private passageway that is not open to the public. However, if you barge your way into Le Paradis Latin, you will find an entire section of an old structure and large blocks of stones that without question predate the seventeenth century: this is a part of the Collège du Cardinal Lemoine. If you bend down to these stones, near the former entrance toward the stairs, you can just make out grooves that were cut out by the hands of the *escholiers:* "3C." This indicates that a student lived on stairway 3C.

The most beautiful of all the colleges still visible today is that of the Bernardines, founded in 1224. Enlarged in the fourteenth century, it offers impressive testimony to the secular medieval architecture of Paris, with its Gothic windows and stonework.

(Cont.)

In 1229, six years after the death of Philippe Auguste and three years after the death of Louis VIII, and while France was living under the regency of Blanche de Castille—who was to remain regent until Louis IX reached his majority—the university rebelled. The students had a terrible reputation by this point; these young people, who were supposed to represent the country's elite, so frightened the bourgeoisie of Paris that at night the streets were deserted. Sometimes with reason, the students were accused of stealing to survive, of kidnapping women from across town and having their way with them, and even, occasionally, of murder. To impose order, Guillaume de Seignelay, the bishop of Paris, threatened to excommunicate anyone who walked around armed. The students sneered at this threat and carried on as before. The bishop became angry and ordered the arrest of the more violent among them and banished others. Let them go hang themselves elsewhere, ran his thinking.

In February of 1229, after the carnival on *Lundi Gras*—Fat Monday—a group of students went to drink at an establishment in the neighborhood of Saint-Marcel. At the end of the evening, suitably tipsy, they got caught up in a lively discussion about the cost of the wine they had drunk; it cost more than they had in their purses. Soon enough words got heated and blows followed. The café owner yelled so loudly that a few stalwart locals from the neighborhood ran to help. The fight between the students and the Parisians went all night, until finally the naughty students were somewhat rudely expelled from the premises.

The next day, humiliated by this defeat, the students came back and surrounded the tavern. Armed with heavy wooden bars, they started to wreck the place and then went from street to street, damaging other shops. Along the way they attacked whomever they happened to come across, wounding and killing at random in their rage.

Outrage spread across Paris, and came to the attention of the regent herself. She declared her support of the citizens against the students and ordered law enforcers to "punish the students of the University."

It is very hard to tell one student from another and the gendarmes didn't make much of an effort to distinguish between them. They simply mounted the ramparts and went after any student they happened to come across, killing

At number 24 Rue de Poissy, the vaults in the basement—an ancient cellar—can still be seen and the ground floor as well, where the convent's refectory was located. The last entirely original structure still standing contains the largest Gothic room in all of Paris—more than 115 feet in length. After five years of restoration, this immense space dedicated to research and study is now open to the public.

At 14 Rue des Carmes, you can find the remains of the College de Presles, founded in 1314. Behind the long ornamented windows, people still live in what once was a sixteenth-century chapel.

At number 17 on this street are the remains of the chapel of the Collège des Lombards, founded in 1334. The main entry dates from 1760 and the other parts of the chapel look somewhat strange, having being washed and eroded by the waters of a fountain that used to be there

The Collège de Cornouailles, founded in 1321, is hidden away in a small alley that leads from the Rue Galende to number 12a Rue Domat. After you reach the first inner courtyard, turn around and you will see before you the entry building of the school, nearly seven centuries old.

The Collège des Écossais—the Scottish School—was located at 65 Rue du Cardinal-Lemoine.

(Cont.)

Transformed into a prison during the Revolution, it was made into an Anglican church in 1806. There one can find a stairway and a *cour d'honneur,* or main courtyard. The façade bears the inscription COLLÈGE D'ÉCOSSE, and an escutcheon with "FCE," which means *"Fief du Collège d'Écosse,"* a sure sign that you are in the heart of a university that wanted to be truly international.

At 9a Rue Jean-de-Beauvais is a chapel dating from the seventeenth century. Entirely surrounded by modern buildings today, it is a remnant of the Collège de Dormans, created in 1365.

At 21 Rue Valette you will find a stairway, yet another vestige. It leads us into the courtyard of the former Collège de Fortet, founded in 1394. Here is a silent and luminous window into history, a place open to the skies and yet right in the heart of Paris. The sight of the stars spreading endlessly out before you may make you want to escape the world. That's exactly what the student John Calvin did when he was being hounded for heresy. The school's most famous student took to the roofs and made his way to Geneva, where he advanced his reforming theory. There is a lovely historic irony to this, for the college was the birthplace of the Counter-Reformation move-
(*Cont.*)

several, wounding others, and robbing everyone.

Now it was the university's turn to feel itself wronged—its privileges trampled upon, its independence contested, and its students under threat. No one seemed to know what to do. To exert pressure on the authorities, masters and students made use of a new method: they went on strike. As soon as the teaching came to a stop, the schools cleared out. The word *grève*—"strike"—would not appear for another six centuries, but all the elements of uncompromising conflict were in place. Students and teachers left Paris to go teach or study elsewhere. The towns of Angers, Orléans, Toulouse, and Poitiers were only too happy to reap to their profit the splendid reputation of the Parisian university. Even England's king, Henry III, welcomed several who were out of favor in the French capital to Oxford.

Neither side would budge. The differences seemed unresolvable. The university fought for its privileges and its independence. The royal authority wanted to establish its right to maintain order. Months went by. The university remained an empty shell.

"One must know when to end a strike," Maurice Thorez, the French Communist leader, would say one day. The problem was no different in the Middle Ages. Happily, Pope Gregory IX found a way to end the stalemate. He wanted Paris to remain a place of higher learning, and particularly religious training. He pushed hard for negotiation, and finally insisted that it take place. For his part, young Louis IX, all of sixteen, sided with his mother.

Finally, however, Blanche de Castille softened her stance and agreed to compensate the students who had been the victims of the gendarmes, restoring to the university its rights and privileges; she also persuaded the city's landlords to offer affordable housing for the students. For their part, the bishop of Paris and the abbots of Sainte-Geneviève and Saint-Germain-des-Prés, along with the canons of Saint-Marcel, spoke in their sermons about the need to respect the teachers and students. This struggle between public authority and academic autonomy endures to our own day.

Pope Gregory IX agreed to recognize the diplomas obtained by the students who had taken refuge in Angers and Orléans, on the condition that they return immediately to Paris. Moreover, the Holy Father confirmed that the students had the right to make their own statutes, and were even authorized the right to use "stoppage"—meaning a strike—in the event that a student was killed and his killer went unpunished. Better still, in the papal bull entitled *Parens scientiarum universitas,* dated April 13, 1231, the pontiff recognized in perpetuity the jurisdictional and intellectual independence of the University of Paris.

The students and their masters returned to Paris. Two years

---

ment: here the Catholic Holy League of the Duc de Guise was created in 1572. As we will see the duke was the instigator of a terrible massacre of Protestants.

Arrayed against such radicalism, the Collège Saint-Barbe, known for its open-minded spirit, taught a discipline that today has mostly been neglected: logic. This college can be found on the Rue Vallette, and absorbed what was formerly the Collège de Coqueret, famous for having educated the Renaissance poets Joachim du Bellay and Pierre de Ronsard.

What remains of the Sorbonne of yester-year?

The Sorbonne's renown spread quickly across all of Europe. Nonetheless, in the fifteenth century, the Sorbonne fell back into the hands of the Church, which finally had recognized the university, principally to gain control of it. With the birth of humanism, new dissident colleges were founded. The Sorbonne lost its influence, becoming as opposed to the new ideas as the old Notre-Dame school had once been.

One event that marked both the extent of its fame and the beginning of its decline was the creation in 1470 of the first printing press in France, which was put within its walls. The Sorbonne was effectively turned into an arm of royal and papal power.

In the seventeenth century, Cardinal Richelieu, though loyal to the pope, tried to rescue the Sorbonne by means of his own private funds. He invested large sums to burnish the old school's coat of arms. The buildings that can still be seen today date not from its beginnings but from Richelieu's efforts (as well as others in the nineteenth century). Inside the chapel one can admire Richelieu's tomb, sculpted by Girardon. Around the chapel whose dome Riche-
(Cont.)

had passed since the strike began. Courses started up again and the city's inhabitants were happy to see the Latin Quarter once again hopping with activity.

Under the reign of Louis IX, better known as Saint Louis, the university expanded yet further. Its seat would depart from Saint-Julien-le-Pauvre, which had become too constraining, and move to the Sorbonne, where it remains to this day. This Sorbonne, on which by now all the faculties of greater Paris depended, started as simply one of the neighborhood's colleges, founded in 1257 by the king's confessor, Robert de Sorbon.

The Sorbonne become so dominant because its founder was a true pedagogue. Other teachers opened colleges to house poor students, mainly with the goal of recruiting some among them to become priests and clerics, or at least to make them indebted to the order or to those who had taken them in. Robert de Sorbon, on the other hand, was not interesting in training servants. He was determined to inculcate in his pupils a sense of discipline, a sense of how to study, and a taste for demanding intellectual challenges.

At the moment when the other colleges were at war over theological and philosophical matters, the Sorbonnards were being armed with arguments and facts. Even today, when you say "Sorbonne" you mean "university." That is how one college among all the others, but not like all the others, eclipsed its rivals.

Saint Louis had no choice but to guarantee the independence of the university. He had acquired for quite a large sum a piece of the true cross from Baudouin II, the emperor of Constantinople, who

lieu had had constructed, with its archetypically neoclassical cupola and its three levels, one finds only modern buildings. Nothing remains of the medieval structures. On the uneven pavement of the main courtyard are white dots that indicate the placement of the first buildings. The rest of the original Sorbonne was buried. Large neo-Renaissance chimneys, intended to recall the medieval originals, were built in the nineteenth century. At the time, "restoration" did not mean the same thing as "reconstruction."

was in bad need of money, as well as the sacred vinegar-soaked sponge that His Roman executioners had given to Christ and the lance that had pierced His side. Along with the crown of thorns, Moses' staff, the blood of Christ, and milk from the Virgin, the collection of relics in the king's possession was truly impressive. The little Saint-Nicolas chapel in the Cité palace seemed insufficient for housing it. Something better, bigger, more beautiful, and more opulent was called for.

Pierre de Montreuil, the architect to undertake this, transformed the modest chapel into a masterpiece of the Gothic style. It was solemnly consecrated on April 26, 1248, two months before Saint Louis left for the Crusades. Today, these relics, which were dispersed or destroyed during the Revolution, are to be found in the vaults of Notre-Dame. The chapel, now called Sainte-Chapelle, remains nearly intact, even if now oddly surrounded by the Palais de Justice.

For five years, Louis IX battled it out under the citadel of Cairo, and reestablished the walls of Cesare and Jaffa, and then finally returned to his realm when he learned of the death of his mother, the former regent, Blanche de Castille.

On his return, the king became concerned about how the city was run. Paris now boasted one hundred sixty thousand inhabitants and there were recurring problems of safety. Citizens were being robbed and murdered with disconcerting ease. The municipal authorities were weakened, because the city's statutes were a little vague. Unlike other cities in the kingdom, Paris had no bailiff, as the sovereign did not want to be represented in his own capital. People worried about what would happen when His Highness went off to do battle at the ends of the earth.

Saint Louis urged the bourgeoisie to organize themselves and asked the merchants to choose from among them a "provost" who would assume governance of the city's business. Exercising his authority from the *parloir aux bourgeois,* a sort of city court, the provost took charge of commercial activity and river traffic.

Moreover, the king named a provost of Paris who would be installed in the Grand Châtelet fortress, from whence he would dispense justice, establish taxes, direct the royal gendarmes, and guarantee the university's privileges. Starting in 1261, Étienne Boileau assumed this important position. A talented organizer, this just and honorable man succeeded in bringing peace to the streets of Paris.

In 1270, Louis left on his second crusade with peace of mind. He had given his city the organization that it still bears to this day. The provost of merchants is the mayor; the provost of Paris is the chief of police.

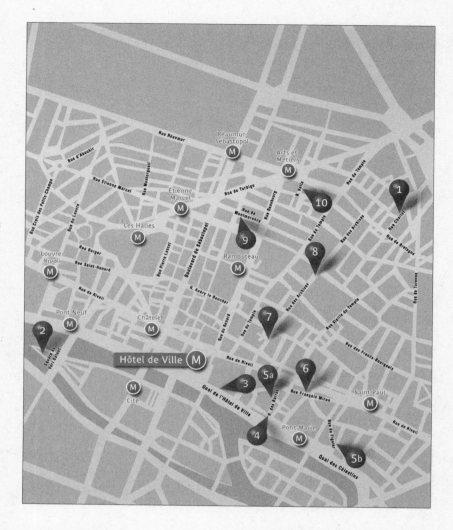

1. At 73 Rue Charlot, a thirteenth-century tower, the last vestige of the Temple Enclosure. **2.** Square Vert-Galant, where Jacques de Molay, the Temple's grand master, was executed. **3.** The statue of Étienne Marcel, in the gardens adjoining the Hôtel de Ville. **4.** The Rue des Barres. **5a.** At the intersection of Rue des Barres and Rue du Grenier-sur-l'Eau, a sixteenth-century house whose fleur de lys at the level of the first floor was engraved during the Revolution. **5b.** The Hôtel de Sens (1 Rue du Figuier), a magnificent example of medieval architecture. **6.** Rue François-Miron. **7.** At 26 Rue des Archives, a medieval cloister belonging to the Billettes Convent. **8.** The door of Olivier de Clisson. **9.** At 51 Rue de Montmorency, the house of Nicolas Flamel. **10.** At 3 Rue Volta, a house that dates from the beginning of the fourteenth century (sometimes said to be the oldest in the city).

Fourteenth Century

Hôtel de Ville

The Birth of the Third Estate

When a Métro stop bears the name "Hôtel de Ville"—city hall—
you really can't expect it to be like the others. It serves a function.
And indeed on the platform of Line 1 you will find a permanent
display, informing subway travelers about the city's major political institutions and their roles. This is a good refresher course for
anyone who needs to bone up on terms such as *préfecture, mairie,*
or *conseil régional.*

We are at the Place de l'Hôtel de Ville, the oldest neighborhood
on the Right Bank. The Saint-Gervais Church, hidden behind the
massive structure of the Hôtel de Ville, was without question the
first place of Christian worship on this side of the Seine.

Beginning in the twelfth century, a powerful corporation of
water merchants, the heirs of the earliest sailors, the masters of
the river traffic, bought the land here to create a port: the Port de
la Grève. Starting at the end of the thirteenth century, this port
served as the people's representative to the king. When Saint
Louis created the first municipal institution of Paris, the "provost
of the merchants" was therefore naturally the product of this corporation, one from whom the city's emblem derives—a church
nave on a river.

Moreover, a statue of Étienne Marcel, a former merchants'

provost whose likeness can be found in more than a few gardens and public spaces, is located here—showing him sitting straight and proud on his charger. The monument was raised in 1888, and in a very particular context, one which turned this homage to the man who once served as the city's provost into an act of political protest. By means of this statue the city fathers demonstrated their opposition to the governmental decision to keep the municipality under the jurisdiction of the prefect. In fact, the government of the Third Republic, influenced by the French Commune of 1871, was designed to prevent new revolutionary sentiment from sweeping across Paris by keeping a close eye on it, and notably by refusing to allow the city to have a mayor. Celebrating Étienne Marcel was a way of protesting this policy. The government of the period and President Sadi Carnot refused to attend the statue's unveiling ceremony. The prefect of the Seine, Eugène Poubelle—whose name now refers to garbage—gave the official speech. Not until 1977 would Parisians be permitted, once again, to elect a mayor, and this was the future president Jacques Chirac.

But to return to the Hôtel de Ville. The colonnaded house where Étienne Marcel once exercised his provost powers was reconstructed two centuries later and in a Renaissance style. It was burned by the Communards in 1871, then rebuilt in the neo-Renaissance style that we know today.

Go along the Rue de l'Hôtel de Ville and you will find yourself facing the statue of Étienne Marcel. On the left the stairs of the Rue des Barres reminds us that we are on higher ground, the first inhabited part of the *marais* on the Right Bank because the floods of the Seine couldn't reach it.

The *barres*—iron bars—evoke Paris's second fortress wall, built during the time of the first Capetians, meaning at the end of the tenth century. In fact they consisted of high palisades of wood overlooking a deep moat. In April of 2009, digs undertaken beneath the Rue de Rivoli definitively established the existence of this wall. The evidence was a ditch about ten feet deep, dug in the form of a V, and which was about sixty-five feet long and forty feet wide. Nothing of this wall remains today—aside from the name of the street, that is.

At the intersection of Rue du Grenier-sur-l'Eau there is a handsome sixteenth-century house whose fleur-de-lys at the level of the first floor was engraved during the Revolution. If you head back to Rue de l'Hôtel de Ville and go all the way to the Hôtel de Sens you will find a magnificent example of medieval architecture.

Now take the Rue Saint-Paul until you find yourself standing before the Saint-Paul-Saint-Louis Church, whose clock, which is located over the main doors, dates from 1627, a vestige of the earlier and more rustic Saint-Paul Church.

While you walk the winding streets of this part of fourteenth-century Paris, observe the Rue François-Miron, on which a good number of the gabled houses recall the Middle Ages. At number 44, the Maison d'Ourscamp has preserved a magnificent Gothic cellar and now is the home of the *Association pour la sauvegarde et la mise en valeur du patrimoine,* or Association for the Safekeeping and Promotion of French Heritage, whose primary mission is to protect Old Paris.

At the end of the Rue François-Miron, take the Rue des Archives, and walk up it on the right to admire the medieval cloister at number 26; it belongs to the Billettes Convent, whose construction dates back to the beginning of the fifteenth century.

You will end up at number 58 and standing before the superb door of Olivier de Clisson, which dates from 1375. Clisson was one of the stalwart soldiers of King Charles V, soldiers to whom credit goes for taking back the country at the end of the fourteenth century. Today this door has been incorporated into the main building of the National Archives, which has been located here since the Revolution, in what was once the Hôtel de Soubise, a truly magnificent example of neoclassical architecture dating from the beginning of the eighteenth century.

Face this building and look left: an iron-grill gate takes you into an older courtyard. In fact, this passageway was part of a chapel from the sixteenth century and the Cour des Marronniers was bordered by buildings of the same period, an ensemble that formed the Hôtel de Guises, whose coat of arms is still visible on the pediment of the venerable Clisson door.

Now go along Rue de Montmorency. At number 51 you will find what once was supposed to have been the home of Nicolas Flamel. It dates from 1407 and would therefore be the oldest in Paris. The mysterious alchemist—now made famous by J. K. Rowling's Harry Potter series—never actually lived here. He generously lent it to peasants who came to work the surrounding fields. Written in Gothic letters on the façade is an indication of this: "We the working men and women lived at the front of this house, which was built in the year of grace 1407, and each kept the right to say each and every day a paternoster and an Ave Maria while praying to God, whose grace might forgive us."

The house at number 3 Rue Volta dates from the beginning of the fourteenth century and is sometimes said to be the oldest in the city. Here lived the bailiff of the priory and of the town of Saint-Martin. The ground floor features two typical medieval shops—the door on the right with all those locks, the edge of it separating the shop from the street, and a bay window with neither tiles nor ironwork. However, some question the authenticity of this construction and believe that it was a re-creation from the seventeenth century.

Ascending to the throne in 1285, Philippe V, called "the Fair," wanted everything. So obsessed was he by the notion of an absolute monarchy that he set out to consolidate every form of power in his hands. His ancestors had come up with the monarchy of divine right; he wanted all earthly rights. As a symbol of centralized authority, he transformed the Cité palace, enlarging it and undertaking major renovation projects, all of which took seventeen years and weren't finished until 1313.

To enlarge his domain nearly to the Seine, the king didn't hesitate to expropriate property from its owners, and built a handsome wall along the length of the river. This wall didn't have a true defensive function; it was meant to stand for royal grandeur. The interior of the palace featured large rooms and the king's quarters were redesigned and filled with beautiful tapestries, silver plate, and the most precious marble.

The house of the king, meaning the administrative body responsible for organizing the sovereign's palace life, involved six functions: the *écurie*, the stables; the *fourrière*, in charge of carriages; the *paneterie*, which saw to the table linen; the *échansonnerie*, which selected and bought the wine; *cuisine*, cooking; and lastly the *fruiterie*. However, for his own private needs the king had a large staff: five chamberlains, three valets, two barbers, one tailor, and a wax-heater (whose job was to heat the wax used for sealing official acts). To these servants, the king added two doctors, three chaplains, fifteen clerics in charge of manuscripts, thirty sergeants at arms, and a crowd of falconers and huntsmen. Attached to the house of Queen Jeanne de Navarre were more than two hundred people, who worked day and night in the palace. Said palace was the center of decision-making, but the king lived there for only a part of the year—during the winter, essentially; the rest of the time

Who was Nicolas Flamel?

As a *libraire-juré,* Nicolas Flamel's job was to scrutinize copies of manuscripts intended for students of the faculties. Suddenly, sometime around 1382, he became fabulously wealthy and gave generous gifts to the churches.

King Charles VI, curious to learn the source of this sudden wealth, asked Lord Cramoisy, who was the master of petitions, to make inquiries about this strange and generous man.

The envoy of the king went to visit Flamel, who admitted that he was an alchemist. He had discovered the basis of the philosopher's stone, which could turn base metals into pure gold.

Flamel's claims have long fired the imaginations of those who sought wealth. It was said that a fabulous treasure was hidden somewhere in his house located on the corner of the Rue des Écrivains. In 1724, Henri Sauval offered an account in his *History and Research into the Antiquities of the City of Paris,* writing that curiosity seekers had spent so much time "rifling and searching through and stewing over this house that all that remained of it was two solid cellars covered in graffiti and fanciful hieroglyphs." The house, the only one in which Flamel and his wife were known to have lived, was

(Cont.)

destroyed in 1852, when the Rue de Rivoli was being constructed. Yet again, nothing was found. The Flamel treasure continues to inspire dreamers and fantasies and the occasional novel.

Philippe V and his court were elsewhere, going from one château to another to hunt in the game-rich forests of the Île-de-France.

The refashioned Cité palace would have been but pretentious show had Philippe the Fair not also sought absolute power. To his way of thinking, two institutions cast a shadow over his power: the Holy See and the Order of the Temple. The first kept insisting that it represented a spiritual power greater than that of temporal kings, and the second was the richest and most powerful religious congregation in the realm. Philippe decided to destroy one and then the other.

In 1304, the sudden death of Pope Benoît XI—from acute indigestion caused by figs—permitted Philippe to gain a foothold and make his wishes clear. In Perugia, the conclave to choose a new pope seemed to go on indefinitely, and was divided along national lines, pitting the French against the Italians. After eleven months of raucous debate, the cry that had been awaited for so long was heard:

"Habemus papam!"

The new pope to mount the throne of Saint Peter was Clement V, a Gascon, and the former archbishop of Bordeaux. King Philippe had bribed and intrigued enough to get his man in, and his new Holiness would deny him nothing. Consecrated in Lyon, then installed in Avignon, the pope lived under the thumb of the king of France.

Having solved the papal side of the equation, Philippe turned to the Knights Templars. At dawn on Friday, October 13, 1307, the king's men surrounded the Temple Enclosure, a group of buildings constructed in the *marais* (which the Templars had themselves drained). The headquarters consisted of a number of buildings used to house the monk-soldiers, very large stables, a church—a Gothic replica of the octagonal cupola of the Holy Sepulchre in Jerusalem—and a solid fortress with a huge square keep and four towers. This vast domain was surrounded by crenellated walls, against which the royal archers had no chance. The rules of the order forbade the drawing of a sword against a fellow Christian. The Templars were therefore taken without protest; they were jurisdictionally dependent upon the pope and had no reason to fear the king of France. They did not know that Clement V was Philippe's puppet.

The trial in which the Templars were judged was purely for show. Under torture, confessions were extracted from those ready to admit to committing every imaginable sin. The Inquisition was called in to help, and they went about their business with consummate skill: they knew how to break bones, pull arms off, dislocate ankles, and crush genitals.

Sodomy and heresy constituted the principal accusations; light punishment was promised to those who agreed to declare their guilt of the crimes.

On March 18, 1314, Jacques de Molay, the Temple's grand master, and three other officials were hauled from their cells and taken to the square before Notre-Dame, where they were to hear the sentence pronounced against them.

How did the Temple Enclosure disappear?

After the eradication of the Templars, their goods were transferred to the Order of the Knights Hospitalers. In 1667, the enclosure's walls, which were no longer tenable, were demolished to permit the construction of private homes and several houses that were designated to be used by artisans.

During the Revolution, the Temple fortress was turned into a prison. Louis XVI and his family were incarcerated there, and little Louis XVII died there on June 8, 1795.

As for the Templar church, it was sold in 1796 to a private citizen, who had it torn down. All that remained was the keep, which became a pilgrimage site for royalists. Napoleon, shocked by the cult that had grown up around the guillotined monarch, issued a decree in 1808 that the tower be torn down.

Today the memory of the Templars depends on plaques, informing passersby that they are on the Boulevard du Temple, the Rue du Temple, the Square du Temple, and the Rue Vieille-du-Temple. Not all is lost. If you go through the entrance of 73 Rue Charlot and head to the left you will find the last vestige of the enclosure—a thirteenth-century tower. Nothing until now has been done to promote it, though

(Cont.)

in September 2009 a leaflet campaign was held around the Carreau du Temple. This helped place the issue of its conservation in the public spotlight.

The four men wore forced to wear filthy robes, and their hair and beards were matted. They bore the marks of seven years of humiliation and torture, and when the crowd saw them a murmur of compassion ran through it. Following the script, the bedraggled Templars confessed their crimes and their sins. In fact, they were merely repeating what they had been taught to say in exchange for that light sentence.

Instead, the judge condemned them to life in prison. When he heard the verdict, Jacques de Molay rose up, no longer the cowering victim; his firm voice echoed across the square.

"The crimes of which you accuse me are lies. The rules of the Templar are holy, right, and Catholic. Yes, I deserve death because in my indignity, from fear of torment and pain, deceived by the pope and the king, I made false confession."

Hugues de Pairaud, one of the other men, emboldened by the example, made a similar statement, swore his innocence, denounced the torturers, and denied his earlier confessions.

A tremor went through the crowd. These men whom the powers had claimed were perverse violators and blasphemers suddenly appeared as who they truly were: helpless men who had fallen into the trap laid by Philippe the Fair.

The crowd swelled slowly but perceptibly enough to make presiding cardinals blanch. The people of Paris moved forward and approached the stage on which the prelates were seated; their expression was not pretty. Parisians did not like being lied to. The cardinals sensed the danger and finished up as quickly as they could. The accused were quickly remanded to the king's provost.

It was important to appease the Parisian anger and to end this business. That same evening, by royal order, Jacques de Molay was burned alive on the Île aux Juifs—the island of Jews—a small spit of land on the Seine that faced the Cité palace.

When the condemned man was tied to the stake he asked whether he could face Notre-Dame Cathedral, such that he might die with his eyes on an image of faith.

"Bodies belong to the king of France, but souls are God's," he said before the flames started to climb.

According to the chronicler Geoffroy de Paris, a witness to the scene, the master of the Templars then cast a curse upon his persecutors.

"God knows well who is in the wrong and who has sinned, and misery will visit those who have wrongly condemned us. God will avenge our death. The Lord knows that in truth all those who are against us and because of us will suffer."

Some believe the curse was effective. Pope Clement V died forty-two days later, from what seems to have been cancer of the intestines. And Philippe the Fair was killed

Where was the Master of the Temple burned?

The Île aux Juifs was one of three small uninhabited islands located at the point of Île de la Cité. Under the jurisdiction of Saint-Germain-des-Prés abbey, the island was likely a place where heretics, witches, and of course Jews were burned.

In 1577, when Henry III decided to create the first stone bridge in Paris—what was to be Pont-Neuf—he decided to rearrange nature a little. The branches of the Seine that separated the three little islands were filled and they became part of Île de la Cité.

Jacques de Molay perished in what is today Vert-Galant Square, meaning the eastern point of today's Île, in front of the bridge and at the level of the statue of Henri IV.

by a fall from a horse eight months later. Fourteen years later the direct royal line of the Capetians came to an end, leaving the throne to the Valois dynasty.

The demise of the Capetians' direct line brought with it interminable conflict between France and England. In 1328, Charles IV, the son of Philippe the Fair, died without a male heir. On the other hand Isabelle de France, the sister of the dead king, had a son: Edward III, the king of England. Edward sought to assume the crown of France, but the French refused to deliver it up to an outsider. Philippe VI of Valois, the nephew of Philippe the Fair, ascended the throne. The Hundred Years War of course had a number of economic and demographic causes, but the business of succession set it off.

A master strategist, Edward earned several significant victories over the French armies. In 1340, at the Battle of Écluse in Flanders, the English naval forces annihilated the French fleet. In 1346 in Crécy, in Picardie, the English archers decimated the French troops.

Throughout all this, Paris remained unperturbed. The big thing at the moment was fashion, which was transforming and adapting. One season the latest thing was the long tunic, and then the next it was all about high-cut jackets. What remained the same were the colors, which were as bright and varied as always, a fixed and joyous rainbow.

Alas, all that was to be changed by the arrival of the Black Plague. Moving up from the south, the plague arrived in the outskirts of Roissy-en-France in August of 1348. Several days later, Paris was struck. The disease ravaged the city and brought it to its knees. Fear was rampant; anyone—parent, friend, neighbor—could be a carrier. At the Hôtel-Dieu—the great hospital that had been in existence for three centuries by this point—five hundred a day were dying; the nuns there worked at risk of their own lives. There were 136 such nuns at the start of the outbreak, and a few months later there were only some 40 left. Bodies were immediately thrown into the ditch at the Cemetery of the Innocents, which was soon full to overflowing. It was necessary to find other burial sites outside the city walls.

Hoping to stop the plague, the houses of those infected were burned and pious processions were mounted to beg for God's mercy. Paris did a great deal of praying, but it seemed to have no effect. The doctors shrugged their shoulders and admitted to their helplessness. Witches filled the vacuum and earned windfall profits from their concoctions, accompanied by rites and prayers that were as strange as they were ineffective.

Finally, at the end of a year, and without any discernible reason, the disease died down and moved away. But by this point Paris had changed; it had been beaten down. At least sixty thousand of its citizens, more than forty percent of the total population, had perished.

From the countryside, crowds of peasants poured into the city, seeking refuge. They had abandoned their fields and farms because of the death of a father or son, or because they lacked the manpower to bring in the meager harvest. These people had come in hopes of finding something to eat; all they found was a haggard, overwhelmed, and unhappy people, and they merely added to the general misery.

The cycle of disasters continued. The war against the English was costly and forced the king to levy new taxes. Henceforth, all manufactured merchandise and foodstuffs sold in Paris and the outlying areas would be subject to a special tax. The price of bread went up, misery deepened.

On September 19, 1356, a new catastrophe was visited upon the realm: the new king of France, Jean the Good, was taken prisoner in Poitiers by the English. After being held for the winter in Bordeaux, the king was taken to England. He was not suffering from this; indeed, he was well treated. But the French people were being forced to cough up three million livres in order to free him.

Meanwhile, in Paris, monarchic power dissipated in the king's absence. The provost of the merchants, Étienne Marcel, took matters into his own hands. First it was urgent that the city's defenses be reinforced, since the unending series of defeats at the hands of the English fed the very real fear that the capital might be attacked imminently. Starting at the end of the month of September, large crowds of workers were at work, restoring, reinforcing, and building. On the Left Bank, some of the old moats were too narrow and shallow to be of much use, so they were dug and enlarged. On the Right Bank, new moats had just completed the existing circuit of walls. On this side of the river, bastions that jutted out over the wall were built, and the walls encircling the Louvre, the Saint-Martin priory, and the Enclos du Temple were also built.

None of this came cheap, of course. The provost was forced to levy yet a new tax, this time on drink. Henceforth, by emptying a flagon of wine or a pitcher of beer, citizens were contributing to the defense of their city.

An army was necessary to hold the city. Étienne Marcel raised a civil guard that he organized not as a military commander but as a civil administrator would. Able-bodied men were recruited and organized according to street and neighborhood. Paris was sectioned off by troops ready to take on the English.

In the Cité palace, eighteen-year-old Charles, the dauphin, tried to maintain the royal line and impose his authority, but the Valois were by this point largely discredited because of their many military defeats. Étienne Marcel and Bishop Robert Le Coq issued an order calling for the monarchy to be controlled by the General Estates, an assembly consisting of the nobility, the clergy, and wealthy citizens.

It was a moment of unrest. A seething mass of humanity went through the streets and turned their attention to the palace. As they approached, they spied Regnault d'Arcy, who had brought the treaty from England signed by the king. Seeing the mob, the man started walking quickly and then began to run before being trapped inside a pastry shop. His throat cut, his body sprawled between the plates of cakes and the sacks of flour.

Étienne Marcel, at the head of his newly raised army, marched toward the palace. Surrounded by his men, the provost entered the building, climbed the stairs to the dauphin's apartments, and broke down the door. Charles seemed barely surprised by this incursion and a fierce argument broke out between the dauphin and the provost. Étienne Marcel accused the king's son of having done nothing to maintain order against the bands of thieves that were prowling the city's outskirts. Charles replied that those who controlled the treasury—meaning the provost—needed to live up to their responsibilities.

The discussion became so violent that two of the country's marshals, Jean de Conflans and Robert de Clermont, tried to come between them. They barely had time to do anything before they were wounded by swords wielded by the provost's allies. Blood flowed and formed large scarlet stains on the dauphin's white shirt. The palace staff took fright and ran off. Charles begged the provost to be spared.

"Sire, you have nothing to fear," Étienne Marcel reassured the king. "My men are at your service and came here to be of use to you."

Saying these words, Étienne Marcel removed his blue-and-white (the colors of Paris) hat and placed it upon the head of the dauphin, a symbol of the protection being accorded the young prince by the city. Then what happened? Actually, nothing. This was, after all, a revolt and not a revolution. Lacking a program, a doctrine, a plan, all the rage ended up being directed nowhere. Blinded by their audacity, the provost and his men felt that they had done the most they could do. They left the palace to join their friends and allies at the Place de Grève. The people of Paris had seized a share of power. The Third Estate was born.

The following day, during an assembly held at the convent of the Augustines on the banks of the Left Bank, Étienne Marcel, who had gathered together the clergy and university officials, decided to push for a system of monarchy that could be controlled by the Estates General, and to reestablish the Council of Thirty-six, magistrates assigned with appointment power. In this way, Étienne Marcel solidified his control of Paris.

The dauphin realized that staying in Paris might not be the best thing for his health. He needed to regroup his forces. A month later, on March 25, Charles left Paris and headed toward Senlis. Étienne Marcel assigned ten prominent citizens to go with him, believing that through them he would be able to keep his eye on the dauphin, and control him. He was mistaken.

While Charles rode around in his provinces and gathered his friends and allies, being a royalist and staying behind in Paris under the thumb of Étienne Marcel was dangerous indeed. Both Matret, the master carpenter of the palace, and Perret, the master of the bridges, were beheaded and their bodies cut up into four pieces.

The provost worked to establish his new order. He welcomed to Paris his ally Charles de Navarre, called Charles the Bad, a great-grandson of Philippe the Fair, and a pretender to the French crown. Charles de Navarre had struck a deal with the English, and this upset the Parisians. Moreover, Charles the Bad actually used English troops as reinforcements. This was tantamount to treason. The people of Paris began to think that they would never be at peace again unless the Valois returned, all the more so since the dauphin had blockaded Paris and the city was beginning to feel the effects. Food was running out. Citizens were beginning to starve.

Something needed to happen. On the late morning of July 31, 1357, Étienne Marcel was surveying the defenses near the Saint-Antoine Gate when a large crowd surrounded him and began chanting with warlike hostility: "Montjoie Saint-Denis! To death! To death!"

Étienne Marcel tried to respond. "Why do you wish me ill? Everything that I did I did for your well-being!"

The provost was jostled and pushed and then fell down. He was hacked to death by axes and swords.

Two days later, the dauphin made his triumphant return to Paris. On August 4, he gathered together the city's population at the Halles and made a speech in which he denounced the plot by Étienne Marcel and Charles de Navarre to allow the English to take Paris.

"On the evening when the provost was killed, he wanted to put to death anyone who he knew remained loyal to the king and his son, and already a number of houses had been marked with signs."

This much is now clear: Paris was the place where rage rises and protest begins. Twenty-five years later, the Parisian revolt still made the throne tremble. In 1383, the young king Charles VI had an order read in the Great Hall of the palace by which he reduced the power of the provost of merchants because of "rebellion, disobedience, monopolies, crimes and misdemeanors, against the crown and others, in deeds and in words." By means of a second order, the king confiscated the "Town Hall and the place that one calls Grève," meaning the very heart and symbol of Parisian protests and strikes. By weakening the job of mayor and closing down city hall, the king hoped to keep Parisians under control. This was an illusion, of course.

1. 38 Rue des Francs-Bourgeois, where the Duke of Orléans was murdered. **2.** On Rue Saint-Paul, the Saint-Paul-Saint-Louis Church, whose clock dates from 1627. **3.** At 20 Rue Étienne-Marcel, the tower that Jean the Fearless built to protect his residence. **7a-7b.** Château de Vincennes. **8.** The Château de Vincennes keep.

Fifteenth Century

Château de Vincennes

Paris at Risk

Now we shall permit ourselves to take a new little excursion outside Paris to have a look at the luminous stones of the Château de Vincennes, a place that as we will see is dominated by its dungeon keep, the home and safe house of kings.

Traumatized by the assassination—in his presence—of his two marshals by Étienne Marcel, King Charles V refused to spend any more time in the Cité palace, where this terrible event had taken place. Instead he focused on finding a place where his power would be safe and with that in mind started building Saint-Pol, located on what is today the Quai des Célestins. This vast assembly of buildings surrounded by beautiful parks—which no longer exist today—afforded greater security than anything within the confines of Paris. Charles V also turned his gaze to the Louvre and had his library, constructed of precious woods, installed in one of the towers; his collection of books was the foundation of what would eventually become the Bibliothèque Nationale.

Lastly, he built the château at Vincennes. The dungeon keep and its wall were completed in 1371; in 1380, he finished the surrounding wall. When he began these construction works, Charles V wanted not to construct yet more new utility buildings, which already existed, but to increase his living space. The design of

214 • Lorànt Deutsch

Vincennes revealed the royal will to change the very nature of construction, and to do more than build still another fortress at the gates to Paris.

This architectural ensemble, which is remarkably well preserved, bears exceptional historical interest. More than anything—more than written texts and archival accounts—it evokes in its very stones the birth of the modern state. In effect Charles V's project was not only to distance himself from Paris, which seemed to be turning into a trap for royal power, but to adopt a new way for authority to function. The king's entourage—advisers, officers, scribes, and secretaries—were assuming a growing importance and starting to form a close and effective team. This new form of "governance" marked a turning point for the monarchy, one which presaged the modern state.

Moreover, there was a need for centralized power: the fifteenth century promised to represent an inexorable plunge into the depths of war, famine, and death. The people trembled because the kings and princes had redesigned the landscape to extend their privileges and holdings. Even religion, the ultimate recourse for a downtrodden population, offered few givens: the Great Schism that divided the West meant that there were two pontiffs on the throne of Saint Peter—one in Rome and the other in Avignon. The disunity of the soldiers of Christ encouraged the conquering ambitions of Islam; the sultan of Turkey hid no longer his eagerness to take Constantinople, the dying flame of the Byzantine Empire. In Europe, King Henry IV of England was facing revolts from the Scots and the Irish, but these did not keep him from continuing to lay claim to Brittany, Normandy, and Flanders.

In France, Charles VI, who ascended to the throne in 1380, seemed to have lost his wits. Staring into space, he wandered around the corridors of his palace at Saint-Pol, poking at the flesh of his thighs with a little iron lancet and crawling on the floor to lap at his bowl like a dog. Then the lunacy seemed to dissipate and the king once again took hold of his mind and the reins of government—at least until the next attack. Successive regents, responsible for the proper functioning of the state during the king's "absences," took advantage of them to pillage the royal treasury. Charles V's achievements, political and geographical, started to melt away like snow in sunshine. Paris was in misery and during the winter nights wolves made their way into the city to devour whatever poor souls they found dragging around the deserted streets.

On November 23, 1407, the war without end with England took a new turn. That evening, Louis, the Duc d'Orléans, the brother of King Charles VI, dined at the Barbette residence with his sister-in-law, Queen Isabeau of Bavaria. The latter had not long before given birth to a weak baby boy who had not lasted more than a few days. Louis had many reasons to find himself at Isabeau's side. It was quite possible that he was the father of the child, whose rapid and silent disappearance was perhaps a good thing, given that it put an end to speculation.

But what if the child had not died, after all? And what if it hadn't been a boy but a girl named Jeanne? Joan of Arc as the fruit of the love between the queen and the brother of the king—this is a seductive and persuasive thesis promoted by a number of historians.

Far from Saint-Pol, where Charles VI was locked up during one of his episodes, the queen had built this private residence at Barbette, a small and discreet little jewel located on Rue Vieille-du-Temple—of which, alas, nothing remains. And it is there that Isabeau, a woman of thirty-six, tried to reignite the dying embers of her ardor. She was still beautiful, with her long, fine face and graceful body, which hardly carried the marks of the eleven children that she had already borne the king. The queen threw herself into a passionate affair with Louis, the "handsome stud ready to whinny before all the ladies," as the rumor had it.

These two loved each other with a passion in which the sweet thrill of the forbidden mixed with political ambition. In effect, understandings, allusions, and diplomatic interests were never absent from their embraces. Each needed the other, or believed that they did.

The king's mental condition had made Isabeau the realm's regent. She presided over the Royal Council without also being able to lead it. Jean the Fearless, the Duke of Burgundy, was seeking to extend his influence, but he was thwarted by Louis d'Orléans. Beyond this struggle between individuals, there was still the war with England, which was at the heart of the central debate: should the truce be renewed, as the Duke of Burgundy wanted, or should the fight against the English continue, as the Duke of Orléans believed?

At Barbette, the evening turned out to be a pleasant one, and in the laughter and carefree atmosphere the death of the child was for the moment forgotten. Then, suddenly, one of the king's valets presented himself to the duke.

"Monseigneur, the king commands that you come to him without delay. He is anxious to speak with you about a matter that concerns you both greatly."

By this point Louis was used to his brother's whims, and to being summoned in the middle of the night to share some delusion with him. Deluded or not, however, the king was still the king. He took his leave of Isabeau.

In the Parisian night, perched on his mule which advanced with small steps, Louis sang gaily along while five or six porters carrying torches lit the way through the dark streets. While Louis was passing by a tavern with a sign that bore the image of Notre-Dame, twenty or so men came hurtling at him.

"What is this? I am the Duke of Orléans!" he protested, believing that he had fallen into the clutches of thieves.

He was not given the time to speak another word. He was toppled from his mount and fell to his knees. Trying to rise he was struck and killed with blows from hatchets, swords, and clubs.

"Murder! Murder!" a cobbler's wife screamed out. She had heard the fracas in the streets and from her window tried to alert people.

"Silence, evil woman!" one of the assailants shouted at her.

With news of the assassination, the Sire of Tignonville, Paris's provost, had the gates to the city closed and ordered his archers to restore order to the streets. It was feared that the victim's allies would seek their revenge.

Two days later, a spectacular procession went from the Blancs-

Where was the Duke of Orléans murdered?

While nothing remains of the Barbette, as I said, the small street that once led to its back entrance is still there. It is in the dead-end street of Des Arbalétriers, at about number 38 Rue des Francs-Bourgeois, that the crime was committed.

Manteaux Church, where the body of the prince lay in state, to the Célestins Church, where he was to be buried. The king of Sicily, the Duc de Berry, the Duke of Bourbon, and the Duke of Burgundy himself—in short, the greatest figures of the realm—carried the coffin, which was covered with blue velvet embossed with the fleur-de-lys.

The provost's investigation tended first toward suspicion that this was a matter of a jealous husband—in other words, the king—but the truth soon became clear. Jean the Fearless, the Duke of Burgundy, had ordered the crime.

Evidence of his guilt made plain, Jean gave up his show of grief and pronounced his pride at having accomplished this act of homicide. He had done it, he maintained, for the good of the realm and the greater glory of France. Who could mourn a man who simply emptied the royal treasury to build himself castles and pay for his numerous mistresses?

The situation soon became untenable. On the one side was Jean the Fearless, who benefited from the support of Parisians because of his promises to lower taxes and control the excesses of the monarchy. On the other was Charles d'Orléans, son of the murdered duke, who clamored for revenge and enjoyed the support of the other noble lords. At thirteen, however, he was a boy rather than a warrior. The next year he was married off to Bonne, the daughter of Count Bernard d'Armagnac, and in his

What remains of the Duke of Burgundy's fortress home?

In the sixteenth century, the duke's home was completely reconfigured, and became an auditorium where one was initiated into the mysteries of the religious vocation. In 1634, under Louis XIII, a royal troupe took residence there. It was here that the main works of Pierre Corneille were created, then nearly all of the tragedies of Jean Racine.

In fact it was in this theater Racine discovered Champmeslé, the young actress who played the role of Hermione in his *Andromaque*. The young woman displayed such tempestuous passion and overwhelming emotion that after the performance the playwright ran backstage, his eyes burning, and fell at her feet, thanking her for giving him such intense happiness. From that point on, Racine never left Champmeslé, and swore to her his undying love. This lasted for a good six years. The Marquise de Sévigné wrote, "When La Champmeslé entered the stage, a wave of admiration swept from one end of the theater to the other, and the entire hall was under her spell, for her to bring to tears whenever she felt like it."

The building remained a theater until 1783, the year in *(Cont.)*

new father-in-law he found his champion. Henceforth the Burgundians and the Armagnacs engaged in a war that would tear the country apart.

Conscious of what would be involved in the fight to take Paris, Jean the Fearless, Duke of Burgundy, decided to transform his private residence on the Rue Mauconseil into a fortress. The setting of the building was ideal for this, for it abutted two solid stretches of the wall that Philippe Auguste had built, a rampart that had been surpassed once the city had outgrown its thirteenth-century limits; twenty-five years earlier, these older walls had been replaced by an even larger wall. The dilapidated fortifications did more than reinforce the duke's residence. Its abandoned towers had become refuges for the homeless, and in the moats emptied of their waters huddled bands of roving mendicants. Meanwhile the round paths were transformed into promenades where the Parisians played at *boules*.

To complete the defense of his house, Jean the Fearless had a solid tower constructed, one that rose proudly nearly ninety feet, and seemed to thumb its nose at the Louvre and the royal residence at Saint-Pol, the two seats of royal authority. Behind the high walls of his fortress, the duke had nothing to fear of the inconstancy of the king or the power of the mob.

While Jean the Fearless was having his tower constructed, the Count of Armagnac was raising an army of mercenaries in the south. These were tough working men who dreamed only of pillaging whatever regions they crossed. They came to Île-de-France and ravaged the farms and the fields, then moved progressively all the way to the moats that protected the suburb town of Saint-Marcel on the Left Bank. They entered Paris but on November 2, 1410, a treaty was signed that immediately arrested their military operations. According to the terms of this treaty, each prince must return to his own lands and not return to the capital except with the consent of King Charles VI.

The winter passed in relative calm. As soon as spring came, the war between the Armagnacs and the Burgundians was picked up in Beauvais and Picardy. But Paris was always the true prize. In the month of August, the Parliament— the city's judicial court—sought to

which the actors invested in the new Comic Opera that had just been built. The old theater became a leather market and then was completely demolished in 1858, to allow Rue Étienne-Marcel to break through.

It was at number 20 Rue Étienne-Marcel where the tower that Jean the Fearless built to protect his residence stood. Here in the middle of Paris is a surprising example of Burgundo-Medieval architecture—and one you can visit. Inside one can find a guardroom on the street level, some apartments on the first floor, a handsome room on the second, the sleeping room of the horsemen on the third, and the wonderful room of the duke himself on the fourth.

From the top of the first spiral staircase are two fascinating reminders of the Duke of Burgundy. First there is the magnificent oak etched into the vaults. The oak has three types of leaves: those to recall the father of Jean the Fearless; those of the hawthorn in memory of his mother; and the leaves of the hops for himself (a leaf from the north, as his mother had been Flemish). Second are two windows, the first bearing the coat of arms of the duke and the second showing a carpenter's plane. This was the response to the danger posed by Louis d'Orléans, who wanted to beat him with a club and was as a result "leveled" by Jean; he was laying claim to his crime.

maintain the peace and to accomplish this called for the arrest of anyone found making speeches deemed dangerous to public safety. To make sure this new order was followed to the letter, the men of the Parliament nominated a governor of Paris, and the man chosen was Valéran de Luxembourg, the Count of Saint-Pol. The count was a loyal vassal of the king, like everyone, but had also formed an alliance with the Burgundians.

The count and his ally Jean the Fearless went after the Armagnacs. They created a militia consisting of butchers, slaughterers, peltmakers, and surgeons; in short, men who were handy with knives and used to the sight of blood. This fierce brigade, which took on the noble-sounding title of "royal militia," had as their mission to arrest anyone in Paris known to be on favorable terms with the Armagnacs.

This inaugurated a season of bloody and blind vengeance. If someone wanted to get rid of a neighbor or a rival, all he had to do was call them an Armagnac. The militiamen would toss the guilty party into a ditch and then pillage his house; most often these supposed Armagnacs were simply drowned in the river. Even the king and his family were not entirely free from suspicion. They left Saint-Pol and moved into the Louvre, which their troops could more easily defend in case this band of butchers turned against the throne itself.

These practices pushed the most prominent Parisians, led by the provost of the merchants himself, to leave town, both to save their necks and so as not to be forced to bear silent witness to these horrors.

No one seemed capable of ending the chaos. A higher power was called for. Thus the canons of Sainte-Chapelle, the Benedictine monks, the Carmelite brothers, and the Mathurin monks gathered together their spiritual forces and processed in bare feet to Saint-Germain-l'Auxerrois, followed in reverent silence by the counselors of the Parliament. It was not a matter of choosing between the Armagnacs and the Burgundians; they simply wanted to create universal accord by universal devotion. Through their prayers, chants, and hymns they asked for princes to make peace among themselves.

The procession, however, convinced no one. In any case, in the month of November 1411, Jean the Fearless entered Paris at the head of English troops. Three thousand Parisians rushed to his side. Henceforth, Paris and its surrounding villages belonged to the Burgundians; the Armagnacs were run out of the kingdom and their goods were confiscated. For its part, Parliament, which was suspected of leaning toward the Armagnacs, was fined a thousand livres, which would be used to pay the English troops for their help and getting them, temporarily at least, to remove themselves. Henry V, the king of England, sought to profit from the civil war in France and take back some of the lands that had been lost.

At the end of April 1413, the popular classes had seen their city and indeed the entire realm suffer enough. They rose up under the leadership of a swindler named Caboche. Caboche's real name was Simon Lecoustellier, but given that his profession was smashing the skulls of cows in order to extract the brain (effectively putting the kibosh on these creatures) he was named Caboche—"head"—and those who followed him were "Cabochiens."

Jean the Fearless thought supporting this rebellion might be a good strategy and lent his support to the Cabochiens, hoping that after they had done the dirty work he could claim the spoils. In the merry month of May, the Cabochiens turned Paris into a horrific scene of violence. They stormed the Bastille and killed the prisoners held within. Anyone who seemed as if he might be allied to the Armagnacs was murdered. The provost of Paris was beheaded. A new law consisting of 258 articles was imposed upon the Parliament to institute strict controls on public expenditure, a complete reorganization of judicial power, and new rules governing crossing fees—which was a no-go and abrogated almost immediately. In the meantime, the city's new masters prowled the streets wearing their white hoods, which is how they identified themselves. Woe to whoever refused to wear it. Even the king was forced to adopt it.

All of this was too much for people of good sense, meaning most Parisians, who wanted only that the excesses of the Cabochiens come to an end. To do that, the Burgundians were in the worst position, since they had, after all, offered their help to this bloody rebellion. That left the Armagnacs. Their troops were stationed near Paris and simply waiting for their moment, and now it had arrived. They attacked and chased out the Burgundians.

Two months later, on August 4, the Cabochiens tried again to start an uprising. At the Place de Grève they gathered, and speakers urged the people to fight back against the Armagnacs. A voice boomed out from among the crowd: "He who desires peace, let him line up on the right!"

Instantly, everyone ran to the right side of the square. This was devastating to the Cabochiens, of course. The most enraged among them made their way to the Hôtel de Ville, and there prepared themselves to fight one last if futile battle. However, in the meantime, both Caboche and Jean the Fearless had already fled Paris and were nowhere to be found.

They would have their revenge at Agincourt on October 25, 1415, when the French army—or more exactly the Armagnac cavalry—was decimated by the English army. Precisely one year after this defeat, a kind of victory for the Burgundians, Jean the Fearless met secretly with Henry V, the English king, at Calais. The two men would share the world and their ambitions: the Burgundians would not oppose the conquest of Normandy by the English, and the English would leave Paris to the Burgundians.

On the night of May 29, 1418, at two in the morning, eight hundred Burgundian knights entered Paris by means of the Saint-Germain-des-Prés Gate and awoke the inhabitants.

"Get up, good people, and arm yourselves! Long live the king and the Duke of Burgundy!"

Jean the Fearless's soldiers made their way into Saint-Pol, nabbed the poor mad king, decked him out, plunked him on a horse, and led him through the streets of the city like a marionette wearing a crown. Only half conscious, Charles VI smiled benevolently at the crowds, seemingly unaware of the terrible events that had shaken the capital. The jubilant crowd welcomed the Burgundians, now sure that they would liberate them of the king's bad ministers, bring about a new prosperity, and push back forever the specter of misery. Hordes of people armed with rusted lances and clubs attacked and pillaged the opulent homes of their former masters with a single cry: "Kill them! Kill the traitorous Armagnac dogs!"

In all the commotion everyone had forgotten about the dauphin, Charles, a boy of fifteen and the sole male heir. In these hours of drama, only one man had kept a cool head and thought about preserving the dynasty: that was Tanguy du Châtel, the new provost of Paris. He rushed across Paris to the Saint-Pol palace, bursting into the room in which the dauphin was lying on his bed, terrified by the events that were taking place all around him. The provost threw a blanket over the shoulders of the prince and took him toward the Bastille, where a number of the evening's survivors were gathering to protect themselves from the wrath of the Parisians. Several hours later, the dauphin emerged from the fortress by exiting through an unguarded side door. The future Charles VII, disguised as an ordinary citizen, wearing a poor, grimy cloak and a simple hat, surrounded by a small troop of loyal soldiers, went through the defenses at a full gallop, abandoning the city to its latest spasm of violence.

A prince without a crown and apparently without a future, Charles could not yet know that he would rebuild his kingdom, but be forced to do it elsewhere, or that he would need to fight for eighteen years before he could reassert his authority over Paris.

In Bourges, which he made into his capital, the dauphin declared himself the sole repository of power.

"Only son, heir to, and successor of his majesty the king and through that by reason and by natural right the rule of the kingdom falls to me."

By letter, he made his stand against the illegal regime in Paris. "We forbid anyone from obeying letters from the rebels, who have murdered the king's chancellor and seized the great royal seal, or any letters aside from our own, sealed with our private seal and signed by our hand."

Charles called himself the "master of the realm," but in Paris Jean the Fearless controlled the crazy king and in Normandy the English king assumed the title of king of France. The country was divided and torn, and no one could predict who would win this war between the princes.

In Paris, it was a free-for-all. Armagnacs or anyone who resembled them were immediately dispatched. The leaders and officers were locked up in the Bastille and there in a nightmare scenario dreamed up by the executioner, a man named Capeluche, the prisoners were called forth one by one by name. They had to exit their cell by means of a low door, forcing them to bend down to pass. With the swing of a well-aimed axe their heads were lopped off and rolled away. Count Bernard d'Armagnac was among those who perished, struck down by Capeluche's axe blow. Down the winding streets of Saint-Antoine ran rivers of blood, which didn't seem to bother the artisans very much. This would not be the last time they would witness this kind of thing.

Jean the Fearless, on the other hand, began to worry about all the blood. He knew from experience that the patience of the Parisians was not inexhaustible. To show his good faith he ordered Capeluche's arrest and had him beheaded, hoping thereby to put a stop to this frenzy on the part of the Burgundian partisans.

The next July 14 was a holiday in Paris. Jean the Fearless and Queen Isabeau of Bavaria entered the city and were greeted by a populace certain that now it would see an unbroken period of peace and security.

Jean the Fearless would not enjoy his victory for very long. A year later, on September 10, 1419, a meeting was organized in

Monterau, in Île-de-France, between the dauphin and the Duke of Burgundy. The tension between them was palpable and the rancor unyielding; voices rose quickly and Tanguy du Châtel, the counselor to the young Charles, drew his sword and plunged it into the stomach of Jean the Fearless.

Premeditated murder? An act of spontaneous passion? A well-organized ambush? This would be discussed for a very long time, but the successive executions of the Count of Armagnac and the Duke of Burgundy canceled each other out. For the moment, it was the king of England who emerged the winner.

By the Treaty of Troyes in 1420, Charles VI agreed to rule with his son the dauphin and offered his daughter, as well as the kingdom of France after his death, to King Henry V.

A little more than a year later, Henry V and Charles VI rode through Paris side by side. One can only imagine the surprise and incomprehension of its citizens. Which one was actually the king of France? It was a viable question, for Charles was only a shadow, barely a symbol, and Henry was his successor, king of France and England, the most powerful monarch of the West. But the dreams of humans are subject to their mortality. In the month of August 1422, Henry, thirty-six years old, was struck down by dysentery. Weakened and suffering indescribable pain, he took to a bed in the keep of the Château de Vincennes; a hermit told him to prepare for the end. He commended his soul to the Lord and passed the governance of France to his brother John, the Duke of Bedford. Having accomplished this, he died. There was some debate as to how to get rid of the body. To return it to Westminster, an embalmer was sought, but no practitioner of this delicate art could be located. So the body was boiled and he made his final trip across the Channel in the form of a disarticulated skeleton, carefully arranged in little packages of whitened bone.

Seven weeks after that, in October, Charles VI died as well, carried off by a mysterious illness. Learning of the death of his father, the dauphin immediately pronounced himself king of France under the name Charles VII. On All Saints' Eve, he entered

Saint-Étienne Cathedral in Bourges, dressed in royal robes, made of vermeil and gold-encrusted ermine, and wearing lace-up boots stamped with fleurs-de-lys.

For the followers of the young king, the realm's true capital remained Bourges, at least so long as the English occupied the banks of the Seine and a good part of their territory. And indeed the list of the territories now controlled by the Duke of Bedford was quite impressive: more than half the kingdom, including Bordeaux, Normandy, Champagne, Picardy, Île-de-France, and Paris. And he kept under his influence the territories of Philippe the Good, son of Jean the Fearless: Burgundy, Artois, and Flanders.

Each of the two enemies, the Duke of Bedford and Charles VII, headquartered in their respective territories, plotted to conquer the entire nation, inaugurating a series of battles, sieges, captured towns, the occupation of forts, all of which submerged the countryside in endless fighting, sowing death and causing famine and disease.

Finally, the boyish and frail Charles VII wisely took advantage of the bravura and tenacity of Joan of Arc—who after all might have been his half sister—who had been transformed from a shepherdess to a warrior inspired by God to accomplish the reconquest of throne and territory.

From Avranchin to Picardy, the provinces rose up against the English occupation. On April 13, 1436, in Paris, alarm bells called the population to revolt and the streets were barricaded. Barrels filled with dirt and overturned carts became barricades and traps, isolating the English troops. Through the neighborhoods bands of enemy archers moved aimlessly, leaderless and looking only to save their own skins.

At the same moment, the soldiers of the king surrounded Paris and liberated Saint-Denis. By carefully orchestrated rumor, the French made it seem as if their army was prepared to attack from the north. The English rushed in that direction while the main body of the French troops made a sweeping movement and entered the city by the Saint-Jacques Gate, in the south.

The city's population enthusiastically welcomed the French soldiers. At last, they thought, the hour of their liberation had arrived. In a dramatic reversal of direction, the English mobilized their last troops around the Bastille, hoping that the thick walls and imposing appearance of this fortress would give them a chance to regroup and counterattack. This was a desperate maneuver as well as a futile one: the proud citadel quickly surrendered.

The officers of the king went to Notre-Dame to hear a Te Deum, while as a sign of a return of abundance, a procession of a hundred carts filled with wheat entered the city. Soon afterward, heralds went through the streets to announce that the peace the king desired was at hand.

"If any among you have been unfaithful to His Majesty the King, all is forgiven. This applies to those absent as well as present."

The forgiving king threw a veil of forgetfulness over all the years that had passed, and those who collaborated with the occupier—those who called themselves "the repudiated French"—were categorically given amnesty. Charles VII rebuilt his kingdom on clemency.

His generosity had limits, however. During all these events, he had not left Bourges, though he consented to receive a Parisian delegation that had come to importune him to come back as quickly as possible to Paris, traditional capital of French kings. The king listened without responding. In fact he had no desire whatever to return to a city of which he had so many terrible memories and that in earlier years he had fled, a city that deep down he believed had been definitively disloyal to the crown.

Still, Paris was Paris. After hesitating for a year and a half, Charles VII finally made his solemn entrance into Paris, on November 12, 1437. To celebrate this reunion so devoutly wished for by the Parisians, and to glorify the union of the sovereign with his historic capital, the church bells rang at full throttle, flowers were strewn in the street, banners hung in the windows, and

What became of the Château de Vincennes?

At the beginning of the year 1661, Cardinal Mazarin, prime minister to the young Louis XIV, was nearing the end. His legs caused him agonizing pain and he coughed frequently. After having purged their patient quite extensively, his doctors determined that the air of Paris was harming him. He was taken to the Château de Vincennes, where it was said that he breathed better. The man nonetheless breathed his last breath in the month of March. At the same moment, the court settled itself there on a temporary basis, the Louvre having burned in part and the roofs over some of the galleries having collapsed.

Louis XIV redid the pavilion that Louis XI had built there, but his heart was in Versailles, and this took him away from Vincennes. During the Revolution, the château was turned into an arsenal. In 1948, the records division of the French military settled there.

In 1958, just after he had been elected president of France, General de Gaulle resisted moving into the Élysée, which he found small and an unworthy place to welcome foreign heads of state. He therefore considered very seriously putting the heart of French political power in the Château de Vincennes. *(Cont.)*

joyous throngs packed themselves along the passage of the brightly colored parade.

To the sound of trumpets, eight hundred archers and crossbowmen entered the city, announcing the arrival of Charles VII, who appeared wearing a long gold-and-azure cape thrown over his armor, seated on a white steed that was covered with a blue velvet blanket covered with fleurs-de-lys. He acknowledged the jubilant crowd with a timid wave of the hand.

The king did not remain long. Three weeks later, he left Paris and returned to Bourges, from whence he continued to organize the war against the English.

Charles VII's successor, Louis XI, also kept his distance from Paris, though he was well aware of the city's strategic importance. Château de Vincennes offered him a place from which the city could be monitored. After Henry V's death in its keep, the tower was deserted, perhaps because it recalled too well the English occupation and the Plantagenet claim over France. Henceforth the keep would serve as a prison. Despite his tough, business-like manner, Louis XI preferred comforts that were of a somewhat less austere nature. In 1470, he had a charming little pavilion constructed on the southwest corner of the wall. He also restarted work on the château's chapel, which is a truly sublime example of late fifteenth-century architecture— *le gothique flamboyant*—featuring a nave of dizzying proportions. The architecture of defense was no longer the thing. The Hundred Years War had concluded twenty

Eventually he gave up on the notion.

The buildings entered a period of obsolescence. The keep seemed on the verge of collapse and was closed down in 1995. A dozen years later, the château was completely restored; twenty thousand blocks of stone were replaced. It reopened to the public as an example of Parisian medieval architecture.

years before and the English holdings in France had been taken back; all that remained in English control was the port of Calais. What remained was the war against Charles the Reckless, the Duke of Burgundy, who lacked powerful allies to back him up and therefore fought a losing battle. In 1477, Burgundy was reattached to the country without a fight.

Moreover, customs now so little involved war that when he was doing a tour of Vincennes, reviewing the gentlemen of his court, Louis XI became aware that not one of them was wearing fighting gear. He determined to give each of them a writing case.

"Since you are no longer in a state to serve me with arms, serve me with your pen," the king told them.

Was this a rebuke or a premonition of the growing importance of communication and hagiography?

Nonetheless, while Louis XI did make war he made even greater use of treaties, alliances, and inheritances. But by the end of his realm France was more or less unified. His son, Charles VIII, would look outside his realm toward Italy, where there were territories to be conquered. Indeed he wanted to take the kingdom of Naples and soon enough would cross the Alps in pursuit of that goal.

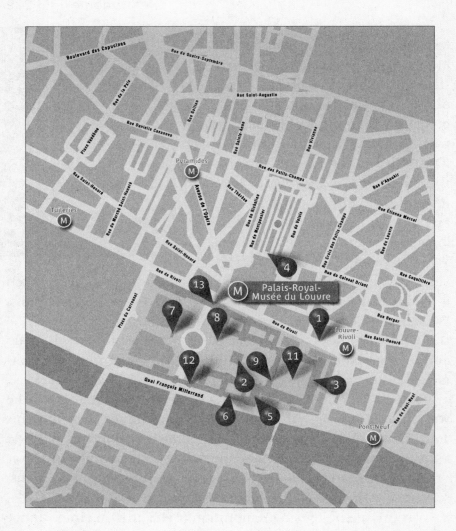

1. The plaque and statue honoring the Admiral de Coligny on Rue de Rivoli. **2.** The transformation of the Louvre. **3.** The colonnade of Claude Perrault. **4.** The Palais-Royal Métro stop. **5.** The Petite Galerie. 6. The Grande Galerie. **7.** The Carrousel. **8.** The Napoleon Court. **9.** The interior of the Louvre. **11.** The marks of the kings on the Louvre. **12.** The backward "N." **13.** Symbols of Napoleon III's republic.

Sixteenth Century

Palais-Royal-Musée du Louvre

The Shadow and Light
of the Renaissance

When you emerge from the Palais-Royal-Musée du Louvre Métro stop, all you have to do is take a look at the *Kiosk des Noctambules*—"Kiosk of the Night Owls"—to understand that you've entered into the realm of art. Constructed in Place Colette in the year 2000 to celebrate the centenary of the Métro, this brightly colored construction by Jean-Michel Othoniel has provoked as much fierce debate as those copper-green Art Nouveau entrances put over the subway entrances over a century ago. Hector Guimard, the champion of the curlycue style, conceived of these designs, which horrified our great-grandparents and today are universally adored. Moreover, there is also a Guimard entryway on the Place Palais-Royal, so you can compare them: one has the glass pearls embedded into a metal stem; and the other is more traditional, with its yellow-and-green signs, its wrought-iron frieze, and its red globes lit up like the eyes of two fanatics.

Palais-Royal-Musée du Louvre. The double appellation is misleading, for the Palais-Royal doesn't designate the Louvre but the home Cardinal Richelieu built in order to be near Louis XII, who lived in the Louvre. After the death of the cardinal and the king, Anne of Austria became regent, and wanted to mark her authority and her taste by moving into the opulent new palace, which was more accommodating than the old Louvre. In fact, she had never been able to abide that austere old fort, with its freezing rooms and dark corridors along which cold breezes blew. The Louvre represented sadness and death. It had been pointed out to her that nonetheless the old place had many qualities and distinct advantages. For example, one could survive a siege there and protect royal prerogative from the power of the masses and invasions of foreign armies. However, the queen was not a military strategist and didn't understand such logic. In 1644, with her two sons, the future Louis the XIV and Philippe d'Orléans, she settled into Richelieu's old home, henceforth called Palais-Royal.

Heavily rebuilt, the main part of the palace is today occupied by the State Department, and its right wing by the Cultural Ministry. The real appeal of the Palais-Royal involved the galleries around the garden, which was one of the most pleasant places in Paris during the eighteenth century. The Palais-Royal theater (the Comédie Française), which sits at the end of the gardens, dates from the end of the eighteenth century and remains one of the most handsome in Paris.

However, let's return to the Louvre, because we are in the sixteenth century and this is where the central events of the period took place. Go into the main courtyard, stand before the Lescot wing, and you will see lines marking where the ancient dungeon once was, as well as the fortress, whose total dimensions did not exceed a quarter of the current space.

Later the Louvre became the largest structure in Paris and the most resplendent museum in the world. All that started with François I, who ordered the construction that ended up taking three centuries and was not completed until Napoleon III's rule in the nineteenth century.

Now for a tour of the palace as it looks today.

Louis XIV, the Sun King, wanted the Louvre's grand entrance to be oriented toward the city, as a way of demonstrating his domination over the Parisians. In 1671, he asked the architect Claude Perrault (the brother of Charles Perrault, the author of the *Mother Goose* fairy tales, including "Cinderella" and "Puss in Boots") to build the sublime colonnade that faces Saint-Germain-l'Auxerrois Church. But it was never finished, in part because having turned his attention to Versailles, the king no longer lived in the Louvre. The work wouldn't be completed until 1811, nearly a century and a half later.

Walk along the Seine and you can see the long building that runs perpendicular to the river and extends the length of the palace. This is the Petite Galerie, which was built upon the moat of Charles V's wall and whose construction Catherine de' Medici ordered to connect the Louvre to the Tuileries, which she was having built. The Petite Galerie was turned into a sad place during the religious wars, as it was long thought that it was from the balcony at the top of the first floor and facing the Seine that Charles IX fired a crossbow at the

H, K, HHH, HDB . . . How do we "read" the Louvre?

Each monarch contributed to the improvement of the palace and added his signature. The H on the front of it stands for Henri II. On the south façade, the HDB refers to Henri de Bourbon, meaning Henri IV. As for the K, it refers to King Charles IX.

The current courtyard was begun by Louis XII with the Sully wing. There you can see the king's sign: the double Greek letter lambda, the A and L interwoven, which stands for Louis and his wife, Anne of Austria. Finally it was Louis XIV who completed the great project, following the plans done by Le Vau for the north and east wings which flank the central courtyard. One can see the royal insignia—the letter L crowned with the letters LB for Louis de Bourbon.

Protestants during the massacre of Saint-Barthélmy. In fact this couldn't be true, as the gallery wasn't finished in 1572, which is when the massacre took place. Today, from the ground floor and particularly from the first floor, which is now the Apollo Gallery, you get a very good idea of the magnificence of the royal apartments during what is called the *Grand Siècle* (Great Century).

The Grande Galerie, which goes along the Seine toward the west, was finished under Henri IV. Hence we see the H and two interlaced Gs, for Henri and Gabrielle d'Estrées, his mistress. Under Louis XIII, here is where the royal coins were minted, the famous Gold Louis. On the first floor of the Louvre, Henri IV organized fox-hunting expeditions in order to initiate his son into the sport.

Starting with the gate leading to the Carrousel, the building that stands there today, extending all the way to the Flore Pavilion, is a reconstruction of the one that disappeared during a mudslide. You can see that the Hs for Henri have been replaced by the N for Napoleon III. The workers of this gigantic site may not have felt deep devotion to the emperor, for if you look at the top of the clock tower on the Lesdiguières Pavilion you can see that the N is backward, a reversal of imperial power.

Turn the corner of the Flore Pavilion and you come upon something no longer there: the Tuileries Palace. Catherine de' Medici's palace, damaged in a fire set by the Communards in 1871, was to have been restored but instead, stupidly, was razed a dozen years later. The Carrousel marked the entrance to the palace beginning in the First Empire and remains the only vestige.

Now let's move on to the Napoleon Court, the one in which the glass pyramid is located today. Above us is an impressive gallery of statues of great men, gazing down upon us. We owe to Napoleon III the construction of these buildings that surround the court and whose function is to correct the absence of parallelism between the buildings along the Rue de Rivoli and the ones along the Seine. On the other hand it was to the first emperor, Napoleon I, that we owe the Rue de Rivoli, with its covered galleries, inaugurating a new century in which Parisians could indulge their passion for strolling. To Napoleon we also owe the buildings of the Louvre right up to the Rohan ticket counters, where, on the pyramid side, the bees recall Napoleon I's sleeping partner, Josephine. On the street side, the marshals of the empire impassively observe the ballet of cars that cross Paris in this great east-west intersection; in order to leave the city these same cars will have to cross beneath the marshals' gaze once again, now on the outer boulevards, before making their way to the *périphérique*.

Starting with the Rohan ticket booth, the buildings that face the Rue de Rivoli date from Napoleon III, the grand architect of this colossal edifice that has seen so many regimes come and go: even his own republic left its trace. If you look at the chimneys and the friezes of the Marsan Pavilion you can see inscribed RF—symbol of the Third Republic.

Now that we've done the tour of the outside, let's go inside by means of the glass pyramid. The Louvre—called the Muséum de la République—first opened its doors in November 1793, during the Revolution. Its holdings vastly expanded by Napoleon's campaigns, it continued to benefit from the generosity of prestigious donors and today possesses nearly three hundred fifty thousand objects. When it opened it had 650.

When they made the transition from palace to museum, the rooms were substantially changed, though a few of them reveal their earlier uses. To limit ourselves to the sixteenth century, Henri II's *chambre de parade* is unchanged, as is the Henri II stairway and the Henri II room in the Hall of the Caryatids. From this magnificent spot, you can still see the back of Saint Louis's chapel's choir, which was integrated into the western wall; as it contains a remnant of Philippe Auguste's Louvre, the wall is twice as thick as the others. This was the tribunal room, meaning where the king sat during festivals and receptions. His throne was set under the central arcade, between the two cannellated columns. There you can also see the four caryatids that date from the beginning of the Renaissance palace. If they could speak, they would doubtless have much to tell us about the *Grand Siècle*.

When François I came back to Paris in 1527, he returned as a vanquished and humiliated king. His expedition in Italy against the Holy Roman Emperor Charles V turned out to be a disaster. He was taken prisoner, and had to spend two million ecus to free

How did the *Mona Lisa* get to the Louvre?

After the death of François I, the portrait left Fontainebleau and was hung in the Louvre. Later, Louis XIV had it removed and put in the Cabinet du Roi in Versailles. In 1798, the painting was brought back to the Louvre, now of course a museum. Not for long, however. First Consul Napoleon Bonaparte had it taken down two years later and placed in Josephine's apartments in the Tuileries. Eventually it was taken back to the Louvre in 1804.

In 1911, Leonardo's painting was stolen by an Italian worker named Vincenzo Perugia, who wanted to return it to his country. For two years, Perugia kept it in the bottom of a suitcase under his bed in his small Parisian room. He would sometimes open the suitcase to have a look at that smile.

Rediscovered, the painting resumed its place in the Louvre. It has taken a few excursions since then—to the United States, Russia, and Japan. Since 2005, this most famous of all paintings has been on exhibit in the *Salle des États*, which was specially designed for the purpose.

himself after a year of captivity. The sum was paid, in part, by the Parisians, rich and poor alike. To show his gratitude, the king decided to move temporarily into the Louvre.

From his Italian defeat François I fashioned a kind of victory—that of bringing the Renaissance to his realm, for from Italy he carried home both artistic treasures and new ideas. This was the continuation of a politics that had been going on for some time. In 1515, after his victory at the Battle of Marignan, he had brought Leonardo da Vinci back with him. The great man had the *Mona Lisa* packed among his things.

As a symbol of the new era, the Louvre's massive old keep was destroyed. Clovis's watchtower disappeared, as did the fortress of the Normans and the Count of Paris's tower. In short, here was the end of the Middle Ages. Other works would follow while the medieval fortress was transformed into a Renaissance château. Starting in 1546, the architect Pierre Lescot built the southern half-wing on the western side, marking the arrival of the Renaissance style in Paris, with its anterooms, columns around the doors, statues, and the rounded or triangular pediments over the windows.

It nearly all added up to François I's artistic last will and testament—he lived only one more year and would not see its completion. In the end, as far as Paris was concerned, however, the artistic promises embodied by the king's return from Italy twenty years earlier didn't really take. The king left the banks of the Seine for the banks of the Loire, where he built the château at Chambord and revamped the ones at Amboise and Blois. Indeed it was at Amboise that Leonardo da Vinci lived until his death; his emblematic painting was hung on the walls of the château at Fontainebleau, which was perhaps the king's favorite residence.

The Renaissance entailed far more than flamboyant art and architecture; there was a darker side, and it involved religious intolerance.

On the morning of October 18, 1534, Parisians awakened to discover posters plastered on the walls across the city bearing these words: "True articles on the terrible, great, and unacceptable abuses of the Papal Mass." "All it takes is a man hiding behind a piece of crust," one author of a pamphlet wrote, referring to the host of the Eucharist, which, to believers, represents the very body of Christ.

This was the work of certain reforming Protestants who wanted to deepen the rupture with Catholic dogma. The result was scandal and indignation, particularly since someone had actually dared to hang one of these in the château at Amboise, near the room of François I himself. This made the king and country, and God himself, tremble with rage.

Paris's three hundred thousand inhabitants—it was the most populous city in Europe—still lived to the rhythm of the Church and its rites. The Protestant community, whose number was at most between ten and fifteen thousand souls, had managed until now to live in a discreet manner. That all changed with this *Affaire des placards*, as it was called, which threw a harsh light on the Reformation and set off violent upheaval. To limit the development of such freethinking, François I banned all printing and ordered bookstores closed. At the very least, this would protect the people from these blasphemous works.

The hunt was on to find the heretics, and in the name of divine truth people were condemned and burned. There were processions through the streets, for the procession was and remained the highest expression of religious loyalty, and took place on every holiday, or to ward off an epidemic, or to avoid a bad harvest, or to seek the blessing of a saint, or to seek a miracle. In general, to calm God's wrath, Parisians were called to join in the holy processions that went from one end of the city to the other.

Occasionally, when the city felt itself in particular danger, the spirit of Saint Geneviève was called upon. The monks of Saint-Germain-des-Prés, their white robes covered with flowers, would carry the relics of the city's patroness saint through the streets, and this would in turn incite a host of processions through the city—starting in the churches, municipal buildings, the royal courts at the Palais de Justice, and Notre-Dame.

Given this outrage on the part of the Protestants, a mere procession wouldn't do. Something far grander was called for. On January 21, 1535, François I joined in a grand parade of expiation in which the city's most holy relics were carried. Sainte-Chapelle was emptied of its treasures, including the crown of thorns, the droplet of Christ's blood, and the droplet of milk from the breast of the Virgin Mary. And to be absolutely certain of appeasing God, six Protestants were burned in the square before Notre-Dame. Caught up in this atmosphere of perfect faith, the king spoke publicly to vilify the errors of the Reformation:

"I desire these errors to be chased from my kingdom and forgive no one. If my own children were implicated, I would burn them myself."

On that day, in Paris and throughout France, the Renaissance, celebrating the arts and human creation, died, supplanted by hatred and suspicion. It would later start up again, more slowly but also irreversibly.

Late in the evening of Saturday the twenty-third of August in 1572, Charles IX, the grandson of François I, convened a meeting with the provost of the merchants at the Louvre and asked him to close the city's gates, to raise chains across the river to prevent river traffic, and to ready the cannons in all the city's main squares.

At dawn on Sunday morning, which was Saint Bartholomew's Day, a group headed toward the building on the corner of the Rue Béthisy and Rue de l'Arbre-Sec, where Admiral Gaspard de Coligny, the main leader of the reformers, was in bed, recovering from a crossbow attack two days earlier.

The Catholic soldiers broke down the doors and did away with the guards barring their way. From his room, the admiral realized what was happening and urged his companions to get out. Jumping from windows and roofs, a number of them managed to get away. Coligny faced his attackers.

> ## What has been the afterlife of Admiral de Coligny?
>
> The building where he lived and died was torn down during the extension of the Rue de Rivoli. But its location is recalled on a plaque at 144 Rue de Rivoli. In 1811, Napoleon gave to the reformed church the Oratory Temple that is located nearby, at 160 Rue de Rivoli. To honor this place of Protestant martyrdom, a statue of the admiral was raised in 1889. Twenty-five feet high and made of white marble, it is the work of Gustave Crauck. The money for it was raised by a national subscription to which both Catholics and Protestants contributed in a spirit of reconciliation.

"Young man, respect my gray hair and my age," said this man of fifty-three to the thug who had broken in.

They were the last words he spoke. A sword came crashing down on his skull. His lifeless body was thrown into the street from the window.

At the moment that the admiral was being dispatched, the lugubrious bell of Saint-Germain-l'Auxerrois began to sound. The massacre was beginning. At the Louvre, Protestant gentry, though guests of the king, were woken, disarmed, and led out into the courtyard. There, with discipline, the Swiss Guards, assisted by the French guard, murdered them one after the other with blows of the halberd. Some of them tried to escape and ran into the galleries, where they were trapped. Blood flowed through the rooms of the palace. Meanwhile, the troop that had led the attack on the Rue Béthisy headed toward Saint-Germain-des-Prés, where there were other Protestants to take care of. The troop had to cross Île de la Cité to reach the Left Bank, and go through the Buci Gate, which was closed due to royal decree. The key was sought, found, and finally the gate was opened. But by now the sun was fully up and the Protestant leaders, alerted as to what was heading their way, had gathered together on the banks of the Seine on a barren piece of land called Pré-aux-Clercs. They saw the soldiers heading toward them and realized that fighting would be useless. They tried to flee on foot or horse. The chase lasted until Montfort-l'Amaury, where some managed to get out and others were put to the sword.

In Paris, in the Cemetery of the Innocents, the flowering of a hawthorn bush that had been stunted and assumed dead for several years was considered a divine sign. Crowds came to witness this amazing event. The little white flower was proof positive that God Himself was smiling down upon the massacre of these heretics.

The Catholic people of Paris gave themselves over to this horrific nightmare—slaughtering men, women, and children. Coligny's remains were found and emasculated, then thrown into the Seine, where they rotted for three days before being hanged from the gallows at Montfaucon. The bodies of the dead were disfigured, for it was imperative to show that these were not human beings but demons that needed to be disposed of like garbage. The king tried weakly to stop the killing, which continued for several days and spread to other cities in the realm.

How many died in Paris? Estimates vary, but most historians put the number at three thousand.

During the course of the years that followed, religious tension remained high, and when it was clear that Henry III would die without an heir, and that the throne might pass to the Protestant Henri of Navarre, French Catholics were again enraged. The Holy League and its leader, Duke Henri de Guise, simply could not accept such an outcome and mobilized their forces. On May

14, 1588, early in the morning, the king, hoping to prevent an insurrection, placed four thousand Swiss Guards in Saint-Denis. They occupied the city's strategic points—the Petit Pont, the Saint-Michel Bridge, the Marché Neuf, the Place de la Grève, and the Cemetery of the Innocents—as well as surrounded the Louvre.

The king planned to arrest and execute the leaders of the Holy League, but before he could do that Parisians rose up to defend them. A citywide militia was formed and led by prominent citizens, representing the city's sixteen *quartiers,* consisting of artisans, merchants, and students. They took up arms—halberds, harquebuses, swords, picks, scythes, anything they could get hold of—and stood ready. By midday the population had blocked the city's main roads by piling up dirt and paving stones. These blockages were called "barricades." Companies of Swiss Guards in the Cemetery of the Innocents were trapped; others were stranded on the Left Bank; shots were fired and tiles thrown from the roofs. Some fifty Swiss Guards were killed and their bodies piled up in the streets. Finally, not willing to get themselves killed for the king, these mercenaries laid down their arms before the armed masses.

"Good France! Show mercy!"

"Vive Guise!" the crowds shouted back.

In Place Maubert, a lawyer galvanized the mob.

"Courage, men! We've been patient long enough! Let us barricade this pathetic excuse for a king in his Louvre!"

Henri III decided to appeal to the leader of the Catholic party, who had spent this "day of barricades" in his home in the Marais. Dressed in his white satin doublet, his rallying sign, the Duc de Guise left his house, took possession of Paris, and deployed his troops before City Hall.

The next day the king emerged from the Louvre. Everyone assumed that he was simply going for his daily walk in the Tuileries. Suddenly he jumped on a horse and galloped out of town, heading toward the cathedral town of Chartres, where he was sure he would find some faithful royalists.

Determined to retake power, Henri III had the Duc de Guise assassinated the following December in Blois; he also arrested the members of the Holy League and laid siege to Paris.

At the end of July 1589, Henri and his troops occupied the heights of Saint-Cloud. Parisians armed themselves, fearing the worst—that the Protestants and the king would seek to avenge Saint Bartholomew. But this fight never happened. On the first of August, a fanatical monk named Jacques Clément plunged his dagger into the stomach of the king.

"You evil monk, you have killed me!" exclaimed Henri III. Though horribly wounded, the king nonetheless took several hours to die.

The sole inheritor of the crown was Henri of Navarre, famous for using the phrase "Paris is well worth a Mass" in order to open the gates of the divided capital. Navarre converted to Catholicism and ascended the throne in 1594, taking the title of Henri IV.

The century ended on a harmonious note. On April 30, 1598, the king of France signed the Edict of Nantes, which, despite its imperfections, recognized Protestantism and represented a step toward religious freedom, putting an end to decades of civil war. Thus did Henri IV give to Paris and to France the most handsome monument of the century, which, despite the agonies and strife, longed to be humanist in character and to be marked by freedom.

It was not to last. A dozen years later, on May 14, 1610, the king's carriage was headed to the Hôtel de l'Arsenal where his minister Sully was in bed with a sudden fever. On the Rue de la Ferronnerie, the carriage was caught in a traffic jam caused by a hay cart and a wine tank that were blocking the road. To get through, the king's valets left the king's carriage, and this was perceived by a fanatical Catholic named François Ravaillac. He believed that God had spoken to him and told him that his mission was to convert the Protestants of the realm to the True Faith.

Ravaillac jumped into the royal carriage and stabbed the king twice (the king's coat of arms scraped the sidewalk and today you can see the mark where the regicide took place). They rushed the king to the Louvre but by then he had lost too much blood. He died the moment he entered the palace.

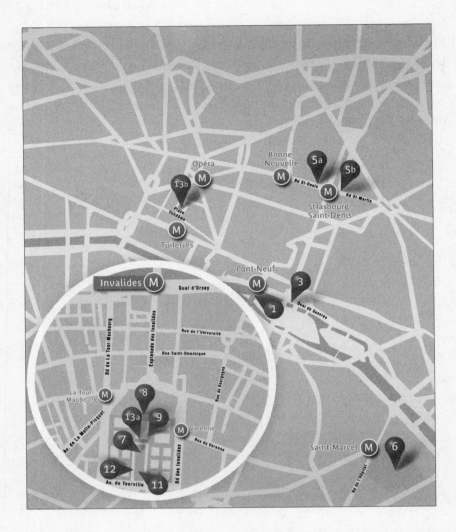

1. The Pont-Neuf. 3. The Quais of the Seine. **5a**. The magnificent Saint-Denis Gate. **5b**. And the modest Saint-Martin Gate. **7**. The church of Les Invalides. **8**. A bas-relief sculpture of Louis XIV on horseback, at the northern entrance to Les Invalides. **9**. The Marquis de Louvois's mark on Les Invalides. **11**. Napoleon's tomb. **12**. And Napoleon's original stone tomb, outside Les Invalides. **13a–13b**. Napoleon's statues.

The Price of the Great Century

The Invalides Métro stop is pretty gloomy. Though it leads us into the magnificence of the *Grand Siècle*, it does so by means of dim and somber corridors. Little matter. Once you reach the surface you discover the grandeur that Louis XIV sought for Paris.

In this part of the Left Bank, somewhat off-center from the city's heart, there was once nothing but mud and swamps that belonged to the Saint-Germain-des-Prés Abbey. The name of the Grenelle field and the subway stop Varenne, which isn't far, designate pretty much the same thing: as we've seen from the days of the Gauls, it was a rabbit warren, a field deemed unfit for farming, which explains why this vast space remained fallow for so long.

Louis XIV himself dismissed putting the Hôtel des Invalides on this spot as the "King's big idea." And when it came to grandeur the Sun King knew a thing or two about big ideas. He understood that a religion that centered on him was a religion for France, and he himself was the most energetic instigator of monuments built to his glory.

In 1669, Jean-Baptiste Colbert, the superintendent of royal buildings, sketched out a few ideas for Paris: "Plans to continue everywhere—Arc de Triomphe, for the earthly conquests—Observatory for the skies—*Grandeur et magnificence.*"

The municipality of Paris financed the two *arcs de triomphe* dedicated to the king, raised up in the place of two gates that were sacrificed to a general program of beautification for the city. The arch over the Saint-Denis Gate was built to honor the victories in Flanders; and the more modest one over Saint-Martin Gate was built in commemoration of the conquest of the Franche-Comté—the former "Free County" of Burgundy.

It would be unfair to see these triumphal arches—whether initiated by the city or by the king—merely as monuments to the grandeur of the monarchy. A true effort was under way to make the city more secure and at the same time a better place in which to live.

In the Paris of the seventeenth century, the most beautiful private homes, ornaments of art and architecture, could sometimes be found on dilapidated streets and muddy lanes, places characterized by misery, crime, and disease. Many Parisian streets were a jungle of haphazard construction of levered wood and precarious chimneys. In their darkened corners gangs of thieves were ready to pounce upon respectable people who had lost their way. They all had their tags. The Rouget Band had their red coats; the Grisons wore gray; the Plumets sported large plumed felt hats. All of them inspired fear among ordinary people.

Paris was a swarm of activity, its ways and byways crammed with hawkers and traffic—water carriers, fowl merchants and their wicker baskets, heavy tipcarts filled with grain. To get anywhere you had to thread your way through all the confusion of wagons, carts, and herds of cattle heading toward slaughter. It was not an easy place to be a pedestrian. An artist named Guérard did an engraving of the streets of Paris and rendered in them the anxieties of the pedestrian.

To walk the streets of Paris, keep your eyes peeled
Listen for every sound, let every nerve be steeled
To avoid being hit, run over, or crushed,

BECAUSE IF YOU CAN'T MAKE OUT IN THE FRAY:
"WATCH IT! WATCH IT! OUT OF THE WAY!"
FROM ON HIGH AND UP FROM BELOW, YOU WILL BE MUSHED.

Construction along the riverbanks had been part of the Parisian landscape since time immemorial: the river quays were an endless work-in-progress. The centuries had brought with them some improvements, and Henri IV and Louis XIII had in their respective times tamed the banks, particularly along the Louvre and on the Place de la Grève, thanks to stone walkways large enough to permit pedestrian traffic and more particularly strong enough to contain the waters in the event of flooding.

On the Right Bank, stretched between the Quai de la Grève and the Quai de la Mégisserie a long stretch of ground became a field of mud in even the lightest rain: the carts that went down to the river there regularly get stuck. To have done with this hazard, the king demanded of the Marquis de Gesvres in 1664 that he build a wharf between the Notre-Dame Bridge and the Pont-au-Change. It carries the name of its builder and the subway stop on the 7 Line, at the Châtelet station, was built using the arches that support it. If you look from here toward Mairie d'Ivry-Villejuif, you will note that the vaults are slightly lower. These are the seventeenth-century foundations.

Eleven years after its construction, the work was completed with another quay, between the Notre-Dame Bridge and the Place de l'Hôtel-de-Ville, which would be given the name Le Pelletier when he was the provost of the merchants (the two wharfs would be joined in 1868 under the single name of Gesvres). On the Left Bank, similar work would be undertaken, as represented in particular by the construction of the Quai de Conti.

As befitted a sovereign, Louis XIV initiated and tracked these projects, though frankly without great enthusiasm. At heart the king didn't much like Paris, and he never had much faith in Parisians. This was one reason that he finally moved away from the capital to set up his court and government at Versailles. He remembered too well how humiliated he had been in Paris as a child. The Fronde—the name given to the civil war that took place in France during the Franco-Spanish War—had nearly toppled the monarchy; no one had believed that a boy of eleven would one day rule the land and members of the nobility took advantage of the uncertainty. His mother, Anne of Austria, the realm's regent, decided to flee Paris.

The night of January 5, 1649, was Epiphany. The streets of Paris were empty, though windows were lit up and everywhere there were celebrations. In the Palais-Royal, the feast went on until late in the evening. The queen had her piece of *galette des rois*—the traditional Epiphany cake—and found the bean, and hence she was given a cardboard crown. Everyone was amused.

Shortly after midnight, the queen retired to her quarters and prepared for bed. A minute after she had lain down she got up, woke up her two sons, Louis and Philippe, and using a back stairway went out into the gardens through a secret door. There were waiting three carriages, ready to take them all far away from Paris.

News of her sudden departure spread quickly through the court and created consternation, for everyone was commanded to follow the queen. Several hours later that same night, long processions of carriages filled with hastily attired men, disheveled women, and sleeping children took them deep into the countryside.

Waiting for them at the end of this exhausting late-night trip was the Château de Saint-Germain-en-Laye, which to sleepy eyes looked like a dark ship with crenellated towers emerging from a frozen sea. Nothing was readied for the royal guests; the rooms had been emptied for winter and were freezing cold. Only the king, his brother, their mother, and Cardinal Mazarin found modest camp beds. Everyone else was forced to make do with rough pallets set on the floor.

In the crowded corridors of the château people milled, including a good many of the kingdom's nobles; everyone was in a foul mood. Worried-looking courtiers, dressed in clothes that were less than fresh, mourned the loss of their comfortable Parisian homes and exchanged the latest gossip from the capital. The royal flight had created stupefaction. Despite his young age, His Majesty was looked upon as the father of his subjects and the protector of his nation, the sovereign with divine right whose mere presence was reassuring and comforting. With him gone, fear filled the vacuum—fear of the unknown, fear of future calamities. For its part the Parliament endlessly debated about how to react. Finally, it was decided to send a delegation to Saint-Germain to beg the regent to return the king to Paris. But when these men arrived at the château the queen curtly refused to receive them, without even attempting to keep up appearances and spare anyone's feelings.

During this time the Hôtel de Ville had become a place where prominent citizens and rebellious nobles came to rub elbows. Feasts and dances took place in the salons, as befitted a society more keen on pleasure than on fighting. But the Parisians also revealed their aggressive nature, in this case by pointing cannons at the walls of the Bastille prison and firing six shells. This was mostly symbolic; the shells did little damage to the thick walls. Having done this, they took over the fortress without further incident. This was deemed a great victory, and in order to celebrate it, the elegantly dressed women and grand-looking men then emptied the prison wine cellar.

The queen's pout lasted for seven months. She then returned to the Palais-Royal.

Two years later, Paris was humiliated yet again. On the night of February 9, 1651, the rebellious princes of the Fronde, appalled by the idea that Anne of Austria and her son the king might once again leave Paris, closed the city gates and mobilized a militia. That night no one would either enter or leave the city. But were the king and his mother even within the city's walls? Might they have already escaped? To reassure everyone, Gaston d'Orléans, young Louis's

Is "boulevard" a typical Parisian word?

In 1670, Louis XIV ordered the demolition of Charles V's ramparts, which were by now doubly useless—both because of the evolution of military technique and because of the urbanization of the neighborhoods outside the walls.

On the Right Bank, the ramparts were replaced by a wide avenue that went from the Bastille to the Madeleine on which people could walk.

The French word *boulevard* belongs to this period and was intended to describe this novelty. It is therefore very typically Parisian. It has a double origin: it comes first from the Dutch *bolewerk*, which means "bastion" (from *bol*, for mortar, and *woerk*, "work"). The term therefore designated ramparts. Later, when the fortress wall was torn down, it gave place to open space filled with trees. The Parisians called these *boules*—from *bol*—*verts*, to acknowledge their greenery. Hence *boulevards* were places to relax, stroll, and daydream.

uncle, sent the captain of the Swiss Guards to the Palais-Royal with the mission of locating the king.

Their suspicions were well placed. The queen had indeed determined to leave Paris again, fearing the return of civil war and a popular revolt among the masses. The arrival of the Swiss Guard had prevented her from executing her plan. The child-king, who was already dressed, was to have gone to bed and pretend to be in a deep sleep, the sheets drawn up to his chin to hide his clothes. At that moment in came the Swiss captain. He looked into the royal chamber and to his profound relief found the young monarch asleep there. By this point a crowd had gathered before the palace and demanded to see their young king in person. They were allowed entry. Silently and respectfully, a line of workers, washerwomen, and porters, their faces animated by concern, filed past the royal bed to observe the sleeping child. Several women made the sign of the cross over the blond curls of the king and murmured prayers on his behalf, before heading back out into the street, reassured.

Louis never forgot the humiliation of all this, and one can understand a little better why he wanted to make Paris seem like less of a prison. This was partly to improve it and partly to weaken it. Ample courtyards and generous boulevards would replace fortifications and impasses. The city would be opened up.

Louis XIV reserved his architectural whims and artistic enthusiasms for Versailles. However, he made one exception in Paris, one that he hoped would benefit the many soldiers wounded or mutilated in the cause of France's military glory. The king did not want to forget those to whom he owed his victories: the rank and file who were mobilized for his costly campaigns. Today you can see the golden dome of his gratitude rising up nearly 350 feet over the vast space, a Gallo-Roman battlefield to which has been restored some sense of serenity: the Invalides.

The Invalides served a practical purpose as well. When Louis XIV, comfortably settled in his carriage, crossed Paris he used the Pont-Neuf, which was crowded with poets, vagabonds, journal salesmen, and bear baiters. And veterans of the wars as well, many of them reduced to begging. The king may have felt his heartstrings pulled by the sight of sleeves without arms, legless cripples, blind or mutilated men—all the poor bastards who had had their bodies broken on the field of honor and now lived a life of misery.

Morally, the king may have been only slightly moved by the sight of these men; politically, he was aware of the danger that they posed. They represented the flip side of the military decoration, and were a little too conspicuous. He who so adored going to war wanted to preserve its image as a grand adventure, and to cover over the fact that it also could lead to misery. His idea was therefore to take these invalids—these shadows on his sunny reign—away from the center of Paris and find a place to hide them from public view.

Eventually, the recommendation was to build the structure on the Grenelle plain. The fact that the plain was so isolated from the rest of Paris suited the king. This way these poor souls would be less visible. A dazzling golden dome would deflect the suffering of those beneath it.

In 1674, Louis XIV formally announced the purpose of the buildings that he had had constructed. They were to be a "royal residence of grandeur and space, capable of receiving and housing all
the wounded officers and soldiers, whether elderly or young, and
to assure sufficient funds to feed and care for them."

The king had good reason to worry about the wounded, for
there was always a war going on in one part of the land or another, producing a seemingly endless crop of them. On August 11
of that year, for example, forty-five thousand men led by the Prince
de Condé battled sixty thousand Dutch and Spanish soldiers under William of Orange. Seven thousand Frenchmen were killed
in this battle, which lasted for a day and a night and took place
near Mons, roughly twenty-five miles from Brussels. Once again,
it wasn't the bodies left on the field of battle that concerned the
king; it was the thousands of survivors who came home without
legs, or eyes, or arms.

Of the eight monumental architectural plans that were proposed, the king selected the one by Libéral Bruant, the architect
who had already designed and built the hospital at Salpêtrière.
The construction of the Invalides corresponds to the same period
as the hospital, which housed some forty thousand indigents, beggars, and sick who, at least according to the king, represented a
threat to public health and security. This reflected a way of thinking that might send chills down the spine of anyone who lived in
mid-twentieth-century Europe. Still, here was Louis XIV's principal legacy for Paris: freed of its beggars, its wounded safely shipped
off to the outskirts.

The plan for the Invalides was simple and magisterial: on these
twenty-five acres would be built a grand court surrounded by
smaller ones, with rectilinear buildings and in the center a church
dedicated both to the king and to the wounded.

In October of 1674, the first men entered their new abode. In a
militarylike ceremony, the veterans were welcomed by the king
himself, accompanied by François de Louvois, minister of war.

The veterans were not bitter; they applauded His Majesty, doubtless relieved to know that henceforth their housing and food would be covered.

Room and board, yes, but not, as it turned out, much freedom. Discipline was strictly enforced at the Invalides. Military exercises were de rigueur, wine and tobacco were forbidden, and religious observance was required. These poor handicapped men were forced to submit even in their retirement to military regulation.

The soldiers were housed four or five to a bare room, while the officers shared a room with one or two others and at least had a fireplace. Designed to house fifteen hundred pensioners, the building was soon home to six thousand, despite a rigorous admissions process and strict regulations.

Today, after passing through the *cour d'honneur* you are immediately plunged into the middle of these men destroyed by war, as the interior has on the whole been remarkably well preserved: the staircase, beams, and corridors remain as they were at the end of the seventeenth century. On the ground floor were the refectories for the wounded soldiers, as well as their dormitories. Today the refectories house the Museum of the Army, but one can still make out in its vast proportions a sense of the original purpose, while admiring the frescoes glorifying Louis XIV's military victories.

Going up to the first floor takes you into the rooms that faced the central gallery. The stairs guiding you there are very gradual, a reminder that they were designed for those who could barely walk. Once you reach the first floor you can see names and drawings engraved onto the walls, as well as the results of the small occupations that were designed to keep the men from being bored. Thus if you head to the northwest toward the Quesnoy corridor, behind the statue of the Grenadier, you will see, drawn over the right parapet, a shoe whose flat heel seems to mock the fashion for red heels reserved for the nobility under Louis XIV. It's a piece of graffiti from the *Grand Siècle*. There's another one next to it, over the parapet to the right as you take the western corridor.

The main entrance is located in the northern pavilion, along

What of Louvois remains in Les Invalides?

Louis XIV, astride his horse, occupies center stage—at the northern entrance to Les Invalides—and though his face was chiseled off during the Revolution it was repaired to perfection under the Restoration.

But the Marquis de Louvois ingeniously found a way to insert himself into the *cour d'honneur.* If you look at the pediments under the roofs you will see that they are comprised of coats of arms dedicated to military glory. On the eastern façade, the one on the right if you turn your back to the statue of Napoleon and move over six pediments, starting with the emperor, you will see an oeil-de-boeuf that represents a wolf observing the courtyard with a fixed stare. That's it: the wolf looks—or, in French, *le loup voit,* hence "Louvois." And that is how the marquis left his mark on the work to which he had dedicated such a large part of his life.

with the administrative offices and the governor's apartments. And in front of this entrance stands the wooden horse, a feared form of punishment for the inmates of Les Invalides. For the slightest infraction, the smallest fault, one was put in it for several hours and subjected to humiliation by fellow soldiers and visitors. For yes, there were visitors. Les Invalides became a favorite destination for excursions and Parisians came here both to be reacquainted with the misery of others and to listen to the old soldiers tell their war stories. At bottom what one found at Les Invalides was an open book of history, ready to be flipped through. The young women who visited sang the latest mournful song:

Tell us pretty lady
Where your husband be.
He's gone away to Holland
The Dutch took him from me . . .

And so the old veterans told their rapt listeners about the war in Holland, where they went to die in the polders of the Low Country or to get shot up by the English while fighting alongside the Dutch (coalitions were always forming and re-forming).

"More than eighty ships and sixteen Dutch firebomb boats bearing a hold filled with powder were involved in the battle," recalled one crippled sailor. "The cannon mouths were moved to the hatches, and the sailors on the fireboats approached the ships, setting fire to the hulls and then scampering off in little dinghies, having set fire to their own ships. It was a sea of fire! And in this furnace the vessels were rammed, their mouths spitting fire and their masts cracking. Good God! Cannonballs filled the air, and the flames were everywhere, and grapple hooks dug deep into the ship rails, and my ears were filled with the cries of the wounded!"

But if Les Invalides were operational, meaning functioning as hospice, hospital, and—the men needed an occupation—uniform manufacturer, one last building completed the ensemble and that was the Church of Saint-Louis. Libéral Bruant, the architect, hesitated and procrastinated over that design; he was never satisfied with the plans and kept coming back to a construction that he always felt was imperfect. Minister of War Louvois was irritated by the delays but waited for two years. Finally he sent the indecisive Bruant packing and replaced him with one of his students, a young man of thirty named Jules Hardouin-Mansart.

In fact, it was not only on the aesthetic front that Bruant faltered but also on the issue of prerogative and precedence. How was he to design a religious space with both

Why does Napoleon lie at Les Invalides?

Transformed into a Temple of Victory during the Revolution, the church still preserves today the sanctuarylike role it played for the army, its men, and its history.

Napoleon had military respect for Les Invalides, which he visited regularly, calling upon the wounded, and organizing within its walls the first award ceremonies of the Legion of Honor; he also allocated to it a significant amount of money.

In December of 1840, brought back from Saint Helena, the remains of the emperor were quite naturally placed in the church in Les Invalides. King Louis Philippe hesitated, however, as to the final placement of the famous tomb. After two years of waffling, His Majesty ordered the architect Louis Visconti (creator of the fountain of Saint-Sulpice Church) to build a monument. A deep pit was dug under the dome. The emperor, wearing the green uniform of the Huntsmen Guard, was not placed there until April 1861, however, under the reign of his nephew Napoleon III.

The tomb, carved from blocks of purple porphyry, the stone of emperors, was placed atop a large green-granite base from the Vosges region and decorated with laurel crowns and inscrip-
(Cont.)

tions of the emperor's victories. Around him in the crypt are the tombs of members of his family, including the Aiglon—the Eaglet—Napoleon's oldest legitimate child, as well as those of other military men who have served France, including the generals Vauban, Turenne, Foch, Juin, and Leclerc.

On the outside of the church, on the western side, you might perhaps see under a tree a modest and neglected stone tomb, which is the original stone tomb in which the emperor was brought back from Saint Helena.

A bronze statue of Napoleon also stands on the first floor of the building, easily visible from the *cour d'honneur*. Commissioned by Louis Philippe in 1833, the sculptor Charles-Émile Seurre designed it to sit atop the Vendôme column. The statue was taken down in 1863 by Napoleon III and replaced by what he felt was a more regal image—that of the emperor wearing a Roman toga. The statue of Napoleon in his two-pointed hat, his hand stuck into his vest, was first exhibited in the Courbevoie traffic circle. After the fall of the Second Empire, this bronze Napoleon was thrown into the Seine, thus escaping the Prussians in 1870 and the Commune in 1871. It was fished out of the water in 1876 and forgotten about for thirty-five years. Finally, in 1911, it was given its place in Les Invalides.

royal and popular functions? How could it accommodate both the Sun King himself and his most humble servants? Hardouin-Mansart found a solution. In his design, the structure doubled, and in an architecturally coherent way. The nave would be dedicated to the religious needs of the common soldier; under the cupola would be housed the royal chapel.

Louvois took matters in hand, allocating more and more funds to the work, and monitoring its progress. Nearly every day he arrived at the worksite and despaired at how slowly it was all proceeding. Every detail had to be seen to—a new element added to the frescoes, a skylight realigned, a correction made to the coats of arms engraved into the stone, a heraldic symbol added.

"You will have to hurry if you want me to see the dome completed," said the minister to the architect.

Alas, he died in 1691, long before the building was finished.

The construction of the church took more than thirty years. After Louvois's death, the king himself took charge of it. He would sometimes visit it incognito; having his carriage stop some distance off and accompanied by only a few courtiers, he would walk the rest of the way on foot. Guided by Hardouin-Mansart, His Majesty came to inspect some effect of the statuary or the deployment of an architectural rib.

Finally, the tallest dome in Paris was finished in 1706, when the Sun King was no more than a toothless old man whose face was the color of yellowed ivory.

But the wish expressed so long before had endured. Les Invalides remained a hospital for soldiers, though the number of pensioners had risen from six thousand to one hundred thousand. The place that the Sun King had wanted as a visible sign of military glory still concealed under its golden dome the sordid and sinister side to war, the misery and the agony of men sacrificed at the altar of the nation's grandeur.

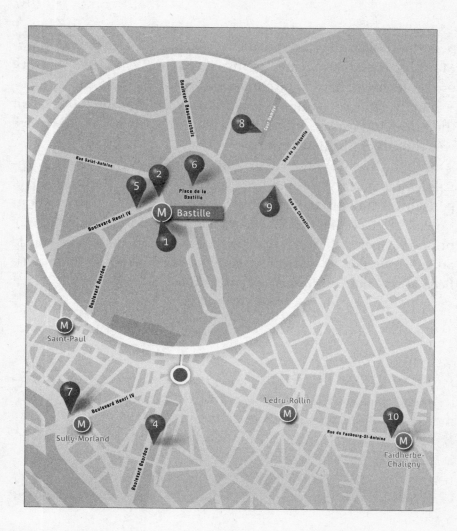

1. The Bastille Métro stop. **2.** The corner of Boulevard Henri IV and Rue Saint-Antoine: a brown paving stone indicates the precise position of the old fortress. **4.** The Arsenal Gate was built on the site of the Bastille; some of its stones are remains of the military fortress. **5.** The last of the Bastille's dungeons. **6.** The Golden Génie. **7.** One of the eight towers of the Bastille, discovered during construction of the Métro and rebuilt in Henri-Galli Square. **8.** The artisans of the Saint-Antoine faubourg. **9.** The house on the corner of Rue de Charenton and Place de la Bastille, where an enormous barricade was set up during the Revolution of 1848. **10.** At 184 Rue du Faubourg-Saint-Antoine, a small fountain dating from the beginning of the seventeenth century.

The Fury of the *Faubourg*

The Bastille Métro stop does a meritorious effort of evoking the Revolution, attempting to inspire revolutionary nostalgia among Parisians on an outing: a brightly colored fresco retraces the great moments and period images evoke the fortress as it looked in former days. Most particularly, on the platform for Line 5, one can see some yellowing stones. These were part of the foundations of a wall from the Bastille, discovered in 1905 when the subway tunnel was being dug. Outside the subway entrance, at the corner of Boulevard Bourdon, you can see another segment of the old fortress wall.

We're lucky that even these modest remains survived, because nothing of the Revolutionary Bastille is left. Today when you say "Bastille" you generally mean the opera house. This heavy glass-and-stone bunker, which has aged prematurely, looms over the square with its inert mass. Built to commemorate the bicentennial of the fall of the Bastille, the opera house has already started to crumble and would not require a revolution to be demolished.

To find what remains of the past, it is useless to look on the opera side of the square or at the *Génie* of the Bastille, a golden symbol of liberty stuck atop its green column. A better bet is to go to the corner of Boulevard Henri IV and the Rue Saint-Antoine and look down: a brown paving stone indicates the precise position of the old fortress. On the façade of the building at number 3 on the square a map indicates its massive form. Toward the Seine, the Arsenal Gate evokes the moat around the walls and some of the older stones are the remains of the military edifice. Finally, at the end of Boulevard Henri IV, also in the direction of the Seine, the base of the Tower of Liberty—one of the eight towers of the Bastille—was discovered during construction of the Métro and rebuilt in Henri-Galli Square.

Let us go back to the Bastille, which was a catalyst for popular hatred well before 1789. Long before that it had been a symbol of opposition to royal absolutism and of princely ambition. As we saw, Parisians had risen up and taken it in 1413.

In 1652, when rebellious princes tried to strip power from the young Louis XIV, the Bastille loomed up in importance for a second time. On July 2, the Prince de Condé, the leader of the princely revolt, marched on Paris at the head of his army. During the early morning hours a savage fight broke out at the Saint-Antoine Gate. Condé troops confronted the firepower of the royal infantry; the result was bodies everywhere. Musket shots rang out and houses were burned. Very quickly the royalist troops, the soldiers of the Fronde rebellion, and the city's inhabitants were caught in a confused melee. Marie-Louise d'Orléans, known as the *Grande Mademoiselle* and a cousin to the king, appeared before the Bastille; its doors opened to her and she was received with honors. She climbed the stairway that led to one of the towers and by means of a telescope observed the scene.

In the distance, toward Bagnolet, she saw the red and blue uniforms of the Royal Army. At her orders the Bastille's heavy cannons were turned toward these troops and fired. The retort was so violent that it shook the walls; the crenellations of the high towers vanished in a cloud of acrid smoke. The shells whistled and landed with devastating effect among the royal divisions, mowing down an entire row of knights. The Bastille bombardment upon the king's men had its effect: in disarray, the marshals loyal to Louis XIV temporarily called a halt to the assault. For a moment Paris was in the hands of the rebellious princes.

Well before July 14, the Bastille had therefore become a symbol—a place either to occupy or to tear down. No one knew exactly what went on inside it, but everyone was quite sure that it represented arbitrary authority and was therefore to be feared and hated.

Generally prisoners held there—never more than forty, sometimes fewer—were treated with respect. These prisoners were often young nobles who had broken certain rules but who had the right to a kind and gentle form of incarceration. To be more at home, they brought in their furniture, gave dinner parties, and occasionally were accorded permission to leave for the day, so long as they returned to sleep in the prison.

Voltaire, the author of a pamphlet that had displeased the authorities, was kept there for eleven months in 1717. Upon his release, he received a pension of a thousand ecus from the regent, Philippe of Orléans.

"I thank your Royal Highness for what you have seen fit to pay for my food, but I pray that you no longer concern yourself with my housing," he responded.

Nonetheless, such largesse was not available to everyone. The archives reveal some pretty awful crimes. "I am sending you this man named F. He is a very bad subject. You will keep him for eight days, after which you can do what you will," wrote Antoine de Sartine, lieutenant general of police around 1760, to the governor of the Bastille, Bernard de Launay. "Have the man named F brought in," Launey wrote on the note, "and after the prearranged time ask M. Sartine under what name he would like himself buried."

What horrors went on in there were only guessed at by the population of the Saint-Antoine *faubourg*. In the neighborhood streets over which loomed the shadow of the gray walls of the prison lived a group of artisans, and they were always quick to express discontent.

The fortress has long since disappeared but one can still walk about the *faubourg* and find a few back courtyards in which hand-made craftsmanship lingers on. You can breathe in the odor of varnish and polished wood, as per the traditions. In the Damoye Court, at number 2 Place de la Bastille, you will find a representative passageway. The house on the corner of Rue de Charenton also offers a handsome vestige of this busy place: here is where an enormous barricade was set up during the Revolution of 1848, sealing off Saint-Antoine.

Everything changes quickly; the old furniture workshops have become popular bars and clubs, for this *quartier* has become one of the trendier spots in Paris. No longer do workers come home to their exposed-beam lodgings, filled with slightly twisted old furniture, but instead young professionals who have turned city living into a lifestyle.

In the eighteenth century the Saint-Antoine *faubourg* wasn't quite like the other *faubourgs*. The term *faubourg* is of course completely Parisian. It dates from the late fifteenth century, derived from the Old French *forsbourc,* which means "outskirts" or "suburbs"—*fors* from the Latin *foris* for "outside." But folk etymology has defined it as *"faux bourg"*—a fake town—to connote its status as a kind of "inner suburb." Since the days of Louis XIV, Saint-Antoine had been the privileged place of poor artisans who had the right to work independently, free of professional organizations or guilds. Cabinetmakers, furniture makers, upholsterers, locksmiths, hatmakers: they all worked side by side and the stores, which often doubled as workshops, followed the shape of the winding streets that eventually emerged into Rue de la Roquette, Rue de Charonne, and Rue de Charenton.

All day long the neighborhood was crisscrossed by wagons and donkeys driven and ridden by farmers from outlying areas who came to sell eggs, vegetables, or fruit; by women who cooked in the open air near the wharves; by swarms of hawkers known for their aggressive vulgarity. The citizens who inhabited Saint-Antoine came from the outside and were always quick to spontaneously express their anger. One epidemic too many, a bad harvest, or an additional tax could lead them down the dangerous path from protest to rebellion.

And so it was that on April 27, 1789, the *faubourg* was in full boil. The source of it was the prosecution being brought against one Jean-Baptiste Réveillon, owner of a large painted-paper factory on Rue de Montreuil. Several days earlier, Réveillon, who was actually quite generous with the 350 workers in his employ, had made a series of propositions to the city of Paris to combat poverty. This businessman and amateur social entrepreneur thought that he had grasped the interconnections between the fates of nations and the lives of the poorest, and had devised a program to change society for the good. More dreamy than wise, more visionary than enlightened, he had proposed doing away with the tax on goods brought into the city, which could therefore be sold at a lower cost. That was fine, except that he also suggested lowering salaries, because the cost of living would now be less. Under the Réveillon Plan, workers who were earning twenty sous a day would have to content themselves with fifteen.

It was in the Saint-Marcel *faubourg*, located on the Left Bank, that a reaction to "Réveillion the Starver" first took place.

"Death to the rich!" shouted the crowd as it made its way to the Place de Grève (of course).

Before the Hôtel de Ville, an effigy of Réveillion was set on fire, and then a procession headed toward Saint-Antoine. Three hundred and fifty guards managed to maintain order during the night, but in the early hours of the morning the tanners of Saint-Marcel and the artisans of Saint-Antoine streamed out onto Rue de Montreuil. Réveillon and his family had long since fled, but his factory was systematically plundered, taken apart piece by piece, and his wine cellar emptied of its bottles.

Finally, after several hours, the police guards, joined by reinforcements, were able to push the crowd back. Stones were thrown from roofs and shots rang out. Soon twelve policemen and hundreds of protesting workers were killed, the bodies of the latter paraded around the *faubourg* and greeted with popular rage. No one yet knew it, but the world was going to be profoundly shaken. The Revolution had now started, and it had just known its most murderous day, despite the horrific violence that was yet to come.

Before number 184 Rue du Faubourg-Saint-Antoine you can still see a small fountain, dating from the beginning of the seventeenth century. More or less situated at the location of the Réveillon factory, it was the center of this *émotion*—to use the language of the *Ancien Régime*. This first "emotion" had claimed more than a hundred lives.

In the weeks that followed, from the sixth floor of the tower of the Bastille in which he was incarcerated, the Marquis de Sade called the people to rise up. Imprisoned by what was called a *lettre de cachet*—or "hidden letter"—written by his mother-in-law to the authorities and outlining his dissolute habits, the marquis wrote his *One Hundred and Twenty Days of Sodom*, a work in which he detailed every possible turpitude of his troubled soul. And when he had had enough of letting the pen run along the paper, he took hold of a long white metal pipe equipped with a little funnel which, when the urge arose, he attached to his bottom—a portable toilet in which he could more conveniently dispatch his excretions down below into the moat. With said instrument Sade formed a kind of bullhorn that he used to harangue the people of the *faubourg*.

"Good people! They are slitting the throats of the prisoners in the Bastille! Come immediately to our rescue!"

These cries for help were taken seriously by passersby, appalled at the thought of what must be happening behind those thick walls. Actually, however, the marquis was living large in prison, quite comfortably situated in two rooms in which he had placed his furniture and his personal library; he was eating so well that he had grown a little potbelly.

On the fourteenth of July, 1789, early in the morning, the storming of the Bastille took place—except that it happened at Les Invalides. For the nearly three months following the attack on the Réveillon factory, popular rage had continued to seethe, and the smell of powder still seemed to float over Saint-Antoine. Rumors true and false were rife. It was said that a plot was being hatched, but a plot by whom and against whom exactly? Against what? It was said that troops were being formed outside Paris to reestablish order. It was said that the harvest had been bad and that there would be severe food shortages.

On the previous evening several bakeries had been broken into and a militia had been formed, and alarms had sounded all night long. The population intended to defend itself against the mercenaries that were threatening to occupy Paris; some workers forged pikes, but it would take more than that; they needed guns. Guns were plentiful at Les Invalides. So that's where people went. The doors were ripped open and the crowd seized thirty-two

What was the Bastille?

To the east of the city, in order to protect the Saint-Antoine Gate, a *bastille*—or "bastion"—was constructed starting in 1370. This fortification offered a place of refuge for Charles V, who generally stayed in his nearby Saint-Pol residence. This "bastille Saint-Antoine" featured eight towers connected by walls that were nearly ten feet thick. The whole thing was surrounded by a moat that was more than eighty feet wide and more than twenty-five feet deep.

By the seventeenth century the Bastille's military function was no longer relevant and Cardinal Richelieu had turned it into a prison in which to put his enemies. There was no need of a judge or jury to be thrown in the Bastille. A king's order or a *lettre de cachet* was more than enough.

In 1788, the Chevalier du Puget, the king's lieutenant at the Bastille, had already planned for the closing of the fortress and estimated that doing so would save forty thousand livres that could be added to the royal treasury, given that the king paid considerable sums to run the place: the salary of the governor, officers, soldiers, doctor, and priest. It was a large staff for a prison population that diminished year by year: nineteen in 1774, nine at the beginning of 1789, and only seven a few months later.

thousand rifles and several old cannons. Now they needed gunpowder.

"There's gunpowder in the Bastille!" someone shouted.

"To the Bastille! To the Bastille!

In a swarm, the Parisians left Les Invalides and headed to the Right Bank, crossing the bridges and marching toward the old fortress. The idea wasn't to take it—no one thought of that—but simply to raid it for its gunpowder and bullets.

When the Marquis de Launay, the governor of the Bastille, saw this human wave heading toward him he kept his cool. He was determined not to give way and simply open up his arsenal to a howling mob. A delegation sent by the Hôtel de Ville came to him and demanded that he give this citizen militia the ammunition they required. The delegation, consisting of the city's highest officials, was received with great courtesy by the marquis, who even invited them to dine (probably as a way of gaining time until royal reinforcements could arrive). It was a pleasant enough meeting but it didn't lead to anything. Launay refused to budge even if he did not also intend to fire upon the crowd, not so long as no one tried to break into the fortress. A second delegation was dispatched several minutes later, and then a third. They met with no greater success.

At one-thirty in the afternoon, the crowd around the Bastille became restless and threatening. The governor knew well that he could not sustain a siege; the proud old place was defended by only ninety-two veterans, most of them with war wounds, and commanded by about thirty Swiss Guards.

Nonetheless it was important that the rule of law be enforced and Launay, a rigid man with a deeply lined face, a poor pawn placed by destiny in a spot that exceeded his capacities, had his men fire on the crowd of enraged protesters who had seized hold of the chains on the drawbridge. A hundred attackers collapsed onto the paved stone.

In the afternoon, two detachments of the Swiss Guard, whose responsibility was to ensure the security of the city, changed sides and joined with the mob. These war-toughened soldiers had five cannons taken from Les Invalides that same day and fired them at the Bastille's doors. A fire broke out, big enough to make the old veterans guarding the fort panic. They forced Launay to raise a white flag. The drawbridge was lowered and the crowd poured into the Bastille. In its joy, it liberated the prisoners, surprised that there were only seven in all, and, on top of that, that they little resembled the heroes of liberty who had been expected; rather they were small-time crooks and forgers. Still, the symbolism was what counted. They were carried out in triumph.

The poor Marquis de Launay was dragged through the streets before being decapitated with a knife by a junior cook. His head was fixed onto a pike and carried around the *faubourg* in triumph. This macabre ritual marked the population's fury and resentment and in their way these were now implacable. There would be no going back.

In Versailles, Louis XVI was woken in the night by the Duc de La Rochefoucauld-Liancourt, and they proceeded to engage in a short scene with dialogue that could easily have been written by actor and playwright Sacha Guitry.

"Sire, the Bastille has been taken, the governor was murdered and his severed head was carried about on the head of a pike."

"Ah, so this is some kind of rebellion, is it?"

"No, sire. It is a revolution."

Two days later the demolition of the Bastille was begun. Eight hundred workers were involved—at twenty-five sous a day—to tear down what still seemed like the "bastion of tyranny." The stones from it would be used to build the Pont de la Concorde— the bridge leading from the Place de la Concorde to the Left Bank—and several others. Some became souvenirs. One resourceful artisan named Palloy even made miniature fortresses out of them and sold them across France.

A year to the day after the storming of the Bastille, to commemorate the anniversary and to bring patriots together in a cause, a Festival of the Federation was organized on the Champs-de-Mars

The last of the Bastille's cells

Everyone now agrees that with the exception of several foundation stones, which are still visible in the Métro stop, nothing of the Bastille remains. Well, that's a mistake. One cell does in fact remain, one of the *cachots*—sordid and lightless holes—that were to be found deep down in the fortress, where royal authority imprisoned the stubborn and the recalcitrant.

One day when I happened to be near the Place de la Bastille, I was talking with a friend who ran a bistro in the neighborhood, and who shared my passion for Paris. He took me down to the cellar of his establishment, which was called La Tour de la Bastille, and which in fact featured one of the Bastille's cells, miraculously saved from revolutionary fervor. Later I verified what my friend had told me. He had been quite right; the stones and the shape of the wall confirmed it. I was deeply moved by the experience of entering this place. Standing amid all the bottles I felt as if I could hear the cries of prisoners and the boom of the July 14 cannons.

Today the bistro has been replaced by a restaurant called the Tête-à-Tête—and that may be gone as well—but the basement still contains the mystery and secrets of number 47 Boulevard Henry-IV.

by La Fayette, commander of Paris's National Guard. Sixty thousand delegates came from the country's eighty-three *départements* to celebrate the unity of all France and King Louis XVI, who was placed atop what was called the *Autel de la Patrie*—the "altar of the country"—from which he swore allegiance to the nation before all the Parisians crowded on the embankment around it.

In 1880, when it was necessary to choose a date to commemorate this festival, it was July 14, 1790, that was chosen, not July 14, 1789; in other words it was the date of reconciliation rather than that of civil war and terrible violence.

After the demolition of the Bastille, the history of the square on which it had once sat was one of failed meetings and missed opportunities, at least from the architectural point of view. On June 16, 1792, the legislative Assembly decreed that the spot where the prison had once stood should become a square with a column atop which would be a statue of Liberty. A month later the first stone was set. Then the project came to a halt due to aesthetic differences. The following year, a fountain that was supposed to represent nature's charms was put in the place of the abandoned column.

In 1810, Napoleon wanted to put up another fountain, a gigantic bronze one made from metal from the cannons taken during the Spanish insurrection. Somewhat oddly, this monument was to represent a giant elephant 260 feet high with water spurting out of his trunk.

The foundation was laid and a life-sized plaster model was made in 1813. After the fall of the empire, this imposing animal—one of the most incongruous constructions Paris had ever known—remained in its plaster form for years. The plaster began to crumble bit by bit, though an elderly guard continued to live inside one of the feet. In *Les Misérables*, Victor Hugo makes it the home of Gavroche, the kid who helps man the barricades.

Happily the plaster carcass was destroyed in 1846, and from the ruins of the pachyderm emerged an enormous pack of rats which terrorized the Saint-Antoine *faubourg* for a number of years.

What lies beneath the column?

History sometimes takes strange turns. To the 540 martyrs of the 1830 Revolution buried under the column were added several Egyptian mummies two or three millennia old.

Napoleon had brought the mummies back from the Egyptian campaign and they had been buried in a garden near the National Library on Rue de Richelieu, on the same spot where, after the Glory Days of July, the bodies of the killed were buried. When it was decided to bury these revolutionary heroes under the column, no one thought about sorting them and the bodies were simply dumped there. And thus it was that several pharaohs also lie under Bastille near the Saint-Martin Canal, which runs beneath it. Did the bark of Osiris, the Egyptian god of the dead, take this watery path that connects the Seine to the Ourcq River to bear these princes and workers into the Realm of the Dead?

In 1833, King Louis Philippe decreed that a column be constructed in the middle of the square, in honor of the fallen heroes of the Three Glories, meaning July 27, 28, and 29, 1830, during which Charles X was thrown off the throne in favor of a constitutional monarchy. The monument, over 175 feet high, was unveiled on April 28, 1840. At the top of the green column the aforementioned golden *Génie*, or "genius," was to represent something that the Assembly's deputies had wanted in 1792: it would stand for "Liberty that broke its chains and flew, and brought with it light."

With cannons firing from the top of Montmartre, the Commune of 1871 tried to destroy the column, which for the radical Republicans represented a symbol of an alliance between a monarch and his people. The column withstood, as did the Republic.

1. Madame la République. **2a**. Boulevard of Crime. **2b**. At 51 Boulevard du Temple, the Théâtre Déjazet. **3a**. The Cirque d'Hiver. **3b**. The Théâtre de la Porte Saint-Martin. **6**. The Ambigu theater was spared, then destroyed in 1966 and replaced by a bank (1 Place Johann-Strauss). **7**. 14 Rue de la Corderie, where the International Workers Association ordered the uprising of February 16, 1871. **8**. Père-Lachaise cemetery, where Communard rebels were lined up and shot on May 28, 1871. **9**. The Nubian Lion Fountain.

In Five Acts and Dramatic Moments

When you come out of the Métro at République you find yourself standing at the foot of the weighty figure of Madame la République. In her revolutionary headgear—the so-called Phrygian hat—holding an olive branch, the Declaration of the Rights of Man at her side, her bronze gaze watches over popular protests for which she has been the guiding spirit for more than a century. Covered in black-and-white flags atop which are inspiring banners, she remains the mother figure for the *Enfants de la Patrie*. At her feet, on the stone pedestal, are the Three Virtues, symbols of the Republic: *Liberté*, symbolized by a flame; *Egalité*, as symbolized by the tricolor flag; and *Fraternité*, as represented by a cornucopia.

This monument, which is now an indispensable part of the Parisian political landscape, was placed here on July 14, 1884, and this secular form of the divine became the apotheosis of the then-new Third Republic, which seemed to have been victorious but which was still somewhat tremulous about what it had survived. The Commune had occurred a little more than a decade earlier, and the memory of what happened at number 14 Rue de la Corderie was very much alive. It was there that the International Workers Association ordered the uprising of February 16, 1871.

Once upon a time the Place de la République had been called the Place du Château-d'Eau, a large intersection at the end of Boulevard du Temple. After the Revolution, Paris's two great fairs—that of Saint-Laurent on the Right Bank and the Saint-Germain on the Left—had declined. Boulevard du Temple then became the place for gatherings and festivals, particularly after the creation of theaters was no longer subject to the whims of official power. New playhouses opened in profusion along the enormous arc of the boulevard, and it became the center for entertainments for all segments of the population, aristocrats as well as proletariats.

The epicenter of the *boul'* (as the boulevards were called) was to be found in the tight perimeter between the triumphal arches at Saint-Denis and Saint-Martin, and the former Rue d'Angoulême, which is today Rue Jean-Pierre-Timbaud; it went all the way to the Cirque d'Hiver, or "winter circus."

This epicenter formed a true border of east and west. The rest of the *boul'*—toward Bastille on the one side, and toward the Madeleine on the other—was less festive. The aristocrats and the bourgeoisie feared venturing too far east into that side of town; and workers were hesitant about entering the western parts of town, which had been the stomping grounds of the *Ancien Régime*. One could easily sense this separation between worlds, so much so that the poet Alfred de Musset would look at the eastern ends of the boulevards from the west and say, "There are the Great Indies."

The Château-d'Eau intersection was surrounded by enormous buildings and home to the fountain that was designed by Pierre-Simon Girard, from which the square and the street derived their name ("water castle"). It was on the Boulevard du Temple—intersection of all pleasures—that the first line of omnibuses, drawn by horses, was established in 1828, leading from Bastille to the Madeleine.

The fountain became too small for the new configuration of

the square; it was dismantled and taken to La Villette in 1867, where it served as a watering trough for beasts being led to the slaughterhouse. Partly transformed, it can still be found in the park in La Villette, under the name Nubian Lion Fountain.

In the 1830s, the Parisian theatrical world was alive with activity and ferment. The heart of this universe of creative illusion was the Boulevard du Temple, which the local population jokingly called the "Boulevard of Crime," because every evening in the various theaters and playhouses any number of actors were involved in stabbing, poisoning, and strangling one another, to the enormous pleasure of the paying public. Among the fifteen or so theaters on the boulevard, a few were so enormous that they could seat more than three thousand spectators. These included the Ambigu, the Porte Saint-Martin, the Théâtre Historique, and the Cirque Olympique; others were more modest in size, only seating around five hundred, such as the Funambules or the Délassements Comiques.

During the day street hawkers shouted out what was on the program that evening, offering a few tantalizing details; when night began to fall, under the trees along the boulevard—which offered a little cover—the ticket lines started to form. Soon it was dark and the cafés lit up, filled with those waiting for the performance to begin. Along the whole line of theaters were shops selling waffles, nuts, spiced bread, apple turnovers, or ices at two sous apiece. The brightly colored lanterns of the merchants threw flickering light on the pavement, and the frenetic sounds of their bells sometimes drowned out the voices of the barkers. And then suddenly the boulevard emptied out and the theaters filled. Not until the intermission would the Boulevard of Crime take life again.

In the playhouses the curtain rose. Audiences were generally noisy and prone to whistle whenever a scene didn't please them, or to let an actor have it.

The uncontested star of the boulevard was Frédérique Lemaître, who triumphed at the Ambigu-Comique starting in 1823 in *The Inn of the Adrets,* a melodrama accompanied by music and ballet that he could turn to his advantage with his gift for improvisation and irony. The play had been a flop when it first opened but Lemaître, a giant of a man with a booming voice, turned his character, the bandit Robert Macaire, into a sort of comic murderer with a heart of gold.

"Killing snitches and police doesn't mean I don't have feelings," he would declaim, to the applause of a delirious audience.

In 1841, Frédérique Lemaître had no male rival on the Boulevard of Crime. As for a female star, her name was Clarisse Miroy; the two of them were destined to meet. Clarisse triumphed in *The Grace of God,* a schlocky vaudeville warhorse which spectators at the Théâtre de la Gaîté had come to love. Each evening the same theatergoer sat in the same seat in the first row of the orchestra. And each evening he waited until Mademoiselle Clarisse had made her entrance before noisily dropping his cane. Invariably the appalled audience would turn toward the clumsy idiot and see Frédérique Lemaître, impassive-looking, his lips pursed under his little black moustache. One night, the cane didn't drop. Clarisse and Frédérique began an affair that lasted for thirteen years.

Their love finally ended in a scene worthy of melodrama. After having left her famous lover, Clarisse wanted to return to him and was rejected in turn. Heartsick and jealous, she put a large dose of laudanum, a popular poison at the time, in his water glass. He managed to survive drinking it, though this act of attempted murder did little to revive his feelings for Clarisse. Frédérique forgave her but would never see her again.

In 1848, the carefree world of the boulevard, like the rest of Paris, was afire with revolutionary fervor. Louis Philippe had ruled the French for nearly eighteen years. The monarchy had gradually lost its grip, mired in economic problems and scandals. Everything seemed to be in league against the king—the harvest had

The Conservatoire National des Arts
et Métiers.

The Dungeon of Phillipe Auguste. The original purpose of the Louvre can still be found deep within it, for when you enter the Louvre's crypt you can make out the walls and find the foundations of the dungeon and the towers of the ancient fortress.

The most beautiful of all the *collèges* still visible today is that of the Bernadines, founded in 1224.

The superb door of the home of Olivier de Clisson dates from 1375. Clisson was one of King Charles V's stalwart soldiers, to whom credit goes for taking back the country at the end of the fourteenth century.

The Chateau de Vincennes, built by King Charles V in the late fourteenth century.

The most famously enigmatic smile in the world.

The armor belonging to François I, displayed in the refectory of the Invalides. The armor was given to François I by Charles V.

Model of the Bastille. After the Bastille was demolished in 1789, the stones from it were used to build several bridges, among them the Pont de la Concorde—the bridge leading from the Place de la Concorde to the Left Bank. Some stones became souvenirs. One resourceful contractor named Palloy even carved the stones into miniature replica fortresses and sold them across France. Here, one of his models at the Musée Carnavalet.

In the 1830s, the Parisian theatrical world was alive with activity and excitement. The heart of this universe of creative illusion was the Boulevard du Temple, which the local population jokingly called the "Boulevard of Crime" (pictured here), because every evening in the various theaters and playhouses any number of actors were involved in stabbing, poisoning, and strangling one another, to the enormous pleasure of the paying public.

Le Grand Palais. The Grand and the Petit Palais were constructed during the Exposition Universelle of 1900, a symbol of exchange and cooperation between peoples.

been poor and the price of bread rose sixty percent, and a disease from Ireland had destroyed the potato crop. Paris feared famine.

Properties fell into disarray, industries were ruined by a stock market crash; intellectuals with dreams of the republic and nostalgic Bonapartists all focused their anger on an elective system that gave only a small minority the right to representation. Isolated and inflexible, Louis Philippe refused to consider any kind of reform agenda.

Public meetings of more than twenty persons were forbidden. That was easily gotten around. Instead of having meetings, people held banquets. The government couldn't forbid that kind of gathering. After a rather frugal dinner came heated revolutionary rhetoric.

The biggest of these banquets was planned to take place on February 22 in Paris. A procession mixing students, workers, and artists was to march from the Place de la Concorde all the way up the Champs-Élysées, where a dinner would be held and after that the usual speeches. East and west were to meet. Starting in the morning, several processions started to make their way through Paris; the police and the army held their collective breaths.

The day passed in relative calm, but the next evening, singing "The Marseillaise," a large group headed toward the Ministry of Foreign Affairs, which was then located on Boulevard des Capucines. The crowd approached the soldiers who were guarding the building and surrounded them. One of the crowd's leaders, a bearded man of some stature, tried to strike an officer with the torch he was carrying. A rifle shot rang out, and the torch shook, then fell to the pavement. Panic ensued. The soldiers started firing in every direction, and in the end sixteen lay dead. Their bodies were piled onto a wagon and paraded around. A menacing crowd followed behind this macabre procession.

"Vengeance! To arms!"

From that moment the throne was doomed. On February 24, while an icy rain fell on the city, barricades were formed on all the city's boulevards; people huddled around braziers, attempting in vain to ward off the cold of a freezing fog that seeped into clothing. The leaden skies were the somber décor of a revolution in progress.

Having taken refuge in his palace in the Tuileries, Louis Philippe sought comfort from his generals, whom he asked whether the city could still be defended.

When no one replied, the king understood. He wearily went to his desk to sign his act of abdication.

The republic was formed. The temporary government asked the theaters to reopen, hoping to have things return to normal as quickly as possible.

But drama was not just taking place on the stages. The fashion now was to form clubs—which were pronounced *cli-oobs*—where people could express their agitation, and they could be found in every *quartier* of the city—home to anarchists, socialists, and neo-Jacobins, who gathered to rub elbows and listen to fiery, anti-bourgeois speeches.

One evening, in one of the biggest of the clubs and also the most extremist—it met in the great hall of the Conservatoire on Rue Bergère and was presided over by the fearsome professional agitator Auguste Blanqui—those gathered showed in great detail how the bourgeoisie were the only ones to benefit from the sweat of the people. It was all a form of theater, and thus somehow fitting that Eugène Labiche, a young writer of vaudeville plays, rose to speak. Standing on the raised platform covered with a green rug, at which also sat the severe-looking members of the club's officers beneath the tricolor flag and its motto, "Liberté, Egalité, Fraternité," he harangued the workers in the audience.

"Citizens, by simple accident of birth, of which I am innocent, I happen to belong to this shameful caste of society that I cannot sufficiently curse. I nonetheless think it an exaggeration to believe that it drinks the sweat of our proletarian brethren. Allow me to cite a personal example that I hope may change your opinion, for if you love justice, O fellow citizens, you should not love truth any the less. I live in an apartment on the fifth floor and lately I had some wood brought in. The virtuous citizen who, for an agreed fee, ventured to climb my stairway to bring said wood to my apartment got so heated in the act of doing so that sweat poured off his features with their manly determination. To put it bluntly he was swimming in perspiration. Well, I happened to taste a little of that sweat and I can tell you that it tasted awful."

A disapproving murmur accompanied the final words of this theatrical declaration. When Labiche, his head held high, slowly descended the steps from the stage, a few were so outraged that they rushed up to him, intending to use their fists to make him understand that they found this kind of humor inappropriate. Luckily the writer Maxime du Camp happened to be in the room, and somehow was able to get his colleague out of there more or less in one piece.

Several months later, in December 1848, the election of Prince Louis Napoleon to the presidency of the new republic cooled tempers. Once he had moved into the Élysée palace, the new chief executive didn't disappoint those who longed for a return to peace. He banned the clubs and leaned on the army to prevent any potential insurrection.

The mandate the prince was given was for a four-year, nonrenewable term. However, by means of a coup d'état he held on to power. On the morning of December 2, 1851, people awoke to find that posters had been put up all over Paris, carrying an appeal and signed Louis Napoleon. "If you believe in me, give me the means to finish the great mission that I have started on your behalf . . ."

The prince's methods were already apparent: the army occupied the city, the Assembly was dissolved, and a number of deputies had been arrested. The speed with which this had happened precluded immediate reaction.

Only the next day did the city shake off its torpor. More than seventy barricades were constructed. The army replied with terror. On the boulevards, drunken soldiers, panicked by the threatening crowd, opened fire. Ten minutes of continuous shooting

What could you find along the Boulevard of Crime?

There is first of all Marcel Carné's 1945 film, *Les Enfants du Paradis*, one of the great film masterpieces of all time, which realistically re-creates all the poetry of the Boulevard of Crime, with its actors and audience and pimps.

There are also more tangible traces. Located at number 51 Boulevard du Temple, the Théâtre Déjazet, built in 1851, escaped demolition by Baron Haussmann. Called in succession the Folies-Mayer, Folies-Concertantes, and Folies-Nouvelles, the playhouse was bought in 1859 by Virginie Déjazet, one of the most celebrated actresses of her time. Closed in 1939, it was turned into a movie house, then in 1976 it would have become a supermarket had the arts community and concerned citizens not mobilized to save it.

To the east, the Cirque d'Hiver on Rue Amelot was another survivor. Built in 1852, it was located at the far end of the Boulevard of Crime. Also turned into a movie theater right at the beginning of the development of the *septième art*, or "seventh art," it became a circus in 1923 and was used by all the great names of the time—Bouglione, Fratellini, Zavatta.

To the west, the Théâtre de la
(*Cont.*)

cut down innocent passersby, children, and old people. Bodies were everywhere, with the wounded trying to crawl away. The crowd howled its reaction. Two hundred and fifteen were killed. The horrified crowd was cowed into submission.

A year passed. Now calling himself Napoleon III, the former president of the republic decided it was time to redesign Paris. His idea was to turn the city into a modern city—open, hygienic—as well as to eradicate the poorer quarters where the ragged people lived and clean up the rough neighborhoods that could so easily turn into revolutionary hotspots. Baron Eugène Haussmann, the prefect of the Seine, aided the cause, creating wide boulevards that made it both more difficult for barricades to be constructed and easier for troops to be brought in should there be a rebellion.

Given the spirit of order and discipline he was trying to instill, the emperor was concerned about the Boulevard of Crime and wanted to have done with the trouble that was always brewing there. The boulevard would be torn up. In 1854, Napoleon III had the Prince-Eugène military barracks constructed nearby. Today they are called the Vérines Barracks of the Republican Guards, named in honor of a lieutenant colonel shot in Germany during the Second World War.

Porte Saint-Martin was also one of the rare survivors of the Boulevard of Crime. First an opera built by Marie-Antoinette, it became a battleground during the Commune. The theater as it looks today was rebuilt in 1873.

The architectural battering ram used by Baron Haussmann turned the city into an enormous worksite. What emerged from it was a city with large avenues. A decree pushed the boundaries of the city all the way to the old fortifications: Auteuil, Passy, Montmartre, and Belleville were integrated into it, bringing the number of arrondissements to twenty. The Place du Château d'Eau, now called Place de la République, was enlarged in 1862. Most of the playhouses on the Boulevard of Crime disappeared.

The biggest theaters refused to die and simply moved elsewhere. The Théâtre Historique became the Châtelet; the Cirque Olympique became the Théâtre de la Ville, also located in the Place du Châtelet; the Gaîté left the Rue Papin and became the Gaîté-Lyrique. The Folies-Dramatiques moved to Rue René-Boulanger, and later housed a movie theater during the 1930s. The Ambigu was spared, then destroyed in 1966 and replaced by a bank. The demolition order was signed by André Malraux.

During its eighteen-year existence, the Second Empire made Paris into a bourgeois playground. Wars took place somewhere else—in the Crimean or in Mexico; the stock market was in full expansion and rewarded bold investors; fortunes were made and industries developed; people went dancing in the Saint-German *faubourg*, which had become the central artery of the luxurious lifestyle.

The greatest moment of this era in France was without doubt the Exposition Universelle of 1867. A palace built of iron, glass, and brick was constructed, covering the entirety of the Champ de Mars. A colossal example of ephemera, with its audacious modern design, the construction was the heart of the new Paris. On April 1, a glorious day, the fair was opened by the emperor, while rays of sun played off the glass. Beginning in the early hours of the morning an immense crowd of people had massed around the entrances. Brought together under one gigantic roof were all the arts and technical achievements of every civilization on earth. There were the latest-model locomotives, Indian teepees, astounding demonstrations of electrical power, and Japanese houses made entirely of paper. Forty-two thousand exhibitors came to show off their creations and inventions. Each country wanted to display its power: the English exhibit took the form of a large golden pyramid, representing the volume of gold extracted from Australian deposits. More worrisome was the Prussian exhibit, which featured an enormous Krupp cannon. In the joyous atmosphere of the exposition, however, no one wanted to acknowledge this menacing note.

The city's dark corners and sordid dead ends were subjected to demolition crews. Now Paris was run through with wide avenues, and glorious streets were bordered with impressive buildings whose stone façades were crowned with slate cupolas. At night, gaslights illuminated Paris and turned it into a perpetual playground. The center of the new nightlife were the great boulevards, charming open spaces that began at the Madeleine and stretched all the way to Château d'Eau, passing through the magnificent neighborhood of the opera house, the ultimate symbol of Haussmannian ambition. Here was a promenade dotted with cafés in which, with their comfortable and upholstered sitting places, one could find both celebrities and true elegance.

With Second Empire Paris in the grip of pure gaiety, balls and feasts were held, each one trying to outdo the other in grandiosity. There was no time to sleep, as was observed with amusement by the worldly chronicler Henri de Pène: "Dinner was set for 7:30, the play at 9 o'clock, and the balls began at midnight, then supper at 3 or 4 in the morning. Then a little sleep after that if it could be had and if there was time for it."

Emperors, kings, princes, and industrial tycoons gathered in this boisterous and fun-loving capital. One was no longer sure to whom to give way when the Russian czar crossed paths with the sultan of the Turks, the queen of Holland met with the king of Italy, and the king of Prussia rubbed elbows with the khedive of Egypt. It seemed in all this euphoria as if mankind was heading toward universal peace.

Three years later, in 1870, the carefree Second Empire was destroyed by the Franco-Prussian war, the product of the Bismarckean dream of a greater Germany. In the month of July, Paris prepared for war with great enthusiasm. The soldiers were wildly cheered as they marched along the boulevards. Women created a pantheon to the heroes of tomorrow; patriotic cafés and inns poured out their cheap wine to the men in uniform.

What lay ahead might have been predicted. The poorly trained French armies were surrounded by the Germans and the emperor himself taken prisoner in Sedan. On Sunday, September 4, the hot sun of late summer made Paris radiate under a deep blue sky. Learning of the military debacle, a huge crowd massed at the Place de la Concorde and seized control of the Second Empire's symbols.

The empress was forced to flee with her last group of loyal followers, the ambassadors from Austria and Italy. This small group crossed the Diana Gallery all the way to the Flore Pavilion and went into the Louvre, immediately engulfed by the museum's enormous Great Hall. Soon she found herself facing Géricault's enormous canvas, *The Wreck of the Medusa*, with its writhing bodies.

"How strange it all is," she murmured, tears rolling down her cheeks.

She exited by the small door onto the Place Saint-Germain-l'Auxerrois. A carriage waited there, and the fallen empress got in and was taken away from the city at a slow trot. For a while Eugénie took refuge with her American dentist, who lived near the Bois de Boulogne. Eventually she went into exile in England.

The republic had proclaimed the end of the war but had not succeeded in stopping it. The capital was bombarded, burying entire families in the remains of their houses. The roofs of Les Invalides and the Sorbonne collapsed. Confusion reigned. The Prussians tightened the vise and soon the city was cut off. The siege had started. Paris being Paris, people still went out to eat in restaurants in which, stuffed and cooked, its tail sticking straight up and a sprig of parsley arrayed about the muzzle, rat was served.

In February, the Prussians arrived and marched down a deserted Champs-Élysées. Paris had put on its cloak of mourning; black crepe floated in the breeze on the balconies of city halls in every neighborhood. The victorious troops did a little tour of the capital and then departed.

Paris was enraged. Starting in the month of March, the Commune rebellion had reached nearly every neighborhood. Red flags were raised up against the gray skies. Exhausted, disoriented, and demoralized soldiers raised their rifles into the air and broke ranks. Soldiers and civilians joined forces as if at a joyous country fair.

However, some French troops remained loyal to governmental authority and they indulged in a debauch of killing. In Montmartre, the Luxembourg Gardens, and elsewhere, people were bludgeoned with rifles and shot; sometimes an entire line of Communard prisoners were simply lined up and machine-gunned. The bodies of the dead piled up in front of the Panthéon. On May 28, the last of the rebels were taken to Père-Lachaise Cemetery, lined up against the back wall, and shot. By the end of May, order was definitively restored, at the cost of twenty thousand dead. Survivors were deported by train.

As Adolphe Thiers put it, "Either the Republic will be preserved or it will not." And thus it was on January 30, 1875, under the presidency of Marshal de Mac-Mahon, that the laws of the Third Republic were adopted by the Assembly—by a single-vote majority: 353 to 352.

Theater in Paris managed to survive the Boulevard of Crime's demise. At the Saint-Martin Gate, the fashion was for grand spectacle. In 1875, *Around the World in Eighty Days,* based on the novel by Jules Verne and adapted for the stage by Verne and Adolphe d'Ennery, enjoyed huge success. People flocked to see the live elephants, boa constrictors, a locomotive made of cardboard spewing out clouds of smoke, a ship on the high seas, an attack against redskins, a Hindu religious ceremony, Javanese dances, and the multitude of figures used in exotic *tableaux vivants*.

Other neighborhoods attracted a new audience. In Montmartre, on Rue Victor-Massé, the Chat Noir cabaret started a shadow theater in 1886 and it became famous throughout Paris.

The *Éléphant* remained the Chat Noir's most famous and celebrated show: a white screen was illuminated and a cartoonish-looking black man approached, pulling a rope; he pulled and pulled and then disappeared, and the rope seemed to stretch out indefinitely; then came a knot, another rope, and finally an elephant deposited what the barker called an "odiferous pearl." From this "pearl" grew a flower that opened right before the eyes of the spectators. Curtain!

From the unexpected success of this theater in miniature arose a new kind of art; an entire room was reserved for it. Henri Rivière, the inventor of the world of silhouettes, was constantly coming up with new ways to animate his shadows. An evening at the Chat Noir became the thing. Balkan kings, British noblemen, and provincial factory owners all religiously attended. Sometimes some illustrious visitor would ask to be allowed behind the scenes after the show. This always upset Rivière, who had provided his crew with a way of responding to the request. They duly informed said illustrious visitor that any false move would release a large cloud of dust that could easily ruin his elegant clothes. A piece of the décor skillfully manipulated would knock his expensive hat off and send it flying. Most often at that point the curious guest pushed matters no further and beat a hasty retreat.

While the Boulevard of Crime was sacrificed to progress and modernity, another kind of crime—a far more real kind—grew up in the vicinity of the future Place de la République. Starting at the end of the nineteenth century, the dance halls on this side of town lined the joyous road to perdition. One could dance at République, forgetting about sorrows in the quadrille of rouge-cheeked young girls. A mixed world of interlopers got caught up in music that was intoxicating. On any given Sunday or holiday, a wide cross section of bourgeoisie, day laborers, working girls, and country hicks all caught sight of bare legs.

Prostitution thrived here. Decked out in vulgar rags, rouge-smeared, exhausted by the endless activity on their bit of pavement, they sold themselves for a few francs. Looks could be deceiving. You could never be sure that beneath the frippery was more than pliant flesh. If she took her client's wallet and he looked like he might protest, she was more than capable of sticking a knife between his ribs.

These tough women, and the thieves, pickpockets, and pimps around them were all called "apaches." With their hats worn at an angle, their tattooed biceps, a cigarette stuck in the corner of their mouths, they terrorized the bourgeoisie and fought each other viciously over the smallest point of honor. These bands were completely hierarchical; daring and defiant, they guarded their turf jealously.

"We in Paris have the advantage of having a tribe of Apaches for whom the Ménilmontant or Belleville heights are the Rocky Mountains," wrote a journalist in 1900. The analogy was clear. The young thugs were like the American Indians at the time in that they refused to be turned into good little workers of the Industrial Revolution, to sacrifice themselves in the name of progress.

The city's poorer neighborhoods were located in the east, which is where Ménilmontant or Belleville were located; the Place de la République was the natural meeting place with the west.

If these poor people sometimes refused to go along with the new social order, it was perhaps because they knew they would be mere pawns—exploited, used up, and spit out by the lords of the *Nouveau Régime*.

The world of the apaches had its heroes and its heroines. In 1902, the newspapers devoted nearly all of their columns to a story that fascinated Parisians. The central figure was a prostitute with almond-shaped eyes and a round face crowned with large curls of dirty-blond hair, which explained her nickname, Casque d'Or ("Goldilocks" wouldn't be a bad translation).

Amélie Hélie—for that was Casque d'Or's real name—was twenty-two in 1900. One night, while dancing the Java in a music hall near the République, she met a young worker named Marius Pleigneur. It was love at first sight—a bond formed by lost children. Marius proved jealous and possessive. To keep Casque d'Or for himself he joined her world. Marius gave up his low-wage jobs and became Manda, the terror of the boulevards, head of a gang known as the Orteaux, named after the street of that name. The unfaithful Casque d'Or drove him to despair. She threw herself into the arms of a Corsican named Dominique Leca, leader of the Popincourt, a rival gang. War broke out along the outer boulevards. As in a classical tragedy, everything unraveled with astonishing speed. On January 9, 1902, Leca was hit with two bullets. The doctors managed to save his life. Several days later, leaning on the arm of Casque d'Or, he emerged from the Tenon Hospital in the Twentieth Arrondissement. Manda was waiting for his rival

And what happened to Casque d'Or?

Amélie Hélie posed for amateur photographers, shacked up with a few millionaire lovers, and worked as a lion tamer in a circus before finally ending up selling women's stockings in Bagnolet. She married a worker whom she no doubt kept entertained with stories of her youth. She died, poor and forgotten, in 1933, at the age of fifty-three.

Neither Manda nor Leca returned from French Guyana, to which they had been sent. Manda died in the penal colony; as for Leca, after paying his debt to society, he worked until his death as a mason in Cayenne.

Casque d'Or took the apaches into legend. A melodrama called *Casque d'Or* or *Les Apaches de l'Amour* had a highly successful run in the playhouses on the boulevard. And in 1952 Jacques Becker produced his immortal film *Casque d'Or*, starring Simone Signoret and Serge Reggiani.

and went after him with a knife, wounding him. The Corsican managed to utter the name of his attacker. Both Leca and Manda were arrested and sent off to a penal colony.

The apaches disappeared in the bloodbath that was the First World War, along with the workers and farmers who made up most of the soldiers.

Casque d'Or, Manda, and Leca lived and loved in the neighborhood around the Place de la République, for that was now its name. In 1879, the year in which the republicans triumphed once and for all over the royalists and the Bonapartists in municipal and senatorial elections, the name of Place du Château d'Eau was changed. It became the home of the imposing-looking statue that still presides over it.

The République had been shaken but had not fallen. Soon it would shape the nature of Paris's institutions.

2a. Across the river from the Place de la Concorde, the Palais-Bourbon, now the home of the National Assembly; its twelve Corinthian columns were intended to reflect those of the Church of the Madeleine (**2b**), as if in a distant mirror. **3**. The Place de la Concorde. **4**. The Place Louis XVI. **5**. The entrance to the gardens of the Élysée palace. **6a**. The Grand and Petit Palais. **6b**. Statues of General de Gaulle, Winston Churchill, and Georges Clemenceau. **7**. At 15 Avenue Montaigne, the art deco façade of the Théâtre des Champs-Élysées. **8a**. At 25 Avenue des Champs-Élysées, the former home of the Marquise de Païva. **8b**. The hotel Marcel-Dassault, home to the Artcurial, is another example of twentieth-century luxury and distinction. For examples of twentieth-century architecture, see: **9a**. The art deco building (formerly the Virgin Megastore) at 56–60 Champs-Élysées; **9b**. The art nouveau façade of the Claridge (74–76, Avenue des Champs-Élysées); **9c**. The former Élysée palace, which became a bank, at number 103. **10a**. The Louis Vuitton store at 101, Avenue des Champs-Élysées. **10b**. The Publicis drugstore at number 133.

The Ways of Power

The Champs-Élysées-Clemenceau stop on the Métro could easily have been called "Champs-Élysées-Clemenceau-De Gaulle-Churchill," since statues of these two great figures of the Second World War are joined here with that of the *Tigre*—"the Tiger"—as Georges Clemenceau was called, transforming the former president of France into a quasi-allegorical character. This stop lies beneath the intersection at the foot of Champs-Élysées, a place that has been the scene of some of the bloodiest conflicts in French history. It should have had a different history, one of harmonious and mutual understanding. The Grand and the Petit Palais, located here, serve as examples, for they were constructed during the Exposition Universelle of 1900, symbols of exchange and cooperation between peoples.

At the top of the avenue, and leaving aside the Arc de Triomphe, which was built to glorify Napoleon, the Champs-Élysées entered into history through the Great War, World War I. In 1920, when the idea of building a tomb for the body of an unknown soldier who had died on the fields of glory first came up, the Chambre des Députés proposed placing the tomb in the Panthéon. The government and the president of the republic, Alexandre Millerand, had another plan, which was to celebrate

Armistice Day (November 11) by taking the heart of Léon Gambetta, the architect of national defense following the fall of the Second Empire, and putting it in the Panthéon. This offered a way of commemorating the second anniversary of the Armistice and the fiftieth of the republic, which was formed in 1870, at the same time.

These two projects, one put forward by the chief executive and one by the Chambre, resulted in a political schism: the Left wanted to glorify Gambetta; the Right wanted to venerate the common French foot soldier, the *poilu*. To avoid open confrontation, President Millerand offered a compromise: the heart of Gambetta would go to the Panthéon and the Unknown Soldier to the Arc de Triomphe in the Place de l'Étoile. This would happen on the same day. No one was really satisfied with the arrangement. The hardcore Left refused to take part in what it deemed a "military festival," and the reactionary wing on the Right howled against the idea of paying homage to the "layman" Gambetta.

Nonetheless, on the morning of November 11, 1920, a solemn procession composed of war-wounded; widows, a mother and an orphan, all of them victims of the conflict, accompanied the coffin of the Unknown Soldier, which was placed on a gun carriage. The procession made a symbolic stop at the Panthéon, where, at that very same moment, Gambetta's heart was being transferred. Then it made its way to the Arc de Triomphe.

Real and symbolic at the same time, the Tomb of the Unknown Soldier permitted the French to express collective grief, allowing families to weep openly over the loss of a father, a son, or a brother, lost somewhere in that great idiocy that was the Great War, a victim of the trenches, or gas, or bombardment. Politics had turned the Arc de Triomphe into a tomb, but also into a powerful symbol: the Tomb of the Unknown Solider closed off the arch. No longer could soldiers march through it. It was a fitting close to the war to end all wars. In September 1940, German troops, marching down the Champs-Élysées, proved that assertion an illusion.

On August 26, 1944, General de Gaulle walked down the same stretch of the Champs-Élysées to the Place de la Concorde.

"Ah, the sea," he apparently murmured when he saw the size of the crowd that was on hand to watch this victory parade.

From windows, balconies, rooftops, hanging from ladders and clinging to lampposts, Parisians wanted to take part in this historic moment, as the wind gently fluttered the *tricouleur*. The cannon salute that erupted in the Place de la Concorde, an echo of the final battle, created a brief wave of panic. People regained their composure and headed toward Notre-Dame Cathedral, where a final gun salute was fired.

In 1970, added to the Place de l'Étoile was the name Charles de Gaulle, who had just died, and in so doing the government mingled together the memory of the Unknown Soldier of the First World War and the founder of Free France. Today, now that the last of the Great War veterans has passed from the scene, all victims of all wars are paid homage to by the relighting of the perpetual flame, so that memory never becomes extinguished.

On July 14, for the length of the Champs-Élysées, the republic gathers together to do honor to its soldiers and to the country they fought for. It is perhaps for that reason that some of France's most significant achievements have been commemorated here. An endless sea of humanity for de Gaulle and the liberation of Paris in 1944; another to express attachment to the *Général* on May 30, 1968, when his government was in trouble; and another to celebrate the soccer player Zidane and the victory of the French national team in the World Cup of 1998. The occasions may change but not the setting.

But the Champs-Élysées, whose commemoration of war is framed by the Étoile and the roundabout, has plenty of other associations, and is now a place where politics and luxury goods merge. Sacha Guitry, the actor and playwright I mentioned earlier, made a film about walking up the Champs-Élysées. Let's follow him.

Across the river from the Place de la Concorde is the Palais-Bourbon, now the home of the National Assembly; its twelve Corinthian columns were intended to reflect those of the Church of the Madeleine, as if in a distant mirror.

The palace was built in 1722 for Louise de Bourbon, the legitimate daughter of Louis XIV and the Marquise de Montespan. Nearly a half century later, the Prince de Condé enlarged the palace and gave it an appearance that was inspired by the Grand Trianon at Versailles.

In 1795, the Revolution took control of the palace, which, with its new semicircle approach, was henceforth home to the Council of the Five Hundred, as the new legislative assembly was called. The *perchoir,* meaning the stage on which the president of the Assembly sits, is a survivor of the revolutionary period, after which the Palais-Bourbon underwent a number of changes and modifications before becoming the home of the current deputies, who number 570 in total.

The northern neoclassical façade dates from Napoleon. Under the emperor, the newly established revolutionary institutions were subject to autocratic power. Reigning from the Tuileries Palace, whose gardens opened out to the Place de la Concorde, Napoleon refashioned Paris. To exalt the victories of the *Grande Armée,* he started construction on the Arc de Triomphe de l'Étoile, and to render homage to his soldiers he ordered built the Madeleine. Finally, to balance everything out, the Palais-Bourbon on the Left Bank was remodeled.

History often presents us with oddities. The building, which embodies the country's republican institutions, carries the most royalist of all names. But it seems appropriate that before it was a symbol of the republic it was the favorite target of protests against monarchic power, in a time when democratic processes were subject to the will of a few.

In February 1934, on the Place de la Concorde, across from the Chambre des Députés, some thirty thousand people gathered together and threatened to launch an assault on the Palais-Bourbon; their goal was to bring down a government. "Against the thieves of this abject administration," extreme right-wing militants—royalists, nationalists, and fascists—had mobilized themselves. Calling themselves variously the Action Française, the King's Camelots, the Patriot Youth, and French Solidarity, they were open about their ambition to overturn *la gueuse*, meaning "the beggar," which is what they called the republic and its left-wing leadership. The Croix de Feu, which was without doubt the largest of these organizations and mainly made up of World War I veterans, was angry at the government but had also no direct political affiliation. Under the orders of a lieutenant colonel named François de La Roque, they gave their speeches and then vacated Concorde, leaving room for the more violent right-wing elements to take over.

As night fell, thousands of protesters tried to march on the Palais-Bourbon, half as expression of public protest and half as attempted coup d'état. Very quickly the police were overwhelmed and fired on the crowd. Clashes continued throughout the night. Sixteen protesters and one policeman were killed; a thousand were wounded.

From his position as tribune of the Chambre, Maurice Thorez, general secretary of the Communist Party, galvanized his forces.

"I call upon all proletarians and upon all our brothers the Socialist workers to come out into the streets and to hunt down these fascist thugs!"

Three days later, on February 9, in the Place de la République, a Communist counterdemonstration took place and they too had lethal run-ins with the police. The result was six dead and sixty wounded.

Leaving behind the Place de la Concorde and moving up the Champs-Élysées, you will see on the right, slightly pushed back, an iron gate on which sits a golden rooster. This is the entrance to the gardens of the Élysée palace. Since the election of Prince Louis Napoleon to the presidency of the Second Republic in 1848, this former home of the Marquise de Pompadour, the pretty mistress of Louis XV, has been the French president's official residence.

As noted earlier, Charles de Gaulle hated the place, which he thought too precious for a soldier like himself. Moreover, it was

How to get from the Revolution to the Concorde

In 1934, Concorde was sardonically referred to as "Place de la Discorde," but it has had other names. In 1789, it was called Place de la Révolution, and the sinister silhouette of the guillotine rose up here. Here are the figures: 1,119 heads were severed in this spot, including those of Louis XVI and Marie-Antoinette. The statue of Louis XV, placed in the square in the mid-eighteenth century, was replaced by a plaster model of Liberté wearing her Phrygian hat. In 1795, after the Reign of Terror had ended, the government, keen to maintain civil order, mandated that it be called "Place de la Concorde."

In 1800 the statue of Liberté was removed. A quarter of a century after that, Louis XVIII wanted to raise a monument to the memory of his brother, the guillotined king. As soon as the first stone was set in place, the square changed its name again and became Place Louis XVI. The work was interrupted by the Revolution of 1830. The square was then called Place de la Concorde once again, this time for good.

Still, if you look at the corner of the square where sits the Hôtel de Crillon, facing the embassy of the United States, you will see a *(Cont.)*

poorly designed; the food arrived cold into the dining room because the kitchen was too far away. And the idea of walking around the former palace of a royal mistress in slippers appalled the austere general.

Not all of de Gaulle's successors have shared his opinion. Georges Pompidou, who was deeply interested in modern art, had the private rooms decorated with the luminous and changing colors of the Israeli artist Agam. But his wife, Claude, hated living in this cold place, which she called an "unhappy house" after the death of the president. She never went back there again, even to visit those who took up residence after she had left.

Valéry Giscard d'Estaing lived alone in the Élysée. His wife, Anne-Aymone, thought the private residence too small and poorly designed for her four children. This left the president with an open field. On October 2, 1974, when he was returning in the company of a pretty young actress, he rammed his Ferrari into the back of a milk truck. This of course caused great hilarity among journalists at the time.

For François Mitterrand, Élysée was a place of work. Torn between his "official" life on Rue de Bièvre with his wife, Danielle, and his other life with the mother of his illegitimate daughter, Mazarine, born six years before his election to the presidency, he never had much of a chance to live in the palace.

plaque, dating from Louis XVIII, and on it you can still read "Place Louis XVI." The king was beheaded several steps away, between the obelisk and the statue of the city of Brest.

In 1836, Louis Philippe had the obelisk, a gift to France by the viceroy of Egypt, Mehemet Ali, placed in the middle of the square.

Jacques Chirac probably appreciated the place more than anyone else. In any case he made the residence quite sumptuous. "Chirac always lived where he worked and worked where he lived," as one of his former associates put it. This was as true when he was the mayor of Paris as when he was president. Bernadette Chirac never attempted to hide her nostalgia for earlier times when she rearranged the palace's flower garden.

Nicolas Sarkozy seemed to appreciate the splendor of the palace enough to marry Carla Bruni there on February 2, 2008. It was an intimate ceremony that took place in the presence of a few dozen people—close family and a handful of friends.

Sarkozy's marriage was actually not the first to take place in the Élysée. On June 1, 1931, President Gaston Doumergue, who had remained a bachelor during his term, got married there as well, twelve days before his last day in office.

Continuing our way up this avenue, which is after all one of the world's most beautiful, we should make a little side trip along the Avenue Montaigne to the Art Deco façade of the Théâtre des Champs-Élysées.

In 1920, under the guidance of Jacques Hébertot, this playhouse represented the avant-garde: operas, ballet, plays, and concerts all took place there. The Swedish Ballet entranced Paris here, with music by Ravel, Debussy, Milhaud, and Satie. Here was where the twentieth century exploded onto the art scene.

Pablo Picasso designed sets. The Spanish-born painter had

married Olga the Russian ballerina he had met in Rome and they had moved into a reassuringly bourgeois apartment at 23 Rue La Boëtie, not far from the Champs-Élysées.

In 1905, fifteen years earlier, Picasso had decided to settle in Paris indefinitely, and could only afford a place in Montmartre—a ramshackle and off-kilter hovel dubbed the Bateau-Lavoir—the "washtub boat," literally. For fifteen francs a month, he lived in a studio on the third floor on the courtyard.

One stormy night, a young woman hurried home, her clothes soaking wet. She had only just moved to La Butte—as Montmartre was called—and was starting a career as a painter and a model, posing for the most celebrated academic artists of the day. Fernande Olivier was her name, and she had noticed Picasso, a timid-seeming and broad-shouldered young Spaniard with burning eyes and jet-black hair that he was constantly brushing away from his forehead. They often crossed paths at the common sink near the entry, their buckets in their hands, sometimes exchanging a few polite words.

That night, Picasso ran into the soaking Fernande in the building's narrow hallway. He was twenty-four, she a few months older. Full-bodied, even voluptuous, she looked charming in her trimmed hat out of which tumbled her blond hair; she was a little taller than he was. Picasso might have felt intimidated by this seductive woman were it not for his dark, devouring gaze. He stood in her way and, laughing, scooped up and offered her a little cat that was always hanging around. Fernande tried to get by him, somewhat coyly, but soon enough had accepted an invitation to visit his studio.

When Fernande entered into Picasso's world for the first time, she was stunned by the agony that the paintings expressed. Happy bird that she was, living in the Butte, she couldn't comprehend their despair and thought these unfinished works morbid. But what most struck her was the chaos of canvases, tubes of paint, and abandoned brushes scattered on the floor. To her horror, a tame white mouse lived in the table drawer.

Fernande gazed at all this strange artistic bric-a-brac and her laughing eyes and luminous face seemed to light up this sad den. Picasso fell in love. Before long pink tints, the color of happiness and hope, would find their way to his canvases.

In the spring of 1906, the Louvre organized a show of Iberian bronze sculptures from the fourth and fifth centuries that had been found in Andalusia. Picasso became obsessed with analyzing the forms and taking in the powerful expression of these statues. Several months later Picasso would make another seminal discovery. One evening in November, he had been invited to dinner at the home of Henri Matisse, the Fauvist painter, on the Quai Saint-Michel. Of course they talked about art. Matisse took a small statue that was sitting on some furniture and handed it to Picasso. It was a wooden figure of a black man, the first that the Spaniard had seen of the kind. He said nothing, but he wouldn't let go of the statuette all evening long, his dark eyes analyzing the dark wood and his fingers gliding over the smooth surface. He felt what he had felt when he first saw those bronze figures in the Louvre.

The next morning, the floor of his studio in the Bateau-Lavoir was littered with pieces of paper, each one featuring a charcoal drawing of a woman's face, sketched furiously and from various perspectives. Each face had one eye and a long nose that ended in a mouth.

Picasso fought with this painting for more than six months, producing innumerable sketches and drawings. The black statuette, the Iberian bronzes, the memory of Cézanne—they all seemed to be taking shape in a work that would be completely and utterly revolutionary.

In 1907, his friends gathered in the Bateau-Lavoir to view the outsized canvas that Picasso was calling *The Demoiselles d'Avignon*. The spectators looked at its twisted curves, its deformed aesthetic, its pink tints emerging from the darkness, and simply shook their heads. No one yet understood that the painting had brought art into the twentieth century. For now, the beginnings of the revolution were limited to the heights of Montmartre. Then it spread to the Théâtre Champs-Élysées, and from there out into the world.

Whatever happened to the Bateau-Lavoir?

On May 12, 1970, at about two-thirty in the afternoon, the central Montmartre firehouse was besieged by phone calls. A fire had broken out in the Bateau-Lavoir.

By the time the smoke had cleared, the place was little more than a smoky ruin among which were calcified remains. The painter André Patureau, one of the residents, was stunned by how quickly it had all happened. "It was horrible. I have lost everything. My paintings, my work, my whole life. I was working on a canvas in my studio on the ground floor when a thick black cloud of smoke poured into the room."

Five years after the fire, the Bateau-Lavoir was reconstructed. The façade was left intact, as it had not been destroyed. Twenty-five working studios and elegant apartments replaced the old heap. Rue Ravignan, a door that is always locked, and an intercom system—these are what greet the visitor making his melancholy quest into the history of a place that once had been open to the four winds.

Let's return to the Champs-Élysées. Once through the Concorde traffic circle, the avenue shoots straight toward the Arc de Triomphe. On the left-hand side at number 25 is the former home of the Marquise de Païva, the Russian courtesan. Here is one of the rare vestiges of the Second Empire, a fashionable neighborhood in which the restaurants and leafy walks attracted an elegant crowd. At the turn of the twentieth century, descending the Champs—on horseback, in carriages, in hackney cabs, and then in the first automobiles—was deemed the height of luxury and distinction.

It is perhaps appropriate that this magnificent palace, completed in 1865, would today be devoted to the world of finance. Going farther up the Champs, someone out for a stroll would be assaulted by a confusion of signs and brands, same sporting feudal coats of arms. The statesmen and the artists have been replaced by businessmen. Today power resides neither in the Élysée nor in the Palais-Bourbon but in this line of storefronts, owned by the great conglomerates of luxury goods and those who pull the strings in the stock market. Seeking architectural souvenirs of the twentieth century we would choose the Art Nouveau façade of the Claridge, at numbers 74–76; that of the former Élysée palace, which became a bank, at number 103; or the Art Deco building, which, until just recently, housed the Virgin Megastore, at numbers 56–60.

Still, the construction of the RER, which has had a station under Étoile since 1970, has somewhat changed the Champs. For forty years, getting from the suburbs to here has been no big deal. The result is the avenue has lost something of its distinguished allure by giving in to chain clothing stores and fast food.

Yet they are still there—Lancel, Lacoste, Hugo Boss, Omega, Cartier, Guerlain, Montblanc. All of them light the sky on the Champs-Élysée, the triumphant procession of the new potentates.

In 2006, Louis Vuitton opened on the avenue, at number 101, and the reconfigured space became subject to all kinds of criticism, mostly because of the kooky window treatments. Yet whatever else you might say about these windows, on display were the original suitcases and bags, the most imitated in the world. And what is there to say about the new building for the drugstore called Publicis at number 133, a veritable institution now for more than half a century? Its transparent and curved design is typical of architecture of the end of the twentieth century and the new millennium. If nothing else, it leaves us perplexed.

Of all these new powers that be, the most obviously visible is the shocking new Versailles with its court, rising up in the distance ahead of you in La Défense, whose Grande Arche has become the Arc de Triomphe of modern times, a literal and figurative distant echo of Napoleonic glory.

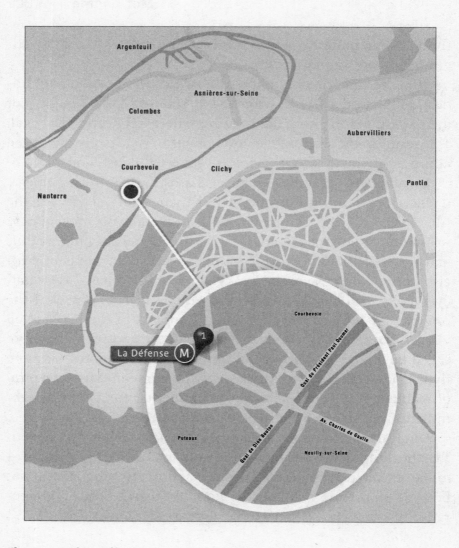

The Statue of La Défense.

Twenty-first Century

La Defénse

Back to the Start

Going down into the terminus of Line 1 in the station at La Défense, you get a clear view of the Grande Arche, framed by the sidereal emptiness that its pretentious form imposes upon the eye. The twentieth century has not been kind to Paris, architecturally speaking: the Montparnasse Tower, the Forum des Halles, the Riverside Expressway (*voies sur berges*), the Centre Pompidou, the Bastille Opera, the François Mitterrand Library. The eyesores inflicted upon the capital are numerous and rather breathtaking. The Grande Arche came into being in 1989 and achieved the culmination of bad taste by being set within the sight lines of the Arc de Triomphe.

I'm being tough, I realize this. Who knows? Perhaps in a hundred years pilgrims will come to La Défense to pay homage to its elegance and power, just as Art Nouveau or Art Deco designs became revered architectural symbols for those living in the second half of the twentieth century. Perhaps they will gather here before this Arc de Triomphe of finance. The neighborhood of La Défense is barely fifty years old, after all. It was General de Gaulle who decided to start construction here in 1958, in the towns of Puteaux, Courbevoie, and Nanterre. He wished to create the economic and financial poles of the France of the Thirty Glories, as the years between 1945 and 1975 have been called. Looking toward the Arc de Triomphe, you will see at the far end of the square, a little lost in all the new construction, the statue of La Défense, erected in 1883 in honor of those who defended Paris against the Prussian invasion in 1870. It is to them that the *quartier* owes its name.

In my heart of hearts, rather than give in to a slightly absurd conservatism, I prefer to accept not the outrageous but the audacious architecture of my time. And then, as we know, time will do its work, history will judge—and better than I can, without question. Because in the end these are future remnants and vestiges, the remains of the century in which I live, and they are indispensable to Paris. Moreover, the magnificent museum on the Quai Branly designed by Jean Nouvel, near the Eiffel Tower, has already become a classic.

Now we can pose the following question: what heritage will the twenty-first century bequeath to future generations?

For the moment I believe these striking new superstructures, built with ephemeral and throwaway materials, will disappear fairly quickly. A number of archaeologists and architects worry openly about the short lives of modern buildings.

Whatever the case, the Paris of our century will be one of dizzying expansion. This will be the century of Greater Paris, a triumph of connective agglomeration that will overwhelm the *périphérique* and swallow up all or at least part of the suburbs and take along with it several districts in the process.

The axes that will need to be redrawn are already clearly visible: the Avenue Charles-de-Gaulle, which goes from Étoile to La Défense and runs through Neuilly like a freeway, will one day be refashioned. Projects are in the works. One day it will become a river of green whose current will end in the esplanade of La Défense, which by then will have lost its confused aspect, the product of haphazard or nonexistent planning.

And developing toward the west, Paris, the Greater Paris of tomorrow, will make this business district, with its thrusting office towers, a part of itself, a witness to its own past, a window open to its future. Then the capital will keep moving, extending farther west, and swallow up Nanterre, which is right behind La Défense.

Thus the city will slowly move back to where it began. As we might remember, the original Lutèce was located on the banks of the Seine in what is today Nanterre. The twenty-first century will perhaps see Paris return to this ancient home of the Gauls and discover again, more than two thousand years later, the bend in the river in whose nurturing confines it was born.